Going Local

Photo by Sergio Cárdenas-Denham.

Going Local

DECENTRALIZATION, DEMOCRATIZATION, AND
THE PROMISE OF GOOD GOVERNANCE

Merilee S. Grindle

PRINCETON UNIVERSITY PRESS

PRINCETON AND OXFORD

Copyright © 2007 by Princeton University Press
Published by Princeton University Press, 41 William Street,
Princeton, New Jersey 08540
In the United Kingdom: Princeton University Press, 3 Market Place,
Woodstock, Oxfordshire OX20 1SY

All Rights Reserved

Library of Congress Cataloging-in-Publication Data

Grindle, Merilee Serrill.
Going local : decentralization, democratization, and the promise of good governance /
Merilee S. Grindle.
p.   cm.
Includes bibliographical references and index.

ISBN-13: 978-0-691-12907-5 (alk. paper)—
ISBN-10: 0-691-12907-X (alk. paper)
1. Decentralization in government. 2. Local government. 3. Decentralization in government—
Mexico. 4. Local government—Mexico. I. Title.
JS113.G75 2007
320.8—dc22   2006051038

British Library Cataloging-in-Publication Data is available

This book has been composed in Sabon

Printed on acid-free paper. ∞

press.princeton.edu

Printed in the United States of America

1   3   5   7   9   10   8   6   4   2

As always,
for Steven, Stefanie, and Alexandra

CONTENTS

ILLUSTRATIONS

FIGURES

MAPS

TABLES

ACRONYMS

AALMAC	Asociación de Autoridades Locales de México, A.C. [Association of Local Authorities]
AAMAC	Asociación de Municípios de México, A.C. [Association of Mexican Municipalities]
CDM	Comité de Desarrollo Municipal [Municipal Development Committee]
CENDI	Centro de Desarrollo Infantil [Center for Children's Development (a generic term for preschool or day-care center)]
CIDAC	Centro de Investigaciones para el Desarrollo, A.C. [Center for Development Research]
CIDE	Centro de Investigaciones y Docencia Económicas [Center for Economic Research and Teaching]
CONAPO	Consejo Nacional de Población [National Population Council]
COPLADE	Comité de Planeación para el Desarrollo del Estado [State Development Planning Committee]
COPLADEMUN	Comité de Planeación para el Desarrollo Municipal [Municipal Development Planning Committee]
DIF	Desarrollo Integral de la Familia [Holistic Family Development]
FAEB	Fondo de Aportaciones para la Educación Básica [Grant Fund for Basic Education]
FAETA	Fondo de Aportaciones para la Educación Tecnológica y de Adultos [Grant Fund for Technical and Adult Education]
FAIS	Fondo de Aportaciones para la Infraestructura Social [Grant Fund for Social Infrastructure]
FAISM	Fondo de Aportaciones para la Infraestructura Social Municipal [Grant Fund for Municipal Social Infrastructure]
FAM	Fondo de Aportaciones Múltiples [Miscellaneous Grant Fund]
FASP	Fondo de Aportaciones para la Seguridad Pública de los Estados y del Distrito Federal [Grant Fund for Public Security]

FASS   Fondo de Aportaciones para los Servicios de Salud
                [Grant Fund for Health Services]
FENAMM   Federación de Municipios de México [Federation
                of Mexican Municipalities]
FORTAMUN   Fondo de Aportaciones para el Fortalecimiento de
                los Municipios [Grant Fund for Municipal
                Strengthening]
GPS   Global Positioning System
IDD   International Development Department (University
                of Birmingham, UK)
IMSS   Instituto Mexicano de Seguro Social [Mexican So-
                cial Security Institute]
INAFED   Instituto Nacional para el Federalismo y el Desar-
                rollo Municipal [National Institute for Federalism
                and Municipal Development]
INAH   Instituto Nacional de Antropología e Historia [Na-
                tional Institute of Anthropology and History]
INDESOL   Instituto Nacional de Desarrollo Social [National
                Institute for Social Development]
INEGI   Instituto Nacional de Estadística, Geografía, e In-
                formática [National Institute for Statistics, Geo-
                graphy, and Information]
NGO   Nongovernmental Organization
PAN   Partido Acción Nacional [National Action Party]
PRD   Partido de la Revolución Democrática [Democratic
                Revolution Party]
PRI   Partido Revolucionario Institucional [Institutional-
                ized Revolutionary Party]
PRONASOL   Programa Nacional de Solidaridad (also known as
                Solidaridad) [National Solidarity Program]
PT   Partido del Trabajo [Worker's Party]
PVEM   Partido Verde Ecologista Mexicano [Mexican
                Green Ecologist Party]
SEDESOL   Secretaría de Desarrollo Social [Social Develop-
                ment Secretariat (ministry)]
SEMARNAP   Secretaría de Medio Ambiente, Recursos Naturales
                y Pesca [Environment, Natural Resources, and
                Fish Secretaríiat (ministry)]
SOLIDARIDAD   Programa Nacional de Solidaridad (originally
                PRONASOL) [National Solidarity Program]
UNESCO   United Nations Educational, Scientific, and Cul-
                tural Organization

ACKNOWLEDGMENTS

SEVEN PEOPLE played a vital part in making this book possible—the researchers who spent the summer of 2004 in thirty different municipalities in Mexico, asking questions, visiting project sites, seeking information, and observing processes of local governance. I owe an enormous debt of gratitude to them and the spirit of commitment and inquiry they brought to the fieldwork.

Orazio Bellettini, Karla Breceda, Alexi Canaday-Jarrix, Elizabeth Coombs, Xóchitl León, and Alberto Saracho-Martínez, graduates of the Kennedy School of Government at Harvard University, and Sergio Cárdenas-Denham, of the Harvard Graduate School of Education, worked long hours, generated important insights, shared their ideas with each other and with me, and persevered in sometimes difficult situations to generate the data on which this book is based. They also read the draft manuscript with care and insight, correcting errors and adding perspective. When we met at workshops, their excitement and good spirits about the project and what they were finding out was infectious. When I visited them in their field sites, they did their utmost to educate me about "their" municipalities. I thoroughly enjoyed working with them and appreciate how much they allowed me to learn. I hope they are pleased with the results of their hard work. Most important, I hope they will long remember the summer they spent "Going Loco."

In the initial stages of the research, Naomi Walcott, a student at the Kennedy School, provided excellent and efficient research assistance. Elizabeth Gewurz Ramírez, also of the Kennedy School, continued in this important role throughout the most intense period of the research. We all gained from her steadfast commitment to the project. During the data analysis phase, Orazio Bellettini, Elizabeth Coombs, Alberto Saracho-Martínez, Xóchitl León, and Emanuel Garza Fishburn served as research assistants, searching for information, combing through data, and generating the tables, figures, and maps that appear in the book. Their expertise and investigative instincts are greatly appreciated. Catherine Fratianni Guevara at the Kennedy School was assiduous in managing the administrative and financial aspects of the project, and she was a great resource for the researchers, the one they could turn to when they needed a problem solved or a friend at "headquarters." Thank you, Katie.

My interest in the idea of local governance was stimulated by Enrique Cabrero Mendoza of the Centro de Investigación y Docencia Económicas (CIDE) in Mexico and the work that he and his colleagues have done in the area of innovation in local government. During the research he was extraordinarily supportive of this initiative and has been its very good friend. The researchers and I also benefited greatly from the experience and contributions of Gilberto García Vázquez.

Also in Mexico, Gustavo Merino Juárez was invariably helpful with ideas and data sources, and Carlos Gadsden was generous with his time. Peter Ward of the University of Texas at Austin shared important ideas and helped shape the project and its outcome. Judith Tendler, a dear friend, encouraged me to undertake this study and provided excellent advice about the fieldwork. Alejandra González-Rosetti, Bertha Angulo Curiel, Mary Hilderbrand, and Lía Limón made traveling to Mexico an unusual pleasure. I want them to know how much I value their contributions and friendship.

I am extremely grateful to the Ash Institute for Democratic Governance and Innovation at Harvard for funding the field research. Without its support, and the interest that Gowher Rizvi and Stephen Goldsmith took in the work, it could not have been undertaken. In addition, the David Rockefeller Center for Latin American Studies (DRCLAS) at Harvard funded the workshops that were absolutely essential to the outcome of the work. I want to thank DRCLAS and its wonderful director, John Coatsworth, for their helpfulness. Steve Reifenberg of DRCLAS was also a great friend who facilitated the work. The Fundación México en Harvard hosted a workshop in Mexico City; its executive director, Barbara Randolph de Rodríguez, and her assistant, Lorenia Villarreal, were welcoming and generous to the research team. I am also grateful to the Center for International Development of Harvard University for covering some of the expenses related to the data analysis. I would like to thank Patrick Florence of the Harvard Maps Collection in the Lamont Library at Harvard University for his assistance in producing the maps that appear in this book.

I had the incomparable opportunity to spend a month as a resident at the Rockefeller Foundation's Study and Conference Center in Bellagio, Italy in the spring of 2005. Exquisite views of water, mountains, and mists, as well as the stimulation of interesting colleagues, encouraged the completion of the first draft of the manuscript. To this extraordinarily beautiful place, to its gracious director, Pilar Palacía, and to its helpful and kind staff, I shall always be grateful.

There are 569 other individuals who also deserve thanks. They are the municipal officials, party leaders, NGO managers, citizens, academics, and others at local, state, and national levels in Mexico who gave generously of their time to discuss their activities and whose perspectives are at the heart of the book. Orazio, Karla, Alexi, Sergio, Eli, Xochi, Alberto, and I want to thank them for the graciousness with which they received us and for their willingness to help us understand their reality. I hope they find it reflected in the book.

As always, Steven Grindle was a source of enormous good humor and encouragement for the project; he particularly appreciated getting to know the team that carried out the work. Although Stefanie and Alexandra have moved on to independent lives, they have continued to follow my travels, offer daughterly advice, and live as deeply engaged people who care about the world of politics and policy. To them, I say again, thank you for being you.

Going Local

Photo by Sergio Cárdenas-Denham.

Chapter 1

GOING LOCAL
Governance on the Line

THIS IS A STUDY of decentralization from the perspective of its local consequences. The book ventures inside town hall, exploring the diverse activities of public officials as they seek to manage a variety of tasks amidst conflicting pressures and new expectations for local government. It explores how, why, and when better local governance emerges—or doesn't—and the implications of structural change for achieving the public good.

. . . .

In April 2004, angry residents of Ilave, Peru lynched the town's mayor and threw his body under a bridge. Less than two months later, citizens of Ayo Ayo in Bolivia dragged their mayor from his home and set him on fire; newspapers carried photographs of his charred remains. Over a number of years, people in Santo Domingo Tehuantepec, Mexico grew accustomed to gathering outside town hall to chant epithets and hurl rocks at the building until incumbent mayors were forced to resign. The people of Santiago Atitlán in Guatemala remember the events of 1997, when the town hall was burned down during a dispute with their mayor. In a more legal vein, seven mayors in the Philippines were taken to court for electoral fraud in 2004, and local party leaders in Gulbarga, India threatened action against two former mayors. The following year, the mayor of Blantyre, in Malawi, was sentenced to three years in prison for stealing funds meant for road repairs. Behind these acts of civic violence and conflict were charges of corruption, malfeasance, lack of accountability, fraud, and failure to respond to the needs of local residents.[1]

Elsewhere, however, local officials were lauded for the innovations they introduced in the governance of their communities and the new spaces they created for civic participation. In a range of countries, mayors became popular candidates for president, and in places as diverse as Argentina, Brazil, Canada, Chile, India, Mexico, the Philippines, South Africa, and the United States, annual awards celebrated local governments that had taken on difficult problems and found inventive ways of resolving them. In some cases, governments became world famous for such innovations, as did Pôrto Alegre, Brazil when it introduced a participatory budgeting process. In Mexico, cities such as Monterrey, León, and Aguascalientes became well-known models for efficient and responsive governance. In municipalities in Kenya, India, the Philippines, South Africa, and elsewhere, citizens shared information, made decisions about resource allocation, monitored policy implementation, and envisioned improvements that would alter the future of their communities.[2]

Why such contrasting experiences? Those who have promoted decentralization during the past quarter century would not predict that places such as Ilave and Pôrto Alegre would be so different in the quality of government that characterized them. These differences matter, because local governments have become newly relevant to the lives of hundreds of millions of people across the globe. Over a span of two and a half decades of decentralization, local levels of government in many countries acquired new responsibilities and more resources for carrying them out. Public officials and public agencies assumed new roles in these governments. Political parties that had long focused on national electoral contests became active in campaigns for the leadership of towns and cities. Citizens increasingly looked to local governments in their aspirations for better and more secure neighborhoods, better health and education services, and programs to enhance economic opportunities.

The rhetoric and theory of decentralization promise better governance and deeper democracy as public officials are held more directly accountable for their actions and as citizens become more engaged in local affairs. Practice over more than two decades, however, suggests that new experiments with decentralization can result in unfulfilled expectations and the emergence of unanticipated problems. Experiences as distinct as those of Ilave and Pôrto Alegre signal the potential for diverse outcomes in local political contexts increasingly characterized by more responsibilities, resources, political competition, and citizen demand making.

In the following chapters, I seek to find answers to several questions: When local governments are charged with new responsibilities and provided with new resources, how are new policy and program agendas set and carried out? How is local governance affected by the dynamics of political competition, the capacity of leaders to mobilize resources for change, the modernization of public administration, the demands and participation of civil society? What is the meaning of decentralization for democratic governance? To find answers to these questions, I use data from a random sample of thirty medium-sized municipalities in a single country, measure their performance as units of government, and seek to explain why they perform as they do.

The findings shed light on complex changes introduced by decentralization and democratization. Together, these two processes increased competition for electoral office in the research municipalities, which in turn provided greater opportunities for the circulation of political leadership. With changes in political leadership came opportunities to initiate improvements in the management of town affairs. Weak institutions of local governance increased the ability of public leaders to introduce significant change in short order, even while the same institutional weakness undermined the sustainability of reform. Thus, electoral calendars often marked the introduction of governance reforms—and their demise. Meanwhile, well-known repertoires for participation made it easier for citizens to extract resources from government than to hold public officials and agencies accountable for their actions. Inside town hall, then, much was set in motion by decentralization and democratization.

Good governance, this book attests, is not simply a function of the structure of intergovernmental relationships. It is, rather, the consequence of new opportunities and resources, the impact of leadership motivation and choices, the influence of civic history, and the effect of institutions that constrain and facilitate innovation. The research reported in the following chapters shows the daily life of municipal governments, public officials, and citizens as they adjusted to complex new roles and realities that were simultaneously political, technical, and historical. The impact of decentralization was tangible in the research communities and, although its impact was not always positive, it held out some promise for better governance in the future.

This work is relevant for researchers and practitioners alike. For those who are concerned about theories that accurately capture political dynamics in new institutional settings, the research reported in this book clarifies the origins of change, adaptation, and the process of political, administrative, and fiscal transitions. Similarly, it illuminates how democratization, accountability of local officials, and participation are encouraged or discouraged by contextual factors at the local level and legacies from the past. For those most concerned about applying the insights of research to real-world conditions, this book suggests ways to redress governance shortfalls in decentralized settings. The site of my research is Mexico, but I believe that the findings of the study are relevant to many other countries that have experienced the consequences of structural change in government and wish to understand its impact on the quality of local governance and democracy.

The Decentralization Revolution

In country after country from the 1980s to the mid-2000s, national governments decentralized.[3] Fiscally, they insisted that subnational authorities become responsible for managing budgets, generating revenue, and rendering appropriate accounts. Politically, they legislated that hitherto appointed officials in provincial and local governments would now be elected by popular mandate. Administratively, they distributed responsibilities for the provision of health and education services to state and local bureaucracies and gave local governments increased duties for physical and social infrastructure. Indeed, decentralization was so widely adopted that it amounted to a structural revolution in the distribution of public responsibilities and authority in large numbers of countries. Like new structures of international governance attendant upon globalization, decentralization helped redefine the role of central government in the development process.[4]

Even though this process of decentralization brought significant new resources and power to local decision makers, it also brought headaches and dilemmas. Long bereft of authority and resources by highly centralized political systems, localities throughout the world grappled with how to take on responsibilities for routine administration, public service provision, and economic development. Institutions for local decision making, in some cases atrophied from decades of centralization, had to be revived to take on complex problems. Service-providing organizations had to be created or restructured; employees needed to be trained and new procedures put into effect. Fiscal management became more exacting even as citizens were increasingly aware that local officials could be appealed to, blamed, or supported for the delivery of a range of public services.

Of course, decentralization can be put into effect in different ways—through devolution, delegation, or deconcentration.[5] While distinctions among forms of decentralization are important in defining the relationship of the center to the periphery and for the management of particular programs and functions, most local governments experience all three types of decentralization at the same time.[6] Thus, for example, a local government may be coping with a devolved education system that continues to vest authority over standards and testing in a national ministry; a deconcentrated health system that requires local governments to be responsible only for the maintenance of local clinics; the full delegation of property tax collection; and the devolution of responsibility over sanitation within norms set by national or provincial governments. Each of these activities involves local officials in redefined relationships with other levels of government, at the same time that it prescribes particular roles for local government.

Thus, from the perspective of local officials and agencies, decentralization means not only a complex of new responsibilities but also a series of different relationships with other levels of government that have to be managed simultaneously. In their terms, then, various types of decentralization are part of a difficult new arena in which they are expected to perform—with new mandates and new rules of the game for being successful. In this context, it may matter less what kind of decentralization characterizes specific policy areas than how local governments and local officials adapt to new demands and expectations and how they manage the full complex of decentralized responsibilities.

Even before the decentralization revolution, of course, local governments often had a range of responsibilities. These tended to be humble ones—garbage collection, parks, road maintenance, local traffic and animal control, school repair. Nevertheless, these services directly affected the quality of life of local residents as well as their sense of order and security. During the period between 1980 and 2005, the new wave of decentralization assigned less humble functions to local governments— education, public health, environmental management, crime prevention and control, local economic development, water supply. Such undertakings had significant ramifications in terms of the opportunities available to poor and middle-income households for social and economic mobility. Structural change meant that local interactions between citizens and the state became more important and more critical to the present life conditions and future opportunities of millions of citizens.

Historically, this era was not the first in which decentralization was advocated as a way to improve political and economic performance; nor was this structural reform without its opponents.[7] Indeed, the histories of numerous countries are punctuated by controversy and even wars over the distribution of power among levels of government.[8] Nevertheless, recent decentralizing initiatives were more widely advocated and more widely adopted than was the case in prior periods, and the emphasis on its promise of improved efficiency, effectiveness, and responsiveness was more marked. Among the most fervent advocates were international financial institutions, particularly the World Bank, which was at the forefront of encouraging governments to devolve authority to local governments, delegate activities and services to quasi-independent organizations or the private sector, and deconcentrate the central delivery of services.

The promise and the practice of decentralization. Scholarship on decentralization initiatives between 1980 and 2005 provides important insights into their central political and economic dynamics. The motivations behind national decisions to decentralize have been assessed and credited to factors as diverse as pressures from international financial institutions, the electoral logic of declining parties, career aspirations of politicians, levels of economic development, and the ideological rationale of neoliberalism.[9] The sometimes surprising reluctance of local and regional governments to take on new responsibilities has been contrasted with the commitment of central politicians to push forward with their reform agendas.[10]

Some research addresses the national consequences of decentralization—the extent to which fiscal discipline may have been imperiled, the degree to which inequality may have increased among regions and localities, and the wins and losses of national political parties in local elections.[11] Others have focused attention on the strategic choices that national states make about the sequence of fiscal, political, and administrative decentralization and their consequences for the effectiveness of such policies.[12] A number of studies illuminate how decentralization can set in motion new conflicts between central and more local levels of government, particularly over demands for increases in power and revenue.[13] Such studies have improved our understanding of why rational politicians would decide to share power downward in their political systems; the factors that combined to create a worldwide trend toward structural reform in government; and the national political and economic effects of this trend.

Yet it is also important to understand the ways in which local governments became new arenas for politics, policy decision making, and governance. A number of studies have broken important ground in this rich field of study. Robert Putnam (1993), for example, explored the causal mechanisms behind good governance in Italy's regions; Judith Tendler (1997) laid out the complex interaction of state and local organizations that contributed to innovative community programs in Brazil; Peter Ward and Victoria Rodríguez (1999) assessed the impact of political competition on the management of cities in Mexico; Blair (2000) explored the extent to which local democracy promoted participation and accountability in several countries; and Stoner-Weiss (1997) described the contextual factors that explained why some regional governments in Russia performed better than others in the wake of decentralization. From such work, we are beginning to understand the divergence between the promise of decentralization and its real-world consequences.

As the decentralization revolution got under way in the 1980s, academics and practitioners alike believed that this structural change was an important way to ensure good governance. Economists, for example, built on the work of Tiebout (1956), Coase (1960), and Oates (1972, 1977) to argue that decentralization would increase allocative efficiency by subjecting public spending priorities to local demand. They indicated that because information on the performance of government institutions is more readily available to citizens in decentralized systems, they are in the best position to make demands for effective services and to reward and punish local politicians; information on local preferences is also more available to decision makers because they are in daily contact with citizens. Moreover, when citizens are taxed for local services, they will have incentives to insist on good-quality services and hold officials and service providers accountable for their actions. For similar reasons, proponents of neoliberal economic reforms argued that decentralization would increase the efficiency of government, mobilize additional public resources, and improve fiscal decision making; it was seen as an important means to redress decades of statist development strategies that had resulted in low growth rates and high levels of corruption in the production of public services.[14]

Political scientists also became advocates for the benefits of decentralization. In the distant past, some had argued in favor of centralization as a response to the threat of participation "overload" and the destructive power of centrifugal conflicts and loyalties in nation building.[15] By the early 1980s, however, many found important reasons for citizen participation in local elections and government decision making as a palliative to overcentralized and authoritarian governments.[16] More effective democratic states needed strongly participatory local democracy, they argued; as citizens have opportunities to participate, they become more effective at rewarding and punishing the behavior of local officials. As a consequence, rational politicians have incentives to be responsive to local needs and local concerns. This kind of participation is, furthermore, an effective "school" for democracy, providing an arena for learning skills of deliberation and the rules that structure conflict resolution in democratic systems.[17] Thus, political decentralization, referring primarily to the popular election of local decision makers and representatives but also incorporating new mechanisms for citizen participation in local government, was expected to promote stronger and better democracies. Among others promoting decentralization for similar reasons were political activists, nongovernmental organizations, and human rights groups. They were vocal in arguing that decentralization increases the ability of citizens to select responsive public officials and hold them accountable for their performance, as well as to participate more effectively in public decision-making arenas.[18]

Similarly, disciples of public management anticipated that decentralization would produce more responsive decision making, higher quality services, and public administrators who would be motivated to perform well.[19] When government administration is brought closer to those who receive services, they argued, beneficiaries of these services would become active in demanding good quality. Because those responsible for the quality of services are local, citizens will be more motivated to complain and demand improvements if services fail or decline in quality. Moreover, civil servants will have incentives to orient their behavior toward good service provision because of the potential for public disruption and complaints from dissatisfied "customers." Corruption would also be more visible at local levels and thus easier to control. Public sector reformers agreed with fiscal decentralizers that services would become more efficient if they were paid for by local taxes and fees. The task for improving government, then, was to strengthen the institutions of local governance, provide local public officials with greater capacity to take on new responsibilities, and develop mechanisms to improve performance and accountability.

Not surprisingly, these high expectations for the decentralization revolution were likely to be disappointed when policies were put in practice to restructure the locus of government decision making and operational responsibility—practice rarely lives up to theory. And indeed, by the early 1990s, those concerned about public finance began to fear that decentralization could lead to increased fiscal deficits and imperil macroeconomic stability.[20] In some cases, local government debt burdens became the responsibility of national governments, causing central bankers to have second thoughts about the wisdom of local officials. Those responsible for national fiscal health often responded to the unanticipated consequences of decentralization by putting in place mechanisms to tighten up central oversight of local revenue and expenditure management. In addition, economists were often disappointed that local governments were not more proactive in generating local revenues. Instead of increasing the robustness of local taxation, many subnational governments increased their demands on central governments for more revenue sharing.[21]

In politics, the practice of decentralization also brought mixed reviews. In some cases, evidence surfaced that local elites could benefit inequitably from decentralization. Scholars found evidence of considerable potential for interest group capture in small electoral arenas and they raised questions about the survival of "authoritarian enclaves" in local settings.[22] Others demonstrated that local governments often reflected the social, political, and economic conflicts that divided local communities; they questioned the view of those who believe that decentralization means more power and equity for ordinary citizens.[23] Some came to the conclusion that there was no inherent reason why decentralized governments should be any more democratic than centralized ones nor any a priori reason why local elections should guarantee the emergence of more effective leadership.[24] Although theoretically citizens should have greater say in the policy and programmatic choices of government under decentralized arrangements, practice suggested that this was not necessarily the case.[25] Instead of a consistent pattern of more responsive and participatory local governments, researchers found wide variability across them in terms of democratic practice.

Those who focused on public management found that the quality of decentralized services also varied significantly across localities. They discovered that the incentive structures of local institutions were not necessarily aligned with pressures to improve performance. Indeed, research indicated that elected municipal authorities were not necessarily motivated to perform any better than their central counterparts in prior periods.[26] Moreover, local corruption could be as invidious and difficult to root out as central corruption. The expectation that privatization and contracting out of local public services would automatically result in great improvements was also dashed; such experiences were often fraught with conflict, performance problems, and corruption.[27] In addition, in the wake of decentralization, citizens, parties, legislatures, and politicians had to sort out many ambiguities in the power relationships and administrative responsibilities among national, state, and local governments.[28] Debates about redefined relationships slowed the impact of change and often left citizens, politicians, and administrators frustrated.

Yet, while expectations about decentralization's benefits for developing countries were modified during a quarter century of experience, the promise of improved governance and democracy was certainly not abandoned. The structural changes introduced through decentralization remained largely in place in the mid-2000s—and they were significant. Power was shared much more widely among levels of government than in the past. Many more officials were elected at state and local levels than was true in prior periods. Political parties were paying more attention to competing in local elections and aspiring politicians saw advantages in beginning or promoting their careers by running for local office. Governors and mayors—and the associations that represented them—became a force that presidents, ministers, and national legislators could ignore only at their peril.[29] They, as well as local and regional legislators and administrators, became more important as front-line representatives of the state when citizens interacted with the political system. Citizens seemed gradually to be developing greater trust in their local governments.[30] While decentralization could be reversed, as it had been in the past history of a number of countries, decentralization and the power and responsibilities that it distributed to local governments were vital economic, political, and administrative realities in the early twenty-first century.[31] These realities had very diverse consequences for local governments.

Explaining Diverse Outcomes: Four Propositions

I use the concept of decentralization throughout this book to refer to the formal and informal mechanisms and rules that allocate authority and resources downward among different levels of government.[32] I am most interested in local (as opposed to regional, provincial, or state) level governments and how they have responded to new responsibilities and expectations. The research reported here confirms that decentralization is a process that unfolds over time; more important, it is neither a linear process nor one that necessarily results in similar outcomes. Decentralization can mean progress toward improved governance and democracy as well as the erosion of local conditions of well-being. My primary goal is to account for these diverse outcomes through the exploration of different causal explanations.

At least four hypotheses have been advanced to explain why local governments might respond differently to new opportunities. These hypotheses center on political competition, public sector entrepreneurship, administrative modernization, and civil society. Each provides a distinct explanation of the factors that encourage and discourage better governance practices in developing country contexts. Because decentralization is a process that proceeds at different paces in different countries, among different policy sectors, and across local governments with distinct histories and competencies, this study sheds light on the conditions under which some hypotheses provide more robust explanations than others.

Political competition. The dynamics of party competition and elections are at the core of one approach to explaining variations in the performance of local government. In this view, democratization and greater competition among political parties to win local mayoral and council elections increase the pressure on incumbents to perform effectively while in office. According to this perspective, where local elections are competitive and opposition parties have real opportunities to win positions of authority, incumbents will be motivated to prove their competence in the management of public affairs and will seek to find new ways of addressing important problems. In the case of Mexico, the site of the research for this book, Rodríguez and Ward have been important proponents of this view.[33]

If partisan political pressures are important in accounting for better governance, it is reasonable to expect that politicians in less competitive environments will rely on traditional methods of mobilizing support—clientelism, accommodation to elite interests, and "jobs for the boys," for example—rather than seeking to improve the way local government works. And, if partisan-political pressures are an important source of performance gains, then we might expect electoral contests to feature promises for improved governance, political discourse to link the quality of governance to particular parties, and to observe some instability in policies and practices when the partisan identity of incumbents changes. We would expect to see considerably less improvement occurring in localities that are less politically competitive.

State entrepreneurship. Another way to explain variations across localities in responding to new mandates and relationships focuses on the activities of agents in public positions of authority who develop ideas, mobilize coalitions, and make strategic choices about how to advance new organizational or policy agendas, regardless of political opposition, public apathy, or capacity constraints. In this view, the state, in the guise of reform leaders and their teams, identifies particular problems and promotes policy, programmatic, or organizational solutions to them, even in the absence of party support or future electoral opportunities and incentives. Ideas, leadership skills, and the strategic choices made to promote a reform agenda and acquire resources play a central role in such an approach.[34]

Public officials and their strategic behavior thus explain what issues are taken up and the political dynamics of promoting them, from agenda setting through decision making to implementation.[35] In this hypothesis, what is adopted as a public initiative would be the result of the behavior and concerns of public officials, the outcome of the motivations of specific individuals, and the extent to which those who are reform-minded select appropriate strategies to move ahead with their ideas. Similarly, it could be anticipated that there would be instability in the focus of change initiatives as those in positions of public leadership come and go, regardless of their partisan identity.[36]

Public sector modernization. Alternatively, variations across local governments might emerge when new incentives for public officials are introduced and when organizations are restructured, governments downsized, services privatized or contracted out, and training and technology introduced to build local public sector capacity. This is, for example, the expectation of the innovations characterized by the New Public Management that has swept countries from New Zealand to Brazil.[37] In this perspective, performance can be expected to reflect inputs for capacity building, organizational reengineering, and restructuring how public services are delivered, regardless of electoral calendars and the partisan identities of incumbents. Where such inputs are missing, we can expect to see poorer performance.

Implicit belief in this public sector modernization model often stimulates international development agencies and central and provincial governments to invest heavily in technical assistance, capacity building, new technologies, and training for local governments.[38] To the extent that such investments are critical for more effective government, a relatively planned, phased, and cumulative process of improvements could be anticipated, mirroring inputs in technology, organizational changes, and training over time. Local governments that are less affected by these interventions could be expected to perform consistently less well. By extension, larger and better off municipalities might be expected to perform better than smaller and poorer ones, on the assumption that they would have more access to technology, well-qualified public officials, training opportunities, and other such inputs.

Civil society activism. A fourth possible way to explain variations in the performance of local government is the extent to which local citizens are mobilized to participate and demand accountability. Thus, according to this perspective, social groups in the local community exert pressure on the public sector to provide better services or more opportunities for participating in policy processes. These groups not only demand good performance, they can also provide models of how improvements can be made, participate in decision making and implementation activities, and take an active role in monitoring the performance of elected and administrative officials—and sanctioning and rewarding them at election time. Through extension of this argument, localities without active civil societies are less likely to take on difficult tasks of providing better services, innovating in their activities, or being responsive to local needs.

Robert Putnam (1993) and others have demonstrated that local government performance is a function of the type and depth of social capital in the community and the extent to which it is mobilized around the idea of good governance.[39] In Mexico, Jonathan Fox and Josefina Aranda (1996) have argued that civil society engagement in local development projects contributes to the positive impact of those initiatives.[40] The assumptions in the model are particularly popular with development practitioners in the NGO (nongovernmental organization) community and with community activists. If such a view reflects the reality of local political dynamics, good governance would be sustained over time due to community pressure and support, and changes would be particularly responsive to the priorities of organized groups in the local community. In communities in which there is little organized pressure, demand making, or efforts to ensure accountability of local officials, we would expect to find much less competent and responsive local governments.

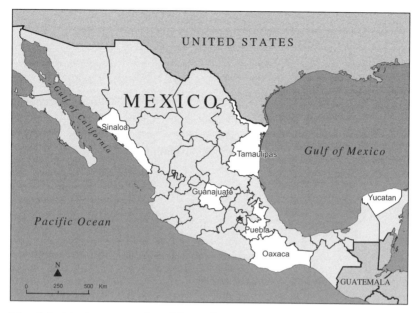

Map 1.1. Mexican states selected for study. Star indicates the capital, Mexico City.

Learning about local realities. These four hypotheses constitute an intellectual agenda for assessing the consequences of decentralization for local governments. *Going Local* traces that experience as it was being lived by a random sample of medium-sized municipalities in Mexico. Most prior studies of local government have been carried out in large cities—national and regional capitals, for example—and have often been limited to research on one site or one state or province.[41] In such contexts, it is more likely that researchers will find a significant number of relatively well-educated voters; local media that provide information on government and incumbent performance, party platforms, and candidate promises; sufficient resources to allow incumbents to follow up on at least some electoral promises; and greater administrative capacity in city hall to be responsive. While such studies are often informative, it is difficult to judge their generalizability. My study is based on a sample of smaller municipalities and comparative analysis across a range of states.

Holding the nature of national decentralization policies constant through a focus on one country, my research makes room for possible regional differences with a random sample of six states, one from each region of Mexico (see map 1.1).[42] In each state, five medium-sized municipalities (25,000 to 100,000 inhabitants) were selected randomly for study, for a total of thirty municipalities in the sample (see table 1.1 and maps 1.2 and 1.3).[43] In 2000, municipalities of this size included 23.6 percent

TABLE 1.1
States and Municipalities Selected for Study

State	Region of Mexico	Municipality	Population (2000)	Area (km²)
Guanajuato	West Central	Abasolo	79,093	534.9
		Manuel Doblado	38,309	801.1
		San Luis de la Paz	96,729	1,816.8
		Santa Cruz de Juventino Rosas	65,479	394.4
		Yuriria	73,820	788.8
Oaxaca	South	Acatlán de Pérez Figueroa	44,579	933.9
		San Juan Guichicovi	27,399	563.9
		Santiago Juxtlahuaca	28,188	583.1
		Santiago Pinotepa Nacional	44,193	719.6
		Santo Domingo Tehuantepec	53,229	965.8
Puebla	East Central	Chignahuapan	49,266	591.9
		Coronango	27,575	37.0
		Ixtacamaxtitlán	28,358	614.9
		Libres	25,719	304.9
		San Pedro Cholula	99,794	51.0
Sinaloa	West	Escuinapa	50,438	1,633.2
		Mocorito	50,082	2,405.5
		Rosario	47,934	2,723.3
		Salvador Alvarado	73,303	1,197.5
		San Ignacio	26,762	4,651.0
Tamaulipas	North	Aldama	27,997	3,655.7
		González	41,455	3,399.1
		Miguel Alemán	25,704	649.4
		San Fernando	57,412	6,096.4
		Tula	27,049	2,660.6
Yucatán	Gulf	Oxkutzcab	25,483	512.2
		Progreso	48,797	270.8
		Ticul	32,776	355.1
		Umán	49,145	434.3
		Valladolid	56,776	867.8

Source: INAFED, Dirección del Sistema Nacional de Información Municipal.

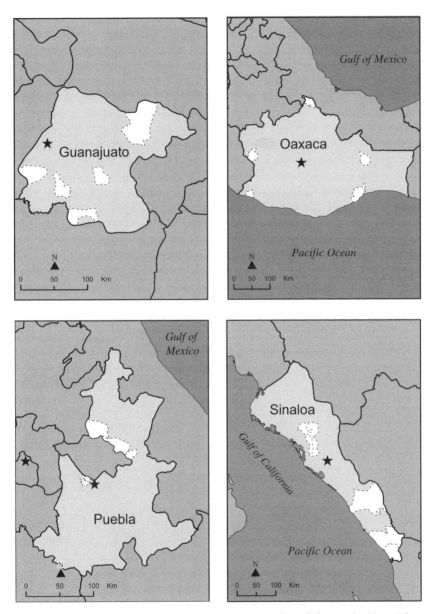

Map 1.2. Top left: Municipalities in Guanajuato selected for study. Top right: Municipalities in Oaxaca selected for study. Bottom left: Municipalities in Puebla selected for study. Bottom right: Municipalities in Sinaloa selected for study. Stars indicate state capitals.

Map 1.3. Left: Municipalities in Tamaulipas selected for study. Right: Municipalities in Yucatán selected for study. Stars indicate state capitals.

of all local governments in Mexico and 25.3 percent of its population; their average population was 46,516 and they ranged in territory from quite small to very large.[44] Despite the search for differences, these municipalities were large enough to have substantial responsibilities and significant resources for attending to them, yet small enough to facilitate understanding complex political, administrative, and fiscal interactions.

A research team collected data in Mexico during the summer and fall of 2004. Researchers interviewed past and present local officials in the thirty municipalities; delved into relevant documents about local fiscal conditions; explored the dynamics of changes in administrative, service, development, and participatory activities of local government; assessed the electoral history of each; generated insights into the relationship of local governments to state and federal ones; and came to know well the localities they were studying. The research team met for an initial training workshop, followed a similar research protocol, received regular feedback, including a site visit, and met for two additional workshops to discuss findings and explore their meaning.

Simultaneously, I carried out research at the national level, among those agencies of government most concerned with the process and mechanics of decentralization, and among academic experts, exploring the role of states, and state governors, in this process. I also interviewed officials in the organizations that represent municipalities and mayors in their interactions with the national government, and reviewed the activities they carry out on behalf of local government. Collectively, we interviewed 569 individuals, including 51 current and former mayors, 113 councilors, 229 local public managers, 98 community leaders and important citizens, 26 local party officials, 48 state and federal level officials, as well as a number of academic experts.

Using the information gathered in the field—and to the extent possible verified with information from survey data—I constructed an index of municipal performance to represent differences among the local governments. National demographic, electoral, and fiscal data on the municipalities also form part of the analysis. In the following chapters, these data are used to explore the four hypotheses and to construct a story of what was happening at local levels in the wake of decentralization.

What was the story that emerged from this study? Very briefly, I discovered that the four distinct hypotheses were actually interrelated and that municipalities that varied significantly in terms of their governance performance were experiencing a series of similar pressures for change:

- Political competition was increasingly important to local politics in all municipalities, even in those that continued to be controlled by Mexico's long-dominant party; greater electoral competitiveness was largely a response to the new opportunities and resources for local government under decentralization and was generally divorced from the ideological or programmatic commitments of political parties. Clientelistic practices did not wither away, but continued to be currency for campaigns and influencing the allocation of public resources. Electoral competition significantly increased the circulation of political elites, but was only indirectly related to the performance of local government. This was largely a result of the increased difficulty of governing in more contentious environments.

- The quality of local governance depended to a significant degree on the entrepreneurial activities of elected and appointed municipal leaders, those brought to public office through newly competitive elections. Among their major responsibilities were acquiring resources from other levels of government and introducing change in the management of local affairs. In fact, these individuals were often able to introduce significant changes in local governance relatively quickly, largely because of the weakness of institutions that could have resisted or slowed the pace of reform. In addition, the politics of getting things done continued to replicate patterns from the more centralized past—personally defined agendas, reliance on other levels of government, and the ability to use personal networks of influence. At the same time, the proscription of immediate reelection significantly limited the durability of change.

- Public sector modernization was widespread, even among relatively un-ambitious governments. Introducing the accoutrements of modern government was primarily a tool of entrepreneurial leadership, however, rather than an independent source of change. Improvements were often rapidly implemented but weakly institutionalized; they changed frequently as administrations changed.
- Citizen engagement was an important factor in extracting resources from local governments; it was much less important in holding public officials responsible for their actions. Interestingly, new accountability mechanisms tended to be introduced from above by government. In the absence of immediate reelection, citizens were denied an important mechanism for bottom-up accountability.
- Innovations in local governance were widespread and public officials took the lead in introducing these improvements; yet their successful introduction was often marred by the failure to sustain them beyond the three-year tenure of political administrations.

These brief points ignore much of the complexity of fiscal, political, and administrative change occurring in the municipalities studied. Subsequent chapters attempt to tell their stories—and to generalize from them—with due regard for the richness of local experience.

The Book in Brief

Mexico was a reluctant decentralizer—the process of sharing power downward in the political system between 1980 and 2005 was protracted and halting. This process coincided with the transition to more open and democratic government in the country, a process that was itself protracted and halting. National administrations shifted emphases back and forth between commitment to decentralize and efforts to recentralize power in the national executive and were reluctant to threaten the capacity of the Partido Revolucionario Institucional (PRI) to continue to win elections. Nevertheless, by the mid-2000s, state and municipal governments in Mexico clearly had more authority and resources to deal with regional and local issues than at any time in the country's history; likewise, citizens enjoyed much more democratic elections and more opportunities to participate in public decision making than had been true in the recent or distant past.

Chapter 2 explores the history of decentralization initiatives in Mexico, describes the relationships among different levels of government at the time of the study, and sets the context for understanding decentralization as it was experienced at the local level. It indicates that federal policy makers' caution about the fiscal and administrative behavior of local governments led to considerable state and national oversight of what local governments were doing, even while responsibilities and resources flowed downward. At the same time, the chapter shows that democratization—in the guise of alternation among parties in power—was initiated at the municipal level, found traction at the state level, and only then was able to gain a foothold in national presidential elections.

This same chapter introduces the thirty municipalities selected for study. These localities shared many characteristics of other medium-sized municipalities in Mexico, and their political histories replicate in important ways the gradual process of democratization experienced by the country. They received much increased fiscal resources from federal sources, witnessed increased political competition, and differed significantly in terms of their performance. As part of this chapter, I introduce and explain the index of municipal performance that is used throughout the book to explore the four hypotheses. The purpose of the chapter is to set the background and provide comparative data to be used in subsequent chapters.

Chapter 3 explores the first hypothesis—that increased political competition can explain differences across municipalities in Mexico. Increased electoral competition was noteworthy in the research sites and highlighted the extent to which gaining control over public office at the local level became newly important in Mexican politics after 1990. The competition for power encouraged the introduction of new parties at the local level, more open forms of candidate selection within parties, and increased interest in local elections. Yet campaigns continued to feature retail promises to groups and individuals and were not characterized by major doctrinal differences among parties, even though the extent of turnover in office increased.

Even where the PRI continued to hold office, local politicians worried about its future as other parties made important inroads in local electoral contests. These contests were important for introducing more opportunities for the circulation of political elites; decentralization clearly brought more options to local voters; and local councils were increasingly pluralist in party representation. At the same time, it was difficult to find systematic differences in the performance of municipalities based on the degree of competition or the identity of the party in power. Increasingly, politicians were aware of the potential threat of election losses, regardless of the political history of the municipality, nor did the penchant for governance reform characterize one party significantly more than another.

If elections increasingly opened up opportunities for the circulation of political elites, to what extent, I ask in chapter 4, could the variable performance of local governments be credited to the activities of entrepreneurial politicians at the local level? They counted for a great deal, as it turns out. In the thirty municipalities studied, mayors and their allies in local government had considerable capacity to set local policy and programmatic agendas, to select officials for local positions of authority, to influence the allocation of local resources, and to structure the administration of public affairs. They had, as a consequence, significant room to maneuver in introducing changes in local government. Their jobs were not easy, however. In order to be effective, municipal leaders had to acquire additional resources, organize and oversee the daily activities of the municipality, and respond effectively to the micro-level concerns of constituents. They had to make trade-offs about priorities and how to focus their time and resources. In particular, mayors differed significantly in their commitments and in their capacity to undertake the complex tasks of leadership.

Almost universally, mayors and other public officials had to find funds for local investments from other levels of government. Across the research sites, municipal leaders relied on traditional forms of political interaction to acquire these resources for their communities. Clientelism, party connections, and personal relationships show the importance of traditional political relationships in accounting for the effectiveness of local leadership and its capacity to make a difference in the performance of local government. To do a good job, local officials had to spend a great deal of time out of their offices, seeking support at state and national levels. Their success was often transitory, however, as the weak local institutions that contributed to their extensive scope for action at the same time exposed their reforms to the short lives of each administration. Political traditions die hard, this chapter suggests, even in contexts in which the structure of authority has moved from authoritarian to democratic.

In the subsequent chapter, the impact of information technology, training, organizational reengineering, and other capacity-building inputs is explored. To what extent did it make a change in the way the public's business was carried out in thirty municipalities in Mexico? Evidence of the introduction of new capacity-building tools and organizational changes was widespread. Almost everywhere, computers managed information and provided officials with new administrative tools; training courses were ubiquitous; more educated people were appointed to public office; and reorganization was a common exercise when new administrations came to office. Many officials spoke of the need to improve the efficiency of local government, and some were conversant with the principles of the New Public Management.

At times, the introduction of new technologies and more effective management practices was mandated by state and federal governments; in some states, for example, municipalities were told to develop Web sites, to make information available to their constituents, and to adopt certain accounting practices. Most commonly, however, improvements in local governance were a result of the choices of local officials, some of whom were particularly concerned about increased efficiency and effectiveness and some of whom chose to ignore even mandates from above. Thus, it was most often the case that public sector modernization was a tool employed by local public leaders as a way to achieve particular goals; it was not an independent force for local change. And, as with the actions of local leaders more generally, some of the changes in the way local public business was done did not outlive the administrations of those who introduced them.

As countries decentralize and democratize, the extent to which citizens participate in local government should expand and their capacity to elicit response and accountability from government should increase. Chapter 6 indicates that citizen engagement in local decisions about resource allocation was considerable in the thirty municipalities. As individuals and as groups, citizens pressed local governments for response to their needs. They had effective strategies for organizing for collective action and for gaining the attention of public officials and access to public resources. Thus, local politics was characterized by considerable demand making by community groups throughout Mexico.

In the research sites, it was much more common to find local groups extracting resources from government than it was to find that they were holding government officials or departments accountable for the quality of the services they were receiving. Where mechanisms for accountability existed, it was likely that they had been introduced by government, and not as a result of pressure from the governed. The expansion of spaces for citizen participation, so much vaunted as part of democratization, was not fully developed in Mexico at the time of the research. Citizens were much better at extracting benefits than they were in demanding democratic accountability. The activism of civil society is important, particularly for the institutionalization of more responsive and effective government, but did not seem to be driving significant differences among the municipalities studied. Indeed, the impact of increased political competition and the interest of public officials in reform provided more robust explanations of differences among municipalities.

In chapter 7, the issue of innovation in local governance is addressed to assess conditions under which positive change is possible. All but two of the municipalities in the sample were able to introduce new policies, processes, programs, or projects that had not been in effect in prior periods. Innovation, then, was not unusual in the medium-sized municipalities in the study and it occurred in administration, municipal services, and programs for economic, social, and environmental development. Some of the changes were quite pedestrian, while others were much more sophisticated. The agents of innovation were overwhelmingly public officials and most of the reforms they undertook were chosen relatively autonomously. These observations confirm the importance of the agency of public officials in local governance and of the relative quiescence of civil society in demanding better local government.

In addition, the generally weak institutional context of local government meant that innovations were subject to considerable change in response to the three-year calendar of local elections. Those that were more likely to be sustained across administrations were those that showed clear benefits in the short term, involved bricks and mortar, were difficult to change once they had been implemented, or were financially self-sustaining. More vulnerable innovations were those that were closely identified with particular administrations, relied on the commitment of particular officials, or were very dependent on outside resources. Innovation was frequent in Mexico's municipalities; its sustainability, however, was often fragile.

This book seeks to analyze and explain how local governments and local public officials were coping with new responsibilities and resources in the wake of decentralizing policies. The answer? They were coping variously. Decentralization in Mexico was a dynamic process, suffering setbacks as well as advances, introducing opportunities for lapses as well as improvements in performance, and calling attention to the diversity of local response to new responsibilities and resources. The dynamic of change was structured by pressures from above and below, as well as from inside town hall, and was affected significantly by changes in the opportunity structure for local political parties and politicians. Importantly, and as the final chapter argues, this dynamic suggests that the four hypotheses do not stand in isolation from each other but are in fact closely interconnected. Public sector entrepreneurship emerged as a critically important factor in explaining what local governments were doing and how well they were doing it, but this in turn was made possible by the expansion of opportunities for competitive elections in a more democratic context and was pursued through a considerable amount of capacity building and citizen demand making.

The results of this study hold important lessons for the comparative politics of decentralization and democratization. Mexico's political system and policies for decentralization, of course, are unique. Nevertheless, the interconnections among increases in competitiveness, elite circulation, capacity building, and citizen participation are likely to be replicated in other settings. Similarly, while local governments are subject to considerable change in their dynamics in the wake of decentralization, the way they carry out business is also embedded in political legacies of the past, and in this, too, the Mexican case is instructive. Local governments everywhere need additional help to avoid dependence, to encourage accountability, and to increase the extent to which they can promote economic development. They are likely to adapt to new challenges and support in different ways, but at times to do so in ways that can strengthen the promise of better and more democratic governance for local communities.

Photo by Xóchitl León.

Chapter 2

DECENTRALIZING MEXICO
A Cautious Journey

MEXICO DID NOT EMBRACE decentralization easily or quickly. Indeed, the country's history during most of the twentieth century was a story of repeated and usually successful efforts to centralize power and resources in the national state, in the presidency, and in a single political party, the PRI (Partido Revolucionario Institucional). By the early 1970s, the federal system was described as one in which "each successive level of government is weaker, more dependent, and more impoverished than the level above."[1] A frequent joke at that time was that the political life expectancy of a governor who displeased central authority—the president—was approximately forty-five minutes; and it was only this long because of the deplorable state of the country's telephone system.[2]

In local parlance, until late in the twentieth century, governors—invariably elected from the PRI—were often referred to as viceroys of the president; elected municipal governments were treated as their fiefdoms. It was frequently acknowledged that governors and senators "belonged" to the president, while mayors and state-level legislators "belonged" to the governors. Indeed, until the mid-1990s, the Mexican political system was considered one of the most centralized in the world, called by some "a perfect dictatorship."[3] It was a civil authoritarian system with regular elections, peaceful handovers of power, and great capacity for conflict resolution without public display of dissent. As such, and despite its inequalities and injustices, it was the envy of politicians in many less stable developing countries. Central to its stability was a no-reelection standard applied to all elected officials, a standard that encouraged mobility for the politically ambitious.[4]

Yet, beginning in the early 1980s, the national government undertook a series of cautious steps toward greater autonomy for state and local governments, shifted significant resources toward them, and put in place a range of programs and policies for strengthening subnational governments. In these decentralization initiatives, governors were more often the beneficiaries of change than mayors. But by 2005, local governments had come to represent a surprising locus for fiscal, political, and administrative decision making. Equally important, Mexico's transition to a more democratic system was initiated and sustained in important ways when opposition parties won local and state level elections. State and local elections for governors, state legislators, mayors, and municipal councilors showed a dramatic shift toward greater pluralism. Through such political advances, in 2000, an opposition party replaced the PRI at the national level, after seventy-one years of uninterrupted rule.

This chapter traces Mexico's journey toward decentralization and greater autonomy for subnational governments, with particular concern for ways in which national policies affected the power and resources of municipal governments. While municipalities were never entirely irrelevant to the country's governance, reforms over a period of twenty-five years greatly expanded their importance for the daily lives of millions and for the future of the Mexican political system. As with all countries, decentralization initiatives in Mexico are embedded in a particular history, and it is this context that is described in the first part of this chapter.

The chapter also lays out the basic structure of municipal government as it existed in the mid-2000s and considers complex fiscal relationships among different levels of government. As will be seen, while local governments received more resources and were given greater responsibilities, the hands of federal and state governments were constraining ones, particularly in fiscal affairs. In addition to changes in these relationships, the chapter shows how political liberalization assisted the process of decentralization. Finally, I present basic information on the thirty municipalities that were part of this study and introduce the index of government performance that is used in later chapters.

THE LONG ROAD TO MUNICIPAL IMPORTANCE

Mexico's local governments are enshrined in Article 115 of the Constitution of 1917 as "free municipalities." This concept of local government does not capture much historical reality, however. Like most other Latin American countries in the nineteenth century, Mexico experienced its share of revolts and rebellions over the extent to which the country would be federalist or unitary.[5] As far back as the constitutional convention of 1856–1857, efforts were made to ensure that municipal rights were recognized. Yet none of these events and conflicts eroded what had been, even before the Conquest, a region of strongly hierarchical power.[6] The Aztec empire ruled from the center and exacted tribute from a wide range of subject tribal states. In a subtle prefiguring of twentieth-century Mexican politics, Aztec rulers began appointing officials to posts that previously had been filled through elections; power grew increasingly absolute before the arrival of the Spaniards.

The *conquistadores* followed suit with a model of centralized government crafted in Spain. Localities were to serve the center, as Spain moved indigenous groups into towns to ensure that they would be instructed in religion and pay tribute to the Crown. The earliest local government, established by Hernando Cortés in Veracruz in 1519, developed a framework for municipal governance that survived the colonial era, almost a century of internecine conflict, and a major social revolution. This model created a local council known as the *cabildo*, with councilors known as *regidores*.[7] These bodies were given responsibilities for tasks such as maintaining order and security, street cleaning and drainage, and overseeing water and food supplies and proper land usage. District agents of the Crown circulated to ensure that tributes were collected and that the local councils did not get out of line, but the practicality of governing the vast province of New Spain left some room for local solutions to problems of control and taxation. Indeed, the seventeenth and eighteenth centuries were punctuated by repeated efforts to centralize control over the province.

In the aftermath of the Wars of Independence (1810–1821), a federalist system was established by the Constitution of 1824, even while religious and military leaders and wealthy landowners opposed this formulation. Debates and revolts were smattered across the nineteenth century between federalists and centralists, presidentialists and legislative supremacists, liberals and conservatives. In efforts to bring order out of considerable conflict, President Porfirio Díaz (1877–1911) resolved the issue and prefigured the future—centralization and presidentialism were institutionalized during his long dictatorship, while the fiction of federalism was maintained.[8]

Yet the tensions between central rule and local autonomy continued to play a role in Mexican history. In the Revolution of 1910, the issue of the free municipality helped galvanize participation in the conflict and resulted in a series of initiatives to inscribe its status into law.[9] Early on, the Plan de Ayala, crafted by revolutionaries from the state of Morelos in 1911, declared the political, economic, and administrative autonomy of local governments. In 1914, the Plan de Puebla put forth the idea of the free municipality as a constitutional principle. And, with the promulgation of the new constitution in 1917, the free municipality was designated to be the basis of the political organization of the country and of the public administration of its states. Municipalities were to have control over taxation powers at the local level and rights of legal recognition.

Despite the declaration, power in the succeeding years lay largely with regional warlords, and then, with the gradual establishment of order in the country, centralizing initiatives were clearly in the ascendance. In 1921, for example, the Ministry of Education, under the leadership of

José Vasconcelos, began a process of nationalizing the education system, which had been the responsibility of the municipalities, as a way of promoting the revolutionary goals of free and secular education. In the estimation of Vasconcelos and other supporters of the Revolution, the municipalities were not doing enough to promote education of the people, particularly those who lived in rural municipalities. The centralization of control over the military was likewise an important foundation of the post-revolutionary political system.

With the establishment of the precursor to the PRI in 1929, centralization of power in the hands of the president became more evident. Under Lázaro Cárdenas (1934–1940), national corporatist organizations to represent major constituencies of the Revolution—workers, peasants, "popular sectors," the military—were created and became the most important pillars of a political party and regime centered in Mexico City.[10] Successive laws and constitutional changes continued to acknowledge the free municipality and a federalist system while consistently undermining the responsibilities and resources of lower levels of government. Over the course of the twentieth century, the national government assumed control even for such local concerns as road maintenance, sewerage, and water provision.[11] Presidents increasingly sat at the apex of a party and governmental system based on the control of resources and patronage.

Fiscal policies were an important instrument in the centralization of an increasingly authoritarian government. A major initiative came in 1947, when the federal government imposed a national sales tax and claimed exclusive rights to an income tax. States, which had fewer taxing powers than municipalities, could impose a sales tax only if it was agreed by and coordinated with the central government. In exchange for these transfers of authority, officials at the state level were given important opportunities to advance their careers within the PRI.[12]

Over the years, municipalities became ever more dependent and the local capacity to fund government became small indeed. According to George Foster's classic account of life in Tzintzuntzan, in the state of Michoacán in the early 1960s, for example, municipal revenues came from "fees for registering land and house titles, for selling livestock, for registering livestock brands, for animal-slaughtering licenses, for marriage acts, and for permits to operate retail establishments."[13] In Tzintzuntzan, this amounted to about $22,000 annually, all but $6,000 of which was used to pay for salaries of public officials. The reach of remaining funds was not great. Foster noted that "other than street lighting *no real community services are provided.*"[14]

Beginning with the policy changes of the 1940s, revenue sharing became the principal mode of financing state and local governments. In 1979, when the sales tax was abolished and replaced with the federally managed value-added tax and states lost the right to impose excise taxes, federal revenue-sharing agreements and transfers to state and local government were specified more clearly.[15] In the context of an oil boom and expansive economic growth, states began receiving larger transfers from the federal government; the strong presidentialist system meant that national executive decisions would largely determine who got what. At the same time, the states were required to distribute to the municipalities at least 20 percent of funds received from federal revenue sharing. The state governments could, however, establish the criteria through which this would be done and, like the political hierarchy of the central/state government relationship, determine who got what at the municipal level. Moreover, compliance with this regulation was often spotty.

This hierarchical and dependent set of relationships began to shift in 1983. In that year, and through the initiative of President Miguel de la Madrid (1982–1988), Article 115 of the constitution was amended to give municipalities greater budgeting and spending autonomy; in particular, they were given control over property taxes—collection and use—which had previously been collected and retained by the states.[16] Local councils were given official responsibilities for basic municipal services including water, sewage, street cleaning and public lighting, garbage, urban transport, public markets, roads and highways, public security, parks, and slaughterhouses.[17] They became responsible for zoning and the creation of ecological zones, and were given greater regulatory power. In addition, municipal councils were instructed to prepare budgets that would be submitted to state legislatures for approval. The amendment also clarified the relationship between employees of municipalities and the council. And, in an important political change, the composition of the elected councils would henceforth be determined by proportional representation.

Beyond the amendment, de la Madrid also declared that national ministries needed to deconcentrate their activities to more local levels.[18] A presidential decree established a national center for municipal research in the interior ministry. It was to serve as a clearinghouse for information on municipal reform; states set up similar centers. In 1987, Article 115 was "cleaned up" by deleting references to governors and state legislators; it became concerned exclusively with municipal governance. Municipal planning committees (known as COPLADEMUNs) were also created at this time.[19] Nevertheless, the changes to Article 115 left the municipalities dependent on state governments; in addition to the power to approve and amend local budget proposals, state legislatures were given the right to remove elected officials and even the entire council if they were deemed to be acting in illegal ways. Moreover, the initiative was promoted from the top down, and did not correspond to demands from lower levels of government that they be accorded greater autonomy.[20]

De la Madrid's actions were taken at a time of deep fiscal and economic crisis in the country, when the burdens of economic policy and managing a complex political system based on the liberal use of subsidies, prebends, and patronage became particularly overwhelming for the central government. Not surprisingly, the 1983 reform has been credited to the desire on the part of central government decision makers to "offload" some of these fiscal and political problems to lower levels of government.[21] Moreover, the president was sensitive to growing political opposition to the authoritarian system of the PRI; decentralization was one way to try to strengthen the flagging legitimacy of the national state.[22] That international financial institutions such as the World Bank and the Inter-American Development Bank became advocates of decentralization in the 1980s may have increased government interest in this "solution" to political, administrative, and fiscal problems. Officially, the changes to Article 115 were linked to the country's development potential. According to the president, "the centralization that in an earlier period allowed the country to accelerate its economic growth and social development has outlived its usefulness and become a serious limitation on the country's national project."[23]

Concern about the legal status and powers of the municipalities was followed by greater recognition of the need to build local governance capacity. In 1989, under the presidency of Carlos Salinas de Gortari (1988–1994), the national government created the Centro Nacional de Desarrollo Municipal. This organization, whose purpose was to strengthen local governments in their administrative capacities and their abilities to manage public services, was created in the interior secretariat (and was later reestablished as the Instituto Nacional para el Federalismo y el Desarrollo Municipal—INAFED).[24]

Also under Salinas, a national social fund program, PRONASOL, was introduced in early 1989. This program was an important way in which the president sought to reassert presidential power and increase the popularity of the regime. Its purpose was to cushion citizens from the immediate and negative impacts of neoliberal economic policies; it provided funds for local social and economic initiatives.[25] In practice, PRONASOL had a paradoxical impact on local governments.

On the one hand, the handsomely funded program was, until 1991, centralized in the president's office.[26] This emphasized the president's personal commitment to the program, but also skirted national and state bureaucracies and the traditional role of the PRI in the allocation of government resources. Thus, the program allowed the presidency to engage directly with local community groups and local governments. From this perspective, PRONASOL was a top-down instrument for local investment and development assistance, with an implicit goal of centralizing more power in the presidential office and reducing the role of the PRI in the allocation of public resources.

On the other hand, in order for local communities and governments to receive funds for projects and development efforts, they were expected to develop proposals and present them to PRONASOL officials. From this perspective, the program introduced an element of local funding entrepreneurship and citizen engagement that had long been lacking in most municipalities.[27] In 1990, PRONASOL created Municipal Solidarity Funds, which were disbursed through Solidarity Committees for projects with collective benefits. These gave many communities an introduction to project development and appraisal and to community-based decision making about project selection.

Additional off-loading of important central responsibilities was also pursued in the name of "federalization" at this time. In 1992, an accord was signed between the federal government, the governors of the country's thirty-one states, and the national teachers' union to decentralize the administration of education to the state level. In this new arrangement, state governments saw their budgets expand two-, three-, or even tenfold as they became responsible for teacher salaries and teachers became employees of the states. While the teachers' union and the federal government negotiated the agreement, the state governors, many of whom were reluctant to take on the financial and political burdens of the education system, were left on the sidelines.[28]

In many ways, then, federalization was a process that continued to reveal the centrist decision-making style of the government. While Salinas spoke consistently of the importance of decentralization and the long tradition of federalism, the activities of his administration demonstrated much greater concern about reestablishing the power of the presidency and addressing the crumbling legitimacy of the national government and the PRI.[29] During this period, for example, the president intervened repeatedly in state level political conflicts; sixteen governors were pressured to resign, were replaced, or were promoted out of office in the period between 1988 and 1994.[30]

After Carlos Salinas, President Ernesto Zedillo (1994–2000) introduced an ambitious agenda of "New Federalism," in part responding to increased pressure for more autonomy from state governors, particularly those representing opposition parties, and mayors of large cities.[31] A national consultation about municipal government in 1995 raised concerns related to local standards, finances, and participation. In 1996, a new law increased from 18.5 to 20 the percentage of total federal revenue allocated to state governments and allowed those governments to raise taxes from new sources.[32] The health sector was reformed in 1996 to give responsibilities to the states to manage primary health and nutritional services, and to control environmental health and contagious diseases. States were also given responsibility for carrying out social assistance policies.[33]

A series of reforms significantly enhanced the revenues of local governments during the Zedillo administration. Vast new resources for social development could be channeled to local government through the Fondo de Desarrollo Social Municipal (formerly Municipal Solidarity Funds), established in 1996. This fund, based on a formula using a number of poverty indicators, was a major step toward increasing the resource possibilities of local governments. Then, in 1997, a new law for fiscal coordination created "Ramo 33" (category 33) of the national budget, including in it several funds for local government. For local governments, the most important one was the Fondo de Aportaciones para la Infraestructura Social (Fund for Municipal Social Infrastructure—FAIS), managed by the social development ministry (SEDESOL), which gave the municipalities resources for creating basic social infrastructure—this latter defined quite broadly. Other funds were earmarked for basic and normal education, health, and strengthening local government, managed by a corresponding ministry.

In general, through the mechanism of Ramo 33, the federal government committed to allocating significantly more resources to local governments.[34] The transfer of funds required that they coordinate with state governments, yet also made clear that transfers of funds would not be subject to political control. In reality, local governments had considerable discretion to decide how the funds would be spent. At the municipal level, Ramo 33 became the most important source for local government resources for social infrastructure, including health and education. Further reforms to Article 115 of the constitution, put into effect in 2000, strengthened the regulatory role of local governments and gave them the right to impose property taxes on parastatal organizations and to assess property values. It also recognized the municipalities as an "order of government," not just of administration, providing them with increased policymaking autonomy.

Another important part of Zedillo's New Federalism included initiatives to strengthen local government and increase the capacity of state governments to contribute to the up-grading of municipalities. Increasingly, the federal government sought to engage states as the primary "tutors" in building municipal administrative and fiscal capacity. In fact, throughout the 1990s, Mexico's central government retained powers of supervision and state governments were empowered to determine what functions would, in fact, be transferred to the local governments.[35] Not surprisingly, there was great variation in the allocation of resources from states to local governments, and state governors continued to have the ability to reward or punish local governments and their leaders. More generally, political, administrative, and fiscal decentralization measures were introduced piecemeal and regularly suffered from a disjunction between policy-as-announced and policy as actually put in practice.[36]

President Vicente Fox (2000–2006) was also a public supporter of the drive to decentralize—within limits. A former state governor, Fox spoke often of the importance of decentralizing power in the country and giving states and localities more control over their fiscal, political, and administrative lives. He called his initiative a "Program for Authentic Federalism," and included in it goals of greater citizen participation, strengthening local government, and improving intergovernmental relations.

During the Fox administration, the treasury ministry established an important committee to oversee coordination of fiscal policy and transfers. In addition, the federal government established laws for public access to information that were also to be enshrined at the state and local levels, and promoted e-government and performance monitoring at all levels. Transfers to local government continued to increase, and the administration introduced a number of capacity-building initiatives. In 2004, the first national treasury convention brought together fiscal officials from all levels of government.

Nevertheless, worried about the potential for fiscal indiscipline, national decision-makers strongly regulated the capacity of municipalities to borrow money without the approval of central fiscal and monetary authorities. In addition, the destination and use of most of the transfers and revenue sharing continued to be determined by central fiat. Moreover, the federal government maintained control over the two most important sources of tax revenue—value added and income taxes.

This checkered history of decentralization with centralizing controls nevertheless had important consequences for local government: it put many more resources in their hands, as is evident from data on fiscal transfers. Figure 2.1 shows the increase in funds provided to local governments from all federal sources between 1990 and 2002. In constant pesos of 1993, municipalities received extremely little funding before 1994; by 2002, they were receiving almost 2 percent of GDP (see table 2.1). In per capita terms, there was an increase from 0.14 pesos per person in 1990 to 311.58 pesos in 2002. The sources of local funding from federal coffers fell into several categories, the most important of which were *aportaciones* (grants) and *participaciones* (revenue sharing) (see table 2.2).

Not only did municipalities receive consistently more resources beginning in the late twentieth century; they were also beneficiaries of a process of political liberalization in the country. In the 1980s, opposition parties

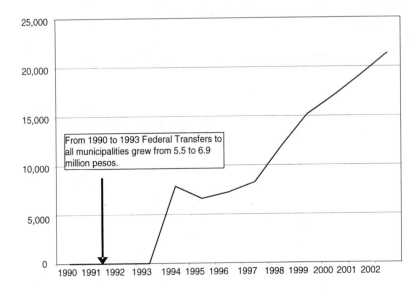

Figure 2.1. Federal transfers to all municipal governments (millions of 1993 pesos). Source: INEGI, Sistema Municipal de Base de Datos, http://www.inegi .gob.mx/prod_serv/contenidos/espanol/simbad/default.asp?c=73.

first began to demonstrate some capacity to contest the hold of the PRI over election results at the local level, in part because of a series of important electoral reforms and in part because of increased mobilization of civil society, particularly in large cities.

In 1973, in one of the first actions of political opening, more political parties were allowed to contest elections. In 1977, another law loosened registration procedures for political parties and opened up at least 25 percent of seats in the national Chamber of Deputies (lower house of congress) to opposition parties.[37] In 1979, a reform increased the representation of opposition parties in state legislatures and local governments. In addition, proportional representation in elections for municipal councils was introduced for local governments with over thirty thousand inhabitants, and then extended to all municipalities in 1983. Three years later, yet another reform limited the majority party to 70 percent of the seats in the national Chamber of Deputies and expanded the number of seats in that body and in the Senate, and divided representation between plurality and proportional representation seats.[38]

Also in the 1980s, a series of events increased the extent to which Mexican citizens became active in local affairs, especially in Mexico City and

TABLE 2.1
Total Funding of Municipal Governments, 1990–2002
(1993 pesos)

Year	Total	As % of GDP	Per Capita (pesos)
1990	11,493,530	0.00	0.14
1991	12,844,330	0.00	0.15
1992	13,957,728	0.00	0.16
1993	15,670,364	0.00	0.18
1994	16,627,876,932	1.27	185.69
1995	13,467,271,150	1.10	147.76
1996	13,593,322,125	1.05	146.84
1997	14,834,650,367	1.08	157.94
1998	19,041,518,428	1.31	199.91
1999	22,914,372,452	1.53	237.25
2000	24,847,462,509	1.55	253.63
2001	27,730,706,387	1.73	279.05
2002	31,412,724,549	1.98	311.58

Source: INEGI, Sistema Municipal de Base de Datos
http://www.inegi.gob.mx/prod_serv/contenidos/espanol/simbad/
default.asp?c=73, and Banco de Mexico, http://www.banxico.org.mx/
eInfoFinaciera/FSinfoFinanciera.html.

other large urban areas. In 1985, a serious earthquake hit Mexico City, and in the chaos that ensued, local communities and citizen groups found they were more capable of organizing and responding to the crisis than were city and federal governments. Concern over quality of life issues, such as pollution and public safety, also helped galvanize urban dwellers in protest against a government whose capacity for corruption and political control had alienated many, particularly among the middle class. This period, in fact, was an important one in terms of the deeper organization of Mexican civil society and its engagement in a variety of social movements.[39]

As a consequence of legal reforms and increased citizen activism, political pluralism in Mexico emerged at the local level, where parties other than the PRI began winning elections in the early 1980s. This was followed by increased capacity for opposition parties, primarily the Partido Acción Nacional (PAN), to win elections at the state level. In 1983, candidates for mayor representing the PAN won elections in several important cities, and in 1989, the first opposition governor in Mexico was elected to office in Baja California. Then, the national congress began to take on a more pluralistic character and in 1997, the PRI lost its majority

TABLE 2.2
Major Sources of Federal Funding for Municipal Governments

Source	Definition	Year Introduced
Aportaciones (Ramo 33) (Grants)	Transfers for education, health, infrastructure, social, and public security policies.	
Fondo de Aportaciones para la Educación Básica y Normal (FAEB)	Transfers to states for new fiscal obligations of a decentralized educational system.[b]	1993[a] 1998
Fondo de Aportaciones para los Servicios de Salud (FASS)	Transfers to states for health-related expenditures.[b]	1996[a] 1998
Fondo de Aportaciones para la Infraestructura Social (FAIS)	Transfers to states and municipalities (usually through the states) for public works and social infrastructure.[c]	1996[a] 1998
Fondo de Aportaciones para el Fortalecimiento de los Municipios y de las Demarcaciones Territoriales del Distrito Federal (FORTAMUNDF)	Transfers to municipalities (through the states) for general expenditure, depending on the number of inhabitants.	1999
Fondo de Aportaciones Múltiples (FAM)	Transfers to states to complement other funds, especially FAEB.[b]	1997[a] 1998
Fondo de Aportaciones para la Educación Tecnológica y de Adultos (FAETA)	Transfers to states for adult and technical education.[b]	1998 1999
Fondo de Aportaciones para la Seguridad Pública de los Estados y del Distrito Federal (FASP)	Transfers to states for public security programs.[b]	1996[a] 1999
Participaciones (Ramo 28) (Revenue Sharing)	Tax income corresponding to each municipality to fund basic expenses, such as payroll, electricity, fuel, etc.	

Source: Guizar Jiménez, José de Jesús, *Evolución de aportaciones federales a entidades federativas y municipios*; and *Programa para un nuevo federalismo 1995–2000, Balance Sexenal*, México D.F., Poder Ejecutivo Federal, 2000; Estados Unidos Mexicanos, Ley de Coordinación Fiscal, 2002.

[a] Dates refer to a previous program with a different name, which was then replaced by the program listed.

[b] States then transfer some of these funds to municipalities.

[c] Potable water, drainage, sewerage, urbanization, rural and low-income community electrification, basic health and education infrastructure, rural roads, and rural productivity investments.

representation in the Chamber of Deputies. In that same year, the Partido de la Revolución Democrática (PRD) won control of the government of Mexico City, the nation's capital. In 2000, of course, this bottom-up competitive growth culminated in the victory of the PAN in the national presidential election, after seventy-one years of PRI governments.[40]

Figure 2.2 shows the growth of non-PRI municipal and state governments from 1985 to 2003. By the 2000s, parties other than the PRI could expect to control about 50 percent of state governments and 30–40 per-

State level

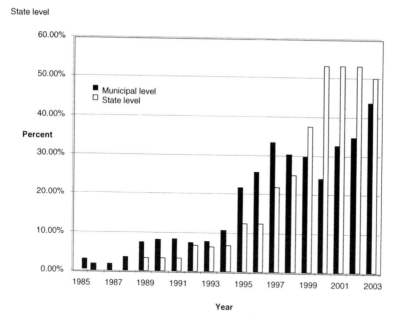

Figure 2.2. Percent of municipalities and states governed by parties other than the PRI, 1985–2003. Source: CIDAC, www.cidac.org.

cent of municipal governments. At the municipal level, this accounted for about 30 percent of Mexico's population (see figure 2.3).

THE SHAPE OF MUNICIPAL GOVERNMENT

Municipalities in Mexico are equivalent to counties in the United States. They are generally composed of a county seat (*cabecera*) and surrounding communities. Often, these communities—variously named agencies, communities, syndicates, colonies, commissions, sections, ranches, or *ejidos*, depending on the state—are rural. The Municipal Census of 2002 reported that Mexico contained 2,429 municipalities. Their size varied greatly, from a municipality that extended for almost 52,000 square kilometers in the state of Baja California to one that measured just 4.3 square kilometers in the state of Tlaxcala. Similarly, their populations ranged from a municipality of 1.65 million people in the state of Jalisco to one of 109 people in the state of Oaxaca. Of the 2,429 municipalities, 61 percent had populations of less than 2,500 people. Nevertheless, the trend

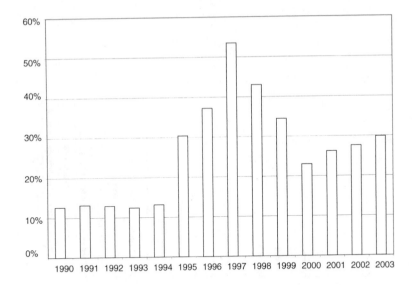

Figure 2.3. Percent of municipal population governed by parties other than the PRI, 1990–2003. Source: INEGI, Sistema Municipal de Base de Datos, http://www.inegi.gob.mx/prod_serv/contenidos/espanol/simbad/default.asp?c=73.

over time was certainly toward greater urbanization. Even though some municipalities remained principally rural, their numbers were declining.

The municipal government is known as the *ayuntamiento*, a term also used to refer to the building that houses local government offices (town hall). The *ayuntamiento* is composed of an elected mayor (*presidente municipal*), elected councilors (*regidores* and *síndicos*), and appointed officials who head up departments or who have other important functions. Elected officials serve for three-year terms and cannot run for the same position again for three years.[41] Collectively, *regidores* and *síndicos* are responsible for the rule-making and oversight functions of local government. In addition, *síndicos* are the legal representatives (in the case of judicial actions involving the municipality, for example) and monitor budgets and expenditures.

Mayors and councilors are elected by party lists, with the first name on the ballot that of the candidate for mayor, the next for positions as *síndico*, and then the names of candidates for *regidor*. The composition of the *ayuntamiento* is determined by proportional representation. Although this electoral system generally ensures the mayor a majority on the council, it is at times necessary to build coalitions among parties in order to ensure the majority; when this happens, the agreement is usually cemented through the distribution of municipal positions by party. Such coalitions are often fragile, and can result in a gridlocked council.

The number of *regidores* and *síndicos* is determined by each state, with small and rural municipalities often having only a few, while larger municipalities may have as many as thirty-six. The thirty research municipalities had an average of twelve councilors (*regidores* and *síndicos*), and the council ranged in size from six to twenty-two elected officials. When the mayor, the councilors, and important appointed officials, such as the municipal secretary, treasurer, head of public works, and others, meet to discuss business, make decisions, and approve rules and regulations, they compose the *cabildo*, the council.[42] Depending on the municipality, the council meets once a week, every two weeks, once a month, or irregularly. Also depending on the locality, representatives of submunicipal divisions are elected by their communities or appointed by the mayor. Their major responsibility is to lobby for resources and projects from the mayor and the council and to manage community-level conflicts.

In the municipal government, mayors have extensive discretion over appointments of officials. Among the most important of these are those who have responsibilities for the various departments of local government—treasury, public works, public safety, culture and youth, public health, urban development, rural development, and so on. In most municipalities, each councilor has oversight responsibility for one or more of these departments. In contrast to department heads, however, the councilors may lack offices or have only cubicles to carry out their activities when they come to the town hall. A common criticism of many of the councilors is that they are rarely to be found in the *ayuntamiento*. Mayors also appoint a chief administrative officer (*oficial mayor*), responsible for managing daily activities, purchases, and petty cash, and the secretary of the *ayuntamiento*, who usually serves as chief of staff to the mayor.[43]

There are important exceptions to this general panorama of local government. In states in which there are significant indigenous populations, municipalities can legally be governed by traditional rules, known as *usos y costumbres* (traditions and customs).[44] Thus, for example, in the state of Oaxaca, where *usos y costumbres* is widespread among municipalities, many local governments are constituted through large community meetings in which participants nominate individuals for particular office, with no reference to party affiliation, and then vote by voice, show of hands, or lining up behind particular nominees. Sometimes *usos y costumbres* involves selecting leaders by acclamation. There are a few municipalities in which a council of elders determines the leadership of local government and some in which women are not allowed to vote. Although official electoral documents and results ascribe political parties to the winners of these traditional practices, in some cases, parties are not an important factor in the decision-making process.

According to a 2000 census, 487,010 people worked for municipal governments. This was up almost 45 percent over the 1990 census, when the process of decentralization was much less advanced.[45] The increase in numbers was in part the result of more responsibilities and resources—more people needed to handle more activities and manage much larger local budgets. Nevertheless, it is also very plausible that some of the increase in numbers is a result of the increases in funding which allowed mayors to appoint more people to local government positions, regardless of responsibilities, in the age-old provision of "jobs for the boys."

As many critics of local government in Mexico argue, the vast majority of municipalities in the country at the time of the research did not have the basic administrative infrastructure to respond to the new challenges of decentralization. According to the municipal census of 2002, for example, only about 60 percent of all municipalities had basic internal administrative regulations, which outline the decision-making process of local government. Only about half had public works regulations, rules about alcoholic beverages, or environmental regulations. Less than a third had basic management regulations (rules about resource use and administrative structures), zoning, land use rules, or codes for public amusements. Even fewer had public security or fire regulations (see table 2.3). These failings were particularly apparent in the large number of municipalities with small populations.[46]

Moreover, municipalities continued to be subject to many constraints imposed by state and federal governments.[47] State governments established a basic law for municipal governments and approved municipal codes; state legislatures had the power to dismiss local governments and local officials if they were found to be in dereliction of duty. Local tax rates were set by national and state governments; local development plans had to be approved by state legislatures; municipal budgets were reviewed and often revised by state legislatures. Municipalities could not borrow without federal government approval, and local planning departments pursued their activities in accordance with state level guidelines and approvals. Municipal finances were monitored by both state and federal ministries, and significant taxing power remained with the central government.

Prior to the decentralization initiatives outlined in this chapter, the federal government of Mexico assumed most formal and informal powers over local government. In the wake of decentralization, state governments took on much more important roles vis-à-vis the municipalities. In addition to legal oversight of many municipal functions, federal revenue sharing and grant funds generally flowed to states first, with stipulations about percentages that had to be passed along to the municipalities. States varied in the extent to which they complied with such regulations, however, and certainly in the extent of administrative and political action surrounding

TABLE 2.3
Institutional Infrastructure in Mexican Municipalities, 2002

Institutional Infrastructure	Number of Municipalities with Item (N = 2,429)	Percent of All Municipalities	Number of Research Municipalities with Item (N = 30)	Percent of Research Municipalities
Municipal development plan (approved)	2162	89.0	27	90.0
Framework for municipal governance[a]	1898	78.1	24	80.0
Internal regulation of the *ayuntamiento*[b]	1451	59.7	20	66.7
Management regulations[c]	796	32.8	9	30.0
Public works regulation	1179	48.5	18	60.0
Zoning and land use regulations	646	26.6	8	26.7
Land division and urbanization regulations	506	20.8	8	26.7
Public security regulation	591	24.3	6	20.0
Civil protection regulation	1087	44.8	17	56.7
Public amusements and events regulation	816	33.6	14	46.7
Alcoholic beverage sales regulation	1307	53.8	14	46.7
Fire regulation	145	6.0	1	3.3
Environmental protection and ecology regulation	866	35.7	11	36.7

Source: INEGI, INDESOL, SEDESOL CONAPO, *Encuesta Nacional para Presidentes Municipales sobre Desarrollo Social,* 2002.

[a] This framework, called the Bando de Policía y Buen Gobierno (or the municipal code), is the basic local document for municipal government. It details the purpose of the *ayuntamiento*, the name and shield of the municipality, its geographic extension, the rights and obligations of its inhabitants, the basic organizaiton of the municipal government, and public services it offers.

[b] This presents the basic structure of the *ayuntamiento*.

[c] This presents the basic administrative rules of the *ayuntamiento*.

the release and monitoring of funds. Similarly, state governments differed in their perspectives about the political and administrative advisability of decentralization to the municipal level, and therefore the extent to which they promoted it and allocated resources for capacity-building initiatives.

The consequence of these structural and political features meant that state governors—increasingly powerful figures in the Mexican political system—and their administrations became centrally important for municipal officials.[48] The amount of resources flowing easily to a municipality was often determined by the quality of the relationship that municipal officials established with the governor and others associated with a particular administration. As we will see, mayors and other municipal officials focused a great deal of time and energy on developing good working relationships with officials at the state level.

Despite such ongoing constraints, municipal government began organizing in the 1990s to increase their representation in national policy discussions and to promote their common concerns through collaboration. In 1994, AMMAC (Asociación de Municípios de México, A.C.), primarily representing municipalities governed by the PAN, was created. PRD and PRI associations of municipalities followed in 1997, the AAM-LAC (Asociación de Autoridades Locales de México, A.C.) and FEN-AMM (the Federación de Municipios de México). While their member-ships varied according to the electoral fortunes of their parties, all succeeded in representing a substantial number of municipalities and insisted that national policy makers listen to their concerns.[49]

Some have argued that decentralization in Mexico, especially through fiscal reform, gave the federal government greater capacity to oversee what local and state governments did by monitoring and controlling their expenditures and distributing revenue shares and block grants in ways that rewarded or punished the activities of local government.[50] According to one expert on municipal governance, "Despite a series of promising reforms launched in 1983, the Mexican government remains one of the most centralized systems of government in the world."[51] Although this may be an overstatement, municipal governments in Mexico were not nearly as autonomous as many official statements implied at the time of the research. Nevertheless, the funds they were receiving and the activities they were responsible for had clearly increased since the early 1980s.

THIRTY MUNICIPALITIES: GOVERNANCE IN ACTION

A Mexican scholar of decentralization commented in 2003 that "Seen from a distance, the theme [of municipal governance] seemed like a puzzle with 2,500 pieces."[52] In many ways, this observation was true of the thirty municipalities selected for this study. Each one had a distinct history, a distinct set of influential local actors, a distinct interaction among political parties, and a distinct level of performance by its government. The munici-pal halls captured some of this diversity—they ranged from simple colo-nial-style buildings with arched colonnades, to baroque wedding cake structures painted white and pistachio green, to modernist arrangements of concrete blocks. Each of these buildings represented a unique world of official business and state–society interaction.

At the same time, there were similarities across the municipalities, and in many ways, they were like medium-sized municipalities elsewhere in Mexico and other countries. With only a few exceptions, all of the *ayunta-mientos* faced a town plaza—usually a shady, inviting place to sit, stroll, and socialize—that was also flanked by the principal church and a number of commercial establishments such as restaurants, bars, pharmacies, and general stores. Within a few blocks of the central plaza, there was usually a covered town market where fruit, vegetables, meat, fish, and other stalls vied for a spot with clothing and shoe booths and small establishments offering a variety of prepared foods. The streets between the plaza and the market were often thronged with people, bicycles, cars, and trucks, particularly in the late morning and late afternoon hours. In the evenings, the central plaza usually served as a meeting place for young and old, a place to discuss the affairs of the day and to relax with friends and relatives.

Table 2.4 provides basic information on the thirty municipalities in the sample, indicating their total population and that of the municipal seat (*cabecera*), area, and an official poverty category, the index of marginalization. The average population for these municipalities was 46,175 and the extent of marginalization ranged from very low to very high. Many of the municipalities were primarily agricultural, and many suffered from extensive out-migration, largely because they could not generate enough employment to meet local demand. Some, however, had significant manufacturing sectors, and almost half had substantial commercial sectors (see table 2.5). Table 2.6 shows the scope of basic social infrastructure, indicating the significant responsibilities each had in education, health, and public health.

These municipalities, then, had relatively complex economies and substantial social infrastructure for local governments to administer and maintain. They also benefited from increased resources, as indicated in figure 2.4, showing significant growth in federal transfers to the thirty municipalities beginning in 1994. Prior to this date, these municipalities had virtually no resources to fund their responsibilities. Figure 2.5, which shows the sources of local government income for the thirty municipalities, indicates the extent of local government dependence on the federal government—these municipalities generated less than 11 percent of their revenue from local sources. Figure 2.6 shows the sources of this locally generated revenue.

In the thirty municipalities in 2002, there were 8,094 local government employees, for an average of 270, but with a range between 36 to 658 employees.[53] On average, about a third of these employees were unionized, meaning that their jobs were not at risk when administrations changed, although twelve of the municipalities had no unionized workers at all. Levels of education of mayors and the directors of various municipal officers were quite high. Half of all mayors in 2002 had university educations, as did two-thirds of the department directors (see table 2.7).

In almost all of these municipalities, the *ayuntamiento* was a busy place. From eight o'clock in the morning until two or three in the afternoon, people arrived at the town hall to carry out important business. Some came to the office of the civil registry to have their legal status and place of residence verified or to register births, marriages, or deaths. Others

TABLE 2.4
Population, Area, and Poverty in Research Municipalities, 2002

Municipality	Population (2000)	Percent of Population in Municipal Seat	Index of Marginalization
Guanajuato			
Abasolo	79,093	30.5	Medium
Manuel Doblado	38,309	31.2	Medium
San Luis de la Paz	96,729	42.3	Medium
Santa Cruz de Juventino Rosas	65,479	53.9	Medium
Yuriria	73,820	29.5	Medium
Oaxaca			
Acatlán De Pérez Figueroa	44,579	12.1	High
San Juan Guichicovi	27,399	15.2	Very High
Santiago Juxtlahuaca	28,188	24.7	High
Santiago Pinotepa Nacional	44,193	55.7	High
Santo Domingo Tehuantepec	53,229	70.7	Medium
Puebla			
Chignahuapan	49,266	28.0	High
Coronango	27,575	45.5	Medium
Ixtacamaxtitlán	28,358	1.0	High
Libres	25,719	46.4	Medium
San Pedro Cholula	99,794	69.3	Low
Sinaloa			
Escuinapa	50,438	55.9	Low
Mocorito	50,082	9.7	High
Rosario	47,934	27.3	Low
Salvador Alvarado	73,303	77.3	Very Low
San Ignacio	26,762	13.5	High
Tamaulipas			
Aldama	27,997	39.7	Medium
González	41,455	23.7	Medium
Miguel Alemán	25,704	89.0	Very Low
San Fernando	57,412	44.6	Medium
Tula	27,049	29.9	High
Yucatán			
Oxkutzcab	25,483	81.0	High
Progreso	48,797	91.1	Very Low
Ticul	32,776	86.6	Medium
Umán	49,145	54.5	Medium
Valladolid	56,776	66.4	Medium

Source: INAFED, Dirección del Sistema Nacional de Información Municipal, CONAPO.

came to pay water bills and property taxes; still others to check up on a scheduled activity; and others to acquire permits to hold a dance or a raffle for a local charity or to get a license for construction work. Representatives from various communities arrived to speak with the mayor, department heads, councilors, and others about road improvements, drainage, or potable water promised during the last electoral campaign.

TABLE 2.5
Economic Activity and Migration in Research Municipalities, 2002

Municipality	Percent Primary Sector	Percent Secondary Sector	Percent Tertiary Sector	Percent Other	Index of Migration
Guanajuato					
Abasolo	38.0	27.9	31.9	2.1	Very High
Manuel Doblado	33.7	31.7	32.7	2.0	Very High
San Luis de la Paz	21.0	27.4	48.5	3.1	High
Santa Cruz de Juventino Rosas	34.7	28.5	34.4	2.4	High
Yuriria	30.1	30.2	36.9	2.8	High
Oaxaca					
Acatlán De Pérez Figueroa	56.4	14.7	27.4	1.5	Low
San Juan Guichicovi	57.7	21.7	18.6	2.0	Very Low
Santiago Juxtlahuaca	54.3	15.7	26.5	3.5	Low
Santiago Pinotepa Nacional	33.8	15.5	48.0	2.8	Low
Santo Domingo Tehuantepec	21.5	24.8	50.9	2.8	Very Low
Puebla					
Chignahuapan	39.4	27.5	31.6	1.5	Very Low
Coronango	27.4	47.1	22.9	2.6	Low
Ixtacamaxtitlán	70.0	13.1	14.9	1.9	Very Low
Libres	39.3	22.4	37.5	0.8	Low
San Pedro Cholula	9.7	38.8	49.3	2.2	Low
Sinaloa					
Escuinapa	38.8	13.0	43.3	4.9	Low
Mocorito	58.1	12.6	26.7	2.6	Medium
Rosario	48.7	13.0	34.3	4.0	Low
Salvador Alvarado	13.7	19.3	62.9	4.1	Low
San Ignacio	53.5	15.9	29.0	1.6	Low
Tamaulipas					
Aldama	47.6	15.1	35.3	1.9	Low
González	43.6	17.7	36.2	2.5	Medium
Miguel Alemán	8.1	27.6	61.4	3.0	Low
San Fernando	30.7	23.6	42.7	3.0	Low
Tula	50.3	18.9	29.2	1.7	Medium
Yucatán					
Oxkutzcab	39.5	16.3	43.3	1.0	Medium
Progreso	16.2	21.7	60.4	1.6	Very Low
Ticul	12.5	41.0	45.6	0.8	Very Low
Umán	6.7	45.5	46.8	1.0	Very Low
Valladolid	19.1	31.8	47.5	1.6	Very Low

Source: INAFED, Dirección del Sistema Nacional de Información Municipal, CONAPO.

In some places, secretaries pecked away at typewriters long out of production and messengers scurried from office to office.

The busiest area was usually the waiting room outside the mayor's office. This was a gathering place for people of humble origins seeking solutions to problems endemic to poverty—money to bury a husband, a chit to use at the local pharmacy for medicines, a job for a cousin who dropped

Table 2.6
Social Infrastructure in Research Municipalities, 2002

Municipality	Primary Schools	Secondary Schools	Universities, Technical, and Professional Schools	Health Units	Percent of Households with Water and Sewerage
Guanajuato					
Abasolo	89	31	7	11	26
Manuel Doblado	89	21	2	9	19
San Luis de la Paz	176	33	13	21	10
Santa Cruz de Juventino Rosas	63	22	9	8	50
Yuriria	95	29	10	15	18
Oaxaca					
Acatlán De Pérez Figueroa	69	18	5	12	31
San Juan Guichicovi	46	16	1	12	23
Santiago Juxtlahuaca	61	14	3	12	11
Santiago Pinotepa Nacional	58	18	4	16	8
Santo Domingo Tehuantepec	67	17	11	1	26
Puebla					
Chignahuapan	71	31	7	20	19
Coronango	11	5	3	2	9
Ixtacamaxtitlán	93	27	2	20	11
Libres	27	11	4	9	20
San Pedro Cholula	49	25	24	9	13
Sinaloa					
Escuinapa	45	15	11	12	23
Mocorito	138	30	7	21	20
Rosario	98	25	11	19	24
Salvador Alvarado	73	17	18	13	14
San Ignacio	79	12	3	18	20
Tamaulipas					
Aldama	98	17	4	9	12
González	61	17	8	11	10
Miguel Alemán	27	6	6	6	8
San Fernando	94	21	8	25	7
Tula	82	23	4	13	8
Yucatán					
Oxkutzcab	26	8	5	6	21
Progreso	27	13	17	10	10
Ticul	15	6	13	5	16
Umán	33	12	4	2	4
Valladolid	82	17	18	22	8

Source: INAFED, Dirección del Sistema Nacional de Información Municipal.

out of school, a free school uniform for a child. Community representatives usually stopped here with project petitions before moving on to the public works department. Employees dropped by to chat with neighbors waiting for a moment with the mayor or the chief of staff. From time to time, self-important people came in, held a hushed conversation with the

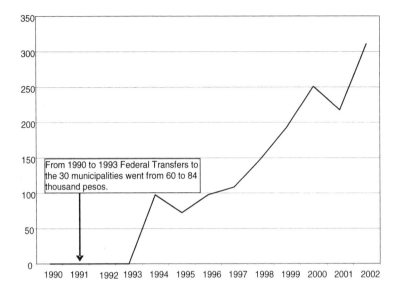

Figure 2.4. Federal transfers to research municipalities, 1990–2002 (millions of 1993 pesos). Source: INEGI, Sistema Municipal de Base de Datos, http://www .inegi.gob.mx/prod_serv/contenidos/espanol/simbad/default.asp?c=73.

person guarding the mayor's door, and were allowed inside. These may have been friends, political allies, those with important businesses in town, or those summoned to a meeting. Whatever their errands, no one questioned their right to see the mayor before the many others waiting for attention. In some municipalities, custom decreed that the mayor spend time circulating in the waiting room, speaking with this individual and that group, making a promise here and dispensing a few pesos there.

Beyond the shuffles and discussions of citizens who needed local officials to resolve problems for them was the routine business of government being carried out behind the scenes. Public works officials would be planning to fill potholes, widen and pave roads, purchase new garbage trucks; establishing specifications for an impressive boulevard for entering the municipality and inventing ways to route trucks away from the town center. The treasurer's office would be working on numerous reports required by the state and national governments, and the police department would be witness to the activities of officers, drunks, and unruly teenagers. In some offices, councilors might be meeting with the department heads of the activities they were responsible for overseeing. Other parts of the *ayuntamiento* might house a day-care center, a center for the elderly, and an Internet center frequented primarily by young people.

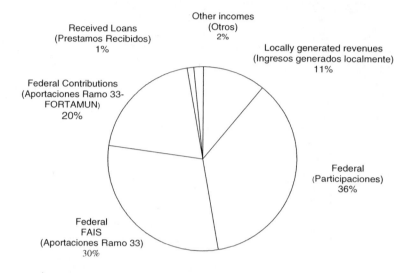

Figure 2.5. Total income of research municipalities, 2001. Source: INEGI, INDESOL, SEDESOL CONAPO, *Encuesta Nacional para Presidentes Municipales sobre Desarrollo Social*, 2002.

Among the activities of local government, the most important one was that of public works. Indeed, governance in medium-sized municipalities in Mexico in the mid-2000s was primarily about public works and their allocation to different parts of the municipality. Roads, drainage ditches, small bridges, potable water, electricity, a new clinic or hospital, parks, basketball courts, ring roads, a new school, tourist facilities, industrial parks—the bulk of what local governments did had to do with physical infrastructure. Mayors focused great attention on the legacy of works they would leave behind when their administrations were over. These, after all, were the most visible signs of efforts by politicians to create public good and to reap the gratitude of citizens. In addition, frequent evidence of poorly constructed works suggested the extent to which municipal contractors and decision makers could reap the benefits of corruption.

Public works usually involved lumpy investments—requiring funds to buy heavy equipment for excavation, for example, or to acquire the lumber, bricks, and cement to build a new school. Finding such resources was an ongoing challenge to public works departments, mayors, and other officials, as will be evident in later chapters. Table 2.8 shows average expenditures on various activities for the thirty municipalities for 2004 and suggests the extent to which public works dominated business in the

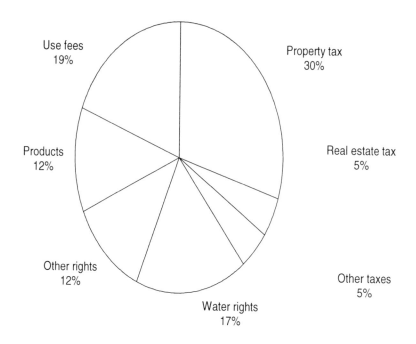

Figure 2.6. Locally generated revenues of research municipalities, 2001. Source: INEGI, INDESOL, SEDESOL CONAPO, *Encuesta Nacional para Presidentes Municipales sobre Desarrollo Social*, 2002.

ayuntamientos—over one-third of all expenditures were used for such investments, while another third was spent on administration.

The civil registry was also an important function of the municipalities in this study. In Mexico, most official interaction and many services required that citizens present proof of citizenship, legal status, and address. Marriage licenses and birth and death certificates were also important documents that had to be acquired through the civil registry. In a country in which there was considerable in- and out-migration, and in which many were poor and marginalized, documenting these conditions could be a major challenge for many citizens—documents might be on record in other municipalities or they simply might not exist, as was frequently the case for birth certificates of the most marginalized people. Computer technology was lessening the burden on citizens and the municipality for these procedures, but it was clear that the civil registry was central to the activities of local government.

To what extent the same can be said for the tax office varied considerably by municipality and by season of the year. The months between January and March, when property taxes were being collected, were the busi-

TABLE 2.7
Level of Schooling Attained by Elected and Appointed Officials in Research
Municipalities, 2002

Level of Schooling Completed	Mayors (N = 30)		Directors (N = 258)	
	Number	%	Number	%
None	0	0.0	0	0.0
Elementary	2	6.7	5	1.9
Junior High	1	3.3	14	5.4
Vocational School	1	3.3	12	4.7
High School	3	10.0	24	9.3
Undergraduate	15	50.0	172	66.7
Graduate	5	16.7	11	4.3
Missing Information	3	10.0	20	7.7

Source: INEGI, INDESOL, SEDESOL, CONAPO, Encuesta Nacional para Presidentes Municipales sobre Desarrollo Social, 2002.

TABLE 2.8
Expenditures by Activity in Research
Municipalities (2002 average)

Activity	Average Share of Expenditures (%)
Administrative	29%
Services	18
Public Works	35
Acquisitions	15
Others	3

Source: INEGI, Sistema Municipal de Base de Datos,
http://www.inegi.gob.mx/prod_serv/contenidos/
espanol/simbad/default.asp?c=73.

est season for this office. At the same time, however, the extent to which
property taxes were collected at all or in part varied considerably by municipality. In some, such taxes were a focus of increased efforts on the
part of municipal government and a site of a number of interesting innovations; in others, they were regularly ignored, the population considered
too poor to make tax collection worthwhile. In most, tax collection was
viewed with ambivalence by elected officials; it might have potential to

increase local public resources but also carried considerable political costs if it was pursued assiduously.

A less formal function of municipal government, but nevertheless an important one, was local conflict management. Conflicts among individuals might involve those related to property lines, to responsibilities for keeping land free of trash, to problems about noise and business hours. Communities might dispute boundaries, rights to particular services, and the distribution of water. Parties might dispute election results and processes of decision making. Areas within the municipal seat might not agree on the location of a new market or the condition of the town slaughterhouse. Disputes among businesses were not uncommon. Much of the activity of the mayor, the department heads, and the council was given over to keeping such disputes at a modest level—occasionally even resolving them.

Municipal governments were required to prepare annual budgets that had to be submitted to the state legislature for approval. In general, the budget was based on calculations about ongoing expenses and a set of priorities for investments, usually public works. Proposals and promises for these investments often emerged during campaigns. Which of these were deemed to be priorities for municipal action could be decided by the mayor, determined in meetings of the council, or result from public consultations. The latter were becoming increasingly attractive to local leaders and heads of public works departments in the 2000s. In addition, different informal decision rules often applied to the determination of priorities—works benefiting the largest group of people, those focused on rural or urban parts of the municipality, or those for underserved populations and areas, for example. At times, community meetings forced citizens to make the difficult choices and trade-offs among priorities— "Would you rather have potable water or a new basketball court?" they would be asked. At times, there were no clear decision rules.

Local governments were also expected to have a set of basic regulations and codes in effect, as we saw before. In fact, many municipalities, particularly small ones, did not have this kind of institutional infrastructure in place. In 2002, for example, 30 percent or less of the research municipalities had administrative regulations, zoning, land management, public security, or fire codes. Table 2.3 indicated the institutional infrastructure for local decision making and resource allocation and hinted at the extent to which decisions could be based on criteria other than those written down in such regulations and codes.

Given constitutional limitations on tenure, broad powers of appointment, and the general weakness of local government institutions, considerable change marked the coming and going of administrations. As each new administration came into office, the paucity of rules of the game for getting things done was often a great surprise to the newly elected. Moreover, it was not unusual to hear that the local treasury had been looted by the outgoing administration, that the capital stock of trucks and machinery had almost been destroyed, that a significant debt had been left by the previous incumbents, and that there was great confusion about what would happen next. Indeed, the first experience of many mayors, councilors, and department heads was shock at what was found—and not found—in the institutional structure left behind by the previous government. With time, new procedures and rules might be put in place, with great expectations about their sensibility and durability, only to be overturned by the next incumbents.

Despite these generalizations, each of the municipalities had its own story to tell. Localities varied in terms of their wealth, urbanity, ethnic composition, class structure, and geography. Their histories contained diverse stories of heroism and villainy, conflict and war, booms and busts. Their citizens, often divided by class and political and economic interests, generally found ways to celebrate the same local heroes, venerate common patron saints, and enjoy shared traditions and landscapes. Their governments responded in different ways to the challenges of decentralization and democratization. As the following thumbnail descriptions of six of the research municipalities reveal, these medium-sized municipalities are probably like hundreds of thousands of other places in the world—unique yet familiar to us.

Six Municipalities, Six Stories

A municipality of 80,000 in Guanajuato. An impressive four-lane highway leads into the *cabecera* of this municipality, which traces its Spanish heritage to 1529. Yet the municipal seat appears poor and is badly maintained; it is dusty and littered with trash. Getting to its outlying rural communities, where 70 percent of the population lives, is difficult because of the bad quality of roads, especially to the poorest parts of the municipality. There are few sources of work, and the area continues to be dependent on agriculture as its primary economic activity. A few years ago, there were four textile mills in the municipality; now there is only one, and people worry about it disappearing also.

Most people know someone in the municipal government who can help them out if they have a problem that needs official attention. But the local government is generally passive, and it does not have many systems in place for planning or monitoring its activities or its personnel; there is little clarity about why particular people occupy particular posts. Corruption is thought to be significant and public security is uncertain. The PAN has won two elections and is the party in power; it is currently faced with serious internal conflicts, many of them related to the distribution of jobs. There is much complaining about alcoholism and drug addiction in the municipality, particularly among the young, but there are no local programs in place to deal with these issues.

A municipality of 55,000 in Oaxaca. This is a lively municipality, with trucks and cars passing through day and night on their way to the state's capital city or the nearby port. It can boast of busy commerce also, with a fish market, restaurants, and stores surrounding the central plaza, itself littered with trash and home to scavenging dogs. The municipal hall and the cathedral are the most imposing structures on the plaza. Traditionally an agricultural center, increasing numbers of workers commute to the nearby port town to work as laborers. About 70 percent of the population lives in the *cabecera*, where carefully maintained differences among communities are marked by local churches, local saints, and distinct festival days—"a small confederation of states," according to one observer.[54] It is a poor municipality, as are most in this southern state. Indigenous groups make up about 11 percent of the population.

Competition for positions in government is fierce, reflecting municipal control over resources for projects and jobs. Of its $7.8 million budget in 2003, $3.3 million was spent on public works and $2.8 million on salaries and operational expenses; local government is the largest employer in the municipality. Mayors have always represented the PRI, although local politicians believe that its loss to some other party is imminent. Few mayors finish their terms of office—they are forced to resign by the council or angry citizens or they become candidates for higher office. Governing is difficult because councilors, even those from the mayor's own party, exact a price in projects and jobs for their support. To make headway in getting things done, the mayor often makes decisions without consulting them. State governors have had to step in from time to time to resolve political conflicts that threaten the stability of the region. Relationships with the governor are extremely important to the mayor and the council; he often uses his control over municipal resources to reward or punish local office holders.

A municipality of 25,000 in Puebla. This municipality in a region of cool, pine-covered mountains and hot, dry valleys is a commercial center for surrounding municipalities. It is a busy place, with traffic jams and heavy truck traffic in the center of the *cabecera*, where about half the population lives. Residents complain of the rising price of land as commerce has grown. In general, its citizens are reserved and careful about strangers.

The town is neither rich nor poor; much of its economy is based on dairy ranches in the outlying areas. Residents are proud of being ranchers, and often sport cowboy boots and hats. There are some local food processing industries and one factory that produces clothing for export.

A local artist has painted a mural celebrating local history and myths on the walls of the colonial-style municipal hall, reflecting local pride. The government works fairly well; basic laws and regulations and a municipal development plan are in place, and the tax office has been computerized. The local government is concerned about economic development and has sought to increase employment opportunities in the area. It has also been active in developing new forms of social communication that are important in a municipality in which there are many dispersed rural communities. Although long dominated by the PRI, this party's margin of victory has been slim in elections since 1995.

A municipality of 50,000 in Sinaloa. Crossing the bridge that leads to the *cabecera* of this coastal municipality, visitors and residents pass under an arch celebrating their arrival. In the center of town, the church, the market, and the recently renovated municipal palace flank a pleasant square. Above the town is a giant Christ figure, still under construction in a park that provides panoramic views of the surrounding mountains and sea. It is a pleasant town, one that supplied gold and silver from the times of the Spanish *conquistadores* to 1945. Yet today, this is a town marked by quiet. There are few people in the streets, and at night there are fewer still. This municipality has a reputation as a crossroads for drug trafficking. Local lore suggests that many families are connected with this business in one way or another; those that are not are fearful of the violence that erupts from time to time. There is a local military base, but its operations seem to have little impact on the drug business or the violence.

Municipal politics and government is dominated by a few families, but even with such centralization of control, violence is common and mayors in the recent past have been killed, many say by drug traffickers. It is common to accuse the local government of extensive corruption, and few citizens have much respect for its activities, even though its accomplishments are equivalent to those of other municipalities of its size.

A municipality of 25,000 in Tamaulipas. This municipality lies across the Rio Bravo from a small Texas town. It is bigger and more prosperous than its U.S. counterpart, and characterized by many U.S.-based retail outlets. In recognition of its international setting, there is a bar on the outskirts of town named Juan Too Many. There are also many medical offices offering services primarily to American patients. It is an urban municipality, with some 90 percent of the population living in the *cabecera*. In the surrounding areas, agriculture is largely irrigated, and watermelon and cantaloupe are exported to the United States. This is a new municipality, having gained its "independence" from the neighboring locality only in 1950. It is built on a well-planned grid, and features a modern municipal hall; the central park is partly given over to a children's playground, with brightly-painted equipment for swinging, bouncing, sliding, and whirling. The municipal building has a center for senior citizens, with an entrance just off the park. While prosperous, few people will comment on sources of employment, beyond the local assembly plant and agriculture, but acknowledge that drug trafficking may be part of the answer.

The local government is generally well-organized and run. Because it is relatively wealthy, the municipality does not receive benefits from many state or federal poverty alleviation programs. Instead, it relies more on local taxation, and has worked hard to modernize its collection system. It has also undertaken a number of longer-term projects for economic development, and is spared the common accusations of corruption. The PRI has always dominated politics in the municipality, but the PAN won an election in 1995, reportedly as a punishment to the PRI because the governor appointed its last candidate for mayor without consulting local opinion. Since then, the PRI has worked hard to maintain its unity.

A municipality of 60,000 in Yucatán. There is a new bus station near the central plaza of this municipality, and the surrounding streets are narrow and uneven. Many of those arriving on the buses are tourists who come for a short while in the afternoons to browse in the souvenir shops and eat in local restaurants. Then they move on to famous archeological sites in other parts of the region. In the evenings, citizens emerge from their homes and walk to the central plaza to escape the heat of the day. On Sundays, there is an open-air band concert sponsored in part by the municipal government. Many local residents commute to work in the hotels and restaurants of the so-called "Mayan Riviera." Belying the calm is the history of the municipality, a central location of the War of the Castes in 1847–1848, when indigenous groups rebelled against the oppression of the mestizo-dominated government.

The PRI lost its capacity to manage the local government in 2004; the PRD won these elections, although most of those supporting this party are thought to be PRIistas in disguise. Outside of election cycles, local parties hardly seem to exist. Clientelism characterizes much of the business of the municipality, including the distribution of jobs and projects.

Overall, the development agenda is limited and most decisions are made unilaterally by the mayor.

JUDGING PERFORMANCE

These descriptions suggest some of the characteristics of the municipalities studied. Each one had its own political and social history, a distinct economic resource base for addressing the needs of its population, and a government that performed at its own level of effectiveness. Given the differences, could the performance of the local governments be assessed comparatively in some meaningful way?

One way of responding to this question would be to measure the development of the different municipalities. The socioeconomic conditions of the thirty municipalities, presented in tables 2.5 and 2.6, certainly suggest considerable differences among them in terms of degrees of poverty and the extent to which citizens had access to basic sanitation, potable water, and schools and health units per population. This approach would be particularly helpful in a discussion of the urbanization and wealth or poverty of the municipalities. At the same time, however, it would focus attention primarily on the level of development of the municipalities, with little insight into how local governments were coping with the responsibilities of decentralization.

Another option for assessing the comparative performance of the municipalities would be to conduct citizen surveys to explore the perceptions of local inhabitants about how well their local governments were doing in providing services and contributing to the general welfare of the population. This approach would be particularly apt if the central questions related to citizen attitudes and behaviors about local governance. This is an important area of research, yet not the one I have chosen as a focus.

Similarly, a study might generate detailed ethnographies of local economic, social, and political interactions and conflicts as well as their roots in history, identity, and culture. This approach would be particularly useful in uncovering the role of local government in the creation and resolution of conflict and its impact on inequalities perpetuated by institutional arrangements, markets, and power relationships.[55] Again, this research would generate valuable insights, but not those that would necessarily address issues of governance.

In this project, I was primarily interested in how *ayuntamientos* functioned as units of government, more interested in the ways in which the business of government was carried out on a daily basis than measures of their development, the attitudes and behavior of their citizens, or their divisions and civic cultures. As indicated, these are all important

TABLE 2.9
Performance Indicators for Municipal Governments

Efficiency
    Basic laws and regulations in place
    Operational plan for municipal development
    Tax system computerized
    "Decision rules" for public works projects
    Low "reputation" for corruption
Effectiveness
    Regular meetings of municipal council
    Operational system for performance monitoring of personnel
    Professionals chosen to head up municipal offices
    Councilors' own office space
    Publicly available budget
Responsiveness
    Signage and equitable access
    Functioning Web site
    Council meetings open to the public
    Regular "citizen days"
    Elected submunicipal officials
Development Orientation
    Undertaking of complex, long-term, or "invisible" public works
    Use of municipal resources to promote economic development
Change Initiative
    Effort to improve indicators mentioned above

aspects of local life, but ones I did not choose as the principal focus of my research.

The approach I selected instead is based on five aspects of local governance performance: municipal (1) efficiency; (2) effectiveness; (3) responsiveness; (4) development orientation; and (5) change initiatives. To measure these factors, I selected conditions within local government that could be observed by researchers and triangulated with other data, at least to some degree.[56] These conditions related to the presence or absence of administrative structures and processes, formal and informal rules that constrained public officials in the pursuit of their responsibilities, the extent to which there was participation in public business, and the degree of effort to promote development and change. These indicators responded to a series of questions, and are summarized in table 2.9.

Efficiency: Factors That Facilitate Timely and Consistent Decision Making

- Was a basic framework for municipal governance in place? State law requires municipalities to have such a framework, usually called a Bando de Policía y Buen Gobierno (but also confusingly called a municipal code in some places), but some had not acted on these requirements.[57]

- Was there an operational plan for municipal development? Again, state law requires a municipal development plan, but some did not have one.[58]
- Was the tax system computerized?
- Were there clear and accepted "decision rules" for allocating public works among communities?
- Did the municipality have a low "reputation" for corruption? Despite its subjectivity, this measure was included because of the consistency with which interviews reflected judgments about the honesty and dishonesty of the local government.

Effectiveness: Factors That Facilitate Professional Orientation among Elected and Appointed Officials and That Make Follow-Up and Monitoring of Decisions Possible

- Were there regular meetings between administrators and the mayor and the council? This is a proxy for intragovernmental coordination and monitoring of programs and projects.
- Was there an operational system for performance monitoring of personnel?
- Were professionals chosen to head up the departments of municipal administration? This is a proxy for performance-oriented behavior and attitudes among appointed personnel.
- Did councilors have their own offices or cubicles? This is a proxy for the extent to which councilors were able to carry out their functions for oversight and monitoring of municipal departments.
- Was the municipal budget publicly available? This indicates a capacity to monitor the allocation of resources and implementation of programs and projects.

Responsiveness: Factors That Encourage Openness/Transparency of Governance and That Facilitate Citizen Participation in Decision Making and Monitoring of Government

- Was there signage and equitable access in the *ayuntamiento*? Equitable access refers to some effective system for queuing and is a proxy for municipal interest in fairness to citizens.
- Was there a functioning Web site for the municipality? This was prescribed by state law, but municipalities varied in terms of whether they were in compliance or not.
- Were council meetings open to the public?

- Were there regularly scheduled "citizen days" or some similar effort to allow citizens direct access to the mayor, the councilors, and the department heads?[59]
- Were sub-municipal officials elected? This is a measure of democratic representation of community concerns in decision making.

Development Orientation: Factors That Indicate Commitment to Improving Potential for Economic Development over the Longer Term

- Was the municipality able to undertake complex, long-term, or "invisible" public works that would increase its attractiveness to potential investors?
- Was there a significant effort to use municipal resources to promote economic development and job creation?

Change Orientation: Initiatives to Bring About Change in Any of the Indicators Listed Above

- During the most recent administration, did the municipality make a concerted effort to improve any of the indicators?

I awarded municipalities one point for the presence of each of seventeen indicators and a zero for its absence. Thus, the indicators are not weighted, reflecting considerable uncertainty about the ease or difficulty of actions needed to carry out the activity. For one indicator—change orientation—I added the number of serious efforts a municipality had made to improve conditions in the other indicators. Thus, each municipality could score up to seventeen points for observed conditions plus additional points equal to the number of change initiatives undertaken.

Table 2.10 presents the results of this scoring process for each of the municipalities, and demonstrates that municipalities varied considerably in their performance, ranging from a low of 3 in the case of Coronango, to a high of 18 in the municipality of Salvador Alvarado; the average score is 9.4. Overall, municipalities in Sinaloa were more apt to score high, while municipalities in Puebla scored relatively low. Both reflect the degree of seriousness with which states assumed regulatory and monitoring roles vis-à-vis the municipalities. It is interesting, however, that the scores within states often varied as much as scores across states. Thus, for example, in Puebla, one municipality scored a high of 15, while another scored 3, and in Guanajuato, scores ranged from 13 to 5. This suggests that municipal performance may be somewhat independent of state policies and capacity to monitor municipal compliance and performance.

TABLE 2.10
Performance of Research Municipalities

Municipality	Total Score
Guanajuato	
Abasolo	12
Manuel Doblado	9
San Luis de la Paz	13
Santa Cruz de Juventino Rosas	12
Yuriria	4
Oaxaca	
Acatlán De Pérez Figueroa	6
San Juan Guichicovi	8
Santiago Juxtlahuaca	9
Santiago Pinotepa Nacional	7
Santo Domingo Tehuantepec	9
Puebla	
Chignahuapan	15
Coronango	3
Ixtacamaxtitlán	4
Libres	8
San Pedro Cholula	5
Sinaloa	
Escuinapa	8
Mocorito	15
Rosario	11
Salvador Alvarado	18
San Ignacio	10
Tamaulipas	
Aldama	7
González	11
Miguel Alemán	13
San Fernando	9
Tula	6
Yucatán	
Oxkutzcab	13
Progreso	11
Ticul	11
Umán	9
Valladolid	6

In subsequent chapters, this index is used to assess the relationship between performance and electoral competitiveness, entrepreneurial leadership, and the mobilization of civil society. It is not used to assess the relationship between performance and state modernization, however, because it proved impossible to separate analytically the measures of performance and what might be used as indicators of state modernization. Instead, in chapter 5, I describe four aspects of state modernization that were evident in many municipalities and analyze how they were introduced into the work of the local government.

CONCLUSION: IMAGES OF LOCAL GOVERNMENT

Two contrasting images attest to different perspectives about how local governments performed in the wake of new pressures implicit in political, administrative, and fiscal decentralization in the developing world. One image—often elaborated in stories about disappointing encounters with local government—was of endemic lack of resources, capacities, and efficiency; of local public officials overwhelmed by new responsibilities; of the failure to respond to public demands; of local politicians building clientelistic networks with public resources; of capture by local elites; of massive corruption; of increasing debt burdens threatening national economic stability; of incompetence, connivance, and mismanagement.

The other—and very different—image was of good governance emerging from the ruins of excessive centralization. This image drew on stories of local governments actively experimenting with new solutions to longstanding problems; of citizens participating in local decision making about the allocation of resources and the definition of public policies; of officials competing with each other to improve the responsiveness of government departments; of new vibrancy infused into local politics by the immediacy of needs for basic services and the resources to respond to them; of impressive actions to stimulate local economic development.

These are the images that encouraged the research in this book.

Photo by Xóchitl León.

Chapter 3

COMPETITIVE ELECTIONS AND GOOD GOVERNANCE

"THERE'S NOTHING SADDER than having to turn power over to the opposition," lamented one municipal official interviewed for this study.[1] However sad for incumbents, turning power over to another political party was an act that happened much more frequently in Mexico's local governments after 1980. Indeed, municipal elections became hotly contested races among parties and partisans; increasingly, the venerable party of Mexico's revolution, the PRI, lost these electoral battles. Where it did not lose, the old hegemonic party had to work harder to win. And, with time, parties challenging the PRI began to face significant electoral opposition once they proved their capacity to win municipal office. Indeed, by the mid-2000s, turning power over to the opposition was the specter behind every local election, one that haunted all parties, not just the PRI.

Proponents of decentralization would be cheered by these changes. Characteristically, they consider greater competition for local government positions a dynamic that will produce more responsive government, higher quality service provision, and greater accountability of local officials for the activities they carry out.[2] According to their view, voters have more information on how local governments perform than they do about those at the national or even the state level; competitive elections give them opportunities to reward and punish those now directly responsible for administration and public services. Not surprisingly, advocates of decentralization believe that political competition also creates strong electoral incentives for politicians to pay attention to the interest that voters have in living in well-governed communities.

Similarly, those concerned about the growth of democracy in many parts of the world would be heartened by the evidence of more locally competitive elections in Mexico. The logic of their case is clear. As voters have more choices, they will increasingly be able to align their preferences with parties responsive to their interests. And, as parties become more aware of the possibility of losing and winning elections, they will be increasingly inclined to consult local preferences in order to win. As local citizens become more aware that their votes matter, they will increase their participation and use the vote not only to signal their policy and programmatic preferences but also their assessment of the performance of incumbents. The outcome of more competition should therefore be more responsiveness to citizen concerns and thus better governance.

Empirically, there is support for anticipating a positive relationship between political competitiveness and better governance. The studies of Rodríguez and Ward in several large municipalities in the north of Mexico consistently found evidence that greater competition, and the incumbency of an opposition party, were associated with better performance of the local governments they studied.[3] Moreover, among the thirty research municipalities, many public officials were convinced that more competitive elections had encouraged better management of public affairs; they believed that citizens had become more likely to use their votes to punish poor performance. A former municipal official in Oaxaca summarized this optimistic view about the consequences of greater electoral pluralism in the context of decentralization. "Decentralization is definitely positive for local governments. There is more competition among parties. The PRI has had to change how it does things."[4] The mayor in the same locale concurred that "with the process of decentralization, we see more citizen participation, in contrast to what happened before."[5] And in Tamaulipas, an elected official opined that alternation in political parties was good because it encouraged the emergence of new ideas and the demise of old habits.[6]

There are, however, those who voice skepticism about the relationship between electoral competition and better governance. In Mexico, for example, Jonathan Fox and Josefina Aranda found that the characteristics of local politics prior to the introduction of decentralization had much to do with the kind of electoral competition that emerged after it and the extent to which competition was linked to improved government performance. Legacies of the past, they argued, have to be factored into assertions about improved accountability of local government.[7] They and other researchers have also been clear about the danger of elite capture of local politics when elections take on more meaning and when local governments have greater resources.[8] In addition, the notion that elections carry clear messages about voter preferences has been questioned, suggesting that politicians face considerable risks in deciding which actions to undertake once they are in office.[9]

In the thirty research municipalities in Mexico, some local officials and citizens were also skeptical. "Now there is a lot of competition, but it hasn't brought us any benefits," complained a prominent and disillusioned citizen in a municipality in Puebla.[10] Nor was increased competition universally characteristic of all municipalities; an important local official in Sinaloa argued that it had passed his municipality by—the PAN had no local presence, he said, the PRI was dominated by inertia, and the PRD had nothing new to propose.[11] Another complained that the PRI continued with its old habits in the municipality, with its candidates selected by the state governor and local elites.[12] In Oaxaca, the president of a local PRI organization and former mayor charged that greater competition had only brought conflict and division to his municipality.[13]

This chapter assesses these competing views about the extent to which greater electoral competition for municipal offices improves the performance of local government. In fact, the findings present an ambiguous picture of stasis and change in the thirty municipalities. Holding local electoral office clearly became more attractive with decentralization, and this was an important explanation for the emergence of opposition parties in many of the municipalities. Moreover, new electoral dynamics were broadly apparent across the research sites, and with them, the increasingly realistic threat of having to turn power over to the opposition. As a consequence, intraparty dynamics changed, emphasizing new and usually more democratic processes of candidate selection and participation. On the other hand, legacies from the past—in particular how campaigns were waged—significantly influenced local policy decision making, despite more competitive local elections. Competition also frequently resulted in increased contention in council decision making.

Overall, evidence from the study sites calls into question a direct relationship between increasing competitiveness and better governance. Increasing competition at times translated into more divided municipal governments in which there was more conflict, significant incentives to spend public resources on patronage goods, and decision-making gridlock. Thus, whereas greater electoral competition encouraged democratization of parties and much wider choice for voters, these factors were often accompanied by increased conflict over resource distribution and patronage in local government. Interestingly, some of the municipalities found ways to deal with these conflicts; others failed miserably to do so. In referring to more democracy in local politics, Enrique Cabrero has drawn attention to what he calls "transition through chaos."[14] For many of the thirty research municipalities, this was an apt description.

ELECTORAL COMPETITION AND ITS CONSEQUENCES: PARTIES, CANDIDATES, VOTERS

In the days of PRI hegemony, Peter Ward tells us, "the exercise of municipal government followed the rationale and orthodoxy of its role as a cog in the Mexican political (that is, PRI) machine."[15] In the vast majority of municipalities, local politics had been controlled by party bosses, or *caciques*, who used their power in the local economy to marshal, and even coerce, votes for their PRI patrons at state and national levels. In the words of a journalist in the *cacique*-ridden state of Puebla, one such local boss "used the municipality's money as if it were his own."[16] Before 1980, explained one mayor, "there was a person who decided what needed to be done. This person belonged to the PRI and he was the person who communicated with the state and federal governments about who would be the next candidate, and consequently, the mayor. The state and federal authorities backed him because he sent them money. . . . In those times there were no [real] elections; he named [mayors] with the *dedazo*."[17]

These were often violent times. *Caciques* and would-be *caciques* fought to control local votes in exchange for the patronage of state and national politicians. In one municipality in Oaxaca, "Someone new would be elected when someone shot the previous [mayor]. These deaths caused a cycle of revenge and violence among families. . . . Politics was really violent in those days."[18] In other places, mayors could suffer grave problems if they did not follow the orders of the local political boss.[19] Not surprisingly, initial electoral forays by opposition parties were often constrained by fraudulent practices that ensured the continuance of the PRI in power. In Oaxaca, a local journalist pointed out that until the late 1980s, "An election not won by the PRI would simply not be recognized."[20]

The spoils of winning local elections in the PRI-dominated past were distributed to *caciques*, mayors, and councilors, who gained recognition at higher levels of government as important to the party's continued power. They also benefited from opportunities for enrichment and impunity for corruption. Municipalities benefited when local bosses were well connected with PRI politicians, particularly at the state level, and used their patronage networks to obtain resources for infrastructure investments. But even the *caciques* were constrained by this clientelist system. Prior to decentralization, the governor and the local representative to the state legislature had extensive control over what investments local governments might expect.[21] In Oaxaca, for example, a former mayor recalled that the state government provided resources to the local offices of its ministries rather than to municipal departments, and that the local representatives of the state government had more power than he did.[22]

The lure of municipal office. This tradition of local subservience and resource scarcity changed dramatically in the 1990s. As was clear in figures 2.2 and 2.3, opposition party victories became increasingly common in Mexico. This was also true of the thirty research municipalities. Figure 3.1 indicates how, over time, there were greater possibilities for parties other than the PRI to win elections.

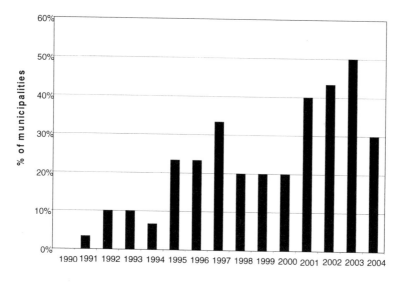

Figure 3.1. Research municipalities governed by parties other than the PRI, 1990–2004. Source: CIDAC, http://www.cidac.org/vnm/db/modules.php?name= Content&pa=showpage&pid=8.

And, even where the PRI continued to reign supreme, its margin of victory was considerably reduced. Table 3.1 shows the increasing threat faced by the PRI at election time in the research municipalities, demonstrating that party's losses and also its decreasing margins of victory. As indicated, in eighteen of the thirty municipalities, the PRI had lost at least one election; in only seven of them had opposition parties *not* come within a 10-point margin of the dominant party. Even in traditional strongholds of the PRI, such as the southern state of Oaxaca and the east central state of Puebla, opposition victories occurred or became more likely by the mid-1990s. Almost everywhere, the PRI became more vulnerable to losing elections.

Two factors are important in explaining this change. First, by the 1990s, it was possible for Mexican citizens to imagine a party other than the PRI winning elections at the local level. At state and national levels, opposition parties became more robust. The PAN, for example, had won governorships and control over state capitals in municipal elections in the 1980s. In 1988, the forerunner of the PRD was created when dissidents broke away from the PRI and contested the presidential election of that year under the banner of the Frente Nacional Democrático. By 1990, there were two viable opposition parties, one to the right of the PRI (the PAN) and one to its left (the PRD).[23]

TABLE 3.1

The Threat of Electoral Loss: Increasing Competition for the PRI
in Municipal Elections, 1980–2004

	Municipio	First Time PRI < 60%	First Time PRI < 50%	First Time with < 10% from Its Closest Opponent	Number of PRI Losses	Parties in Office at Time of Research
Guanajuato	Abasolo	1982	1991	1991	2	PAN
	Manuel Doblado	1991	2003	2003	1	PAN
	San Luis de la Paz	1988	1991	1988	2	PAN
	Santa Cruz de Juventino R	1991	1997	2000	1	PVEM
	Yuriria	1991	1997	1997	2	PAN
Oaxaca	Acatlán de Pérez Figueroa	1992	1992	1992	1	PRI
	San Juan Guichicovi	1992	1995	1995	0	PRI
	Santiago Pinotepa N.	1995	1995	1995	1	PRI
	Santiago Juxtlahuaca	1995	1995	1995	0	PRI
	Santo Domingo T.	1980	1995	1995	0	PRI
Puebla	Chignahuapan	2001	2001	—	1	PAN
	Coronango	1983	1992	1995	1	PRI
	Ixtacamaxtitlán	1995	2001	2001	0	PRI
	Libres	1995	1995	1995	0	PRI
	San Pedro Cholula	1992	1995	1995	1	PRI
Sinaloa	Escuinapa	1992	1992	1992	2	PAN
	Mocorito	1995	1995	1995	0	PRI
	Rosario	1995	1995	1998	1	PRD
	Salvador Alvarado	1992	1992	1995	1	PRI
	San Ignacio	1998	—	—	0	PRI
Tamaulipas	Aldama	1995	1995	—	0	PRI
	González	1995	1995	1998	0	PRI
	Miguel Alemán	1995	1995	1995	1	PAN
	San Fernando	1995	1995	—	0	PRI
	Tula	1995	—	—	0	PRI
Yucatán	Oxkutzcab	1993	1995	1995	3	PRI (PAN)
	Progreso	1993	—	—	0	PRI (PRI)
	Ticul	1993	1995	1995	2	PRI (PAN)
	Umán	1990	1995	1995	1	PRI (PRI)
	Valladolid	1993	2001	1995	1	PRI (PRD)

Source: CIDAC and Local Electoral Institutes

Note: In the case of Yucatán the results of the 2004 election that was held in the middle of the research period are shown in parentheses. These are accounted for in the *number of PRI losses.*

Second, as indicated in figures 2.1 (all municipalities) and 2.4 (the thirty research municipalities), and table 2.2, local governments began to receive significantly increased fiscal transfers in 1994. Very simply, there was more to contest by the mid-1990s. In the words of one town councilor, "Municipalities have gone from not managing anything to being millionaires."[24] Potential and actual politicians at local levels were clearly able to see the benefit of holding office when such sums were at stake. An academic studying local governance in Oaxaca argued that prior to the surge in resources available to local governments, no one was interested in being mayor because there were no resources to manage nor was there any prestige associated with holding local office.[25] In another municipality, a former mayor recalled, "When I was a councilor . . . in 1975, the municipality subsisted on what it could collect from fees for slaughtering livestock and commercial taxes, as well as fees for marriage licenses and registering births. If I'm not mistaken, about 500 pesos a month was managed. Before, no one wanted to be municipal president. Why would anyone want to be?"[26]

Increased resources translated into tangible benefits for municipalities, for parties, and for individuals. Clearly, more resources meant that municipalities could invest in improvements like paved roads, parks, better garbage collection, more extensive electricity and potable water systems, and job-creating industrial parks. And, indeed, most of the research municipalities boasted more investments in infrastructure and services; public officials were consistent in indicating the importance of having control over resources in order to "attend to local needs." One municipal councilor acknowledged that because of increased federal funds for social infrastructure, "it was possible to construct 80–100 percent more [public] works than in past administrations."[27]

Increased resources also proved to be a bonanza for patronage opportunities. Municipalities that could now be more active in providing local infrastructure, social service provision, and economic development generated more jobs in town hall. As indicated in the previous chapter, like presidents and governors, mayors had much discretion in terms of filling jobs in the executive. In the research municipalities, they selected the directors of all municipal offices—chief administrative officer, municipal secretary, public works, police, rural development, markets and slaughterhouses, public health, urban development, economic development, youth and sports, and so on.

Their powers of appointment generally extended much beyond directorships to subdirectors, office workers, and others. A majority of officials interviewed indicated that they were hired for their jobs because they had been active in the winning candidate's campaign or were friends of the mayor. A common criticism by non-majority party councilors was that the mayor had filled town hall with relatives, friends, and opportunists. One councilor in Yucatán referred to the personnel change after a recent election as a "purge," and in Guanajuato, a town treasurer reported a 50 percent turnover in her office after the election.[28] Of course, unionized public servants in these municipalities—one-third of the total—were immune from such changes, although their responsibilities might be shifted around with the advent of a new administration. Even with this exclusion, however, the extent to which mayors could dispense employment opportunities expanded rapidly.

Moreover, mayors often had considerable influence over who would hold positions on the council. Particularly in cases in which parties were unified behind a single candidate for mayor, this person had much to say about those who would be on the party lists for councilor positions and in what order they would appear on those lists. Repeatedly, when councilors were asked about how they got on lists for the elections, they reported having been recruited by their party's candidate for mayor. In cases in which there was less internal party agreement on who would head the list, the party's nominee was still in a strong position to negotiate over positions on it.

Combined, executive and legislative positions added up to significant numbers. With some 500 workers, for example, a municipality in Oaxaca was the largest local employer, giving the *ayuntamiento* considerable weight in the local economy.[29] In another municipality, the treasurer suggested why local elections were so important. "People live from politics [because . . . they] . . . don't have any other important sources of income.[30] In a municipality in Yucatán, a councilor complained of an "explosion" of high-paying positions in recent years.[31] At times, the creation of new jobs was inventive. In one large municipality, each councilor was assigned a substitute, thus doubling the number of positions on the town council.[32] "Jobs for the boys" was an important way in which parties were able to build support during election campaigns. As one former mayor explained, candidates and their allies promised people during campaigns, "If I can't give you a job, I'll give you a recommendation for one."[33]

Control over town hall also offered benefits to individual incumbents. In the research municipalities, the subject of corruption was regularly part of political discussions. Although there are no data to assess the extent of personal enrichment, a number of the municipalities had reputations for high levels of corruption, admitted even among municipal officials. Citizens regularly commented on the appearance of new cars, new houses, and lucrative business ventures owned by local public officials. In Puebla, the president of a local Rotary Club spoke of the importance of "the prize" that politicians got for winning office, investing a lot of money in running for office and, when they won, having an opportunity to realize a return on this investment.[34] A former mayor was remembered in one municipality for the cars, motorcycles, taverns, and grocery and other stores he accumulated while in office.[35] Elsewhere, narcotrafficking and influence over municipal funds was cited as a primary reason for becoming a candidate for mayor.[36] In Tamaulipas, competition was explained by the fact that politicians knew how much money could be made in the *ayuntamiento*.[37]

Of course, not all mayors or municipal governments were corrupt, and some were well known to be examples of probity. Even then, however, salaries of mayors and councilors were widely reported to be high—often $1,200–$1,600 per month—quite a sum for these medium-sized, mostly poor municipalities. "Mayors become *riquísimos*," explained a former local party president.[38]

Equally important, winning control of town hall provided an important "trampoline" for individuals to move on to more important public offices. Assessments of political careers in large cities indicate a general trend across many countries for mayors of national capitals to become strong contenders in presidential elections.[39] In Mexico, becoming mayor was also an important step toward political mobility. Because elected officials cannot immediately succeed themselves in office, to remain active in politics, they must seek other offices. Characteristically for mayors, this meant becoming the local deputy to the state legislature or standing for election to the national congress. Locally, being mayor was often referred to as a stairway or trampoline for political ascendance, a factor recognized by one respondent, who argued that "Currently, being a mayor is one of the most rapid ways to be taken seriously as a future candidate for positions of greater importance, such as a state or federal deputy."[40]

The formation of an opposition. The increased lure of public office, particularly in the second half of the 1990s, was important in explaining the emergence and growth of opposition parties at local levels. Although in a few cases the mobilization of parties to oppose the PRI in the research municipalities was a result of the incursion of nonlocal partisans working to organize local affiliates, in most cases, the creation of an opposition responded to local dynamics. In a large number of the research municipalities, in fact, factionalism within the PRI was responsible for creating the opposition.

A good example of this occurred in the early 1980s in a Oaxacan municipality, when a group of young teachers within the PRI banded together to challenge the local *cacique*, who controlled the economy through his monopoly on regional transport and his role in coffee marketing, and who dominated local politics through his relationships with patrons at the state level.[41] The insurgents ran him out of town, and when the state government stepped in to manage the conflict, a deal was struck that the *cacique* and the leader of the insurgents would both move elsewhere. For a period, the PRI was infused with new ideas as the remaining teachers took control of the local party apparatus and the PRI recaptured some legitimacy among local voters. In 1989, however, internal party elections pitted a candidate of the old guard against a candidate of the insurgent group. When the former won by only four votes in intraparty elections, the reformers suspected fraud.[42] At that point, they defected from the PRI to affiliate with the PRD, which had just been organized at the national level.

This was not an isolated dynamic. In another municipality in Oaxaca, opposition emerged within the PRI because one important community was consistently denied resources by the town government. Discontented leaders decided to form a local chapter of the PAN to contest elections.[43] In yet another Oaxacan site, a former PRI leader ran for office under the PRD label when he was not chosen by the PRI to head its party list in the election. The PAN emerged in two Guanajuato municipalities when disaffected PRIistas decided that their party was not going to reform itself.[44] The importance of party change in town hall motivated political leaders in two other municipalities in the same state to join the PAN in the first half of the 1990s.[45] A PRD candidate in Tamaulipas had been an official in a prior PRI administration but left the party when it chose someone else to be its standard-bearer for municipal president.[46]

Whatever the motivation, the emergence of opposition parties at the local level at times posed considerable risk for the initial members. The chief administrative officer of one municipality commented that he had been one of the first PANistas in town, "at a time when being a PANista was like if you were Catholic and you became a Protestant." And another official in the same town echoed that "it was considered practically a crime to support the PAN" in the 1980s.[47] When a PRIista turned-PRDista in the same town became a candidate for mayor in 2000, he was attacked at gunpoint and told to stay out of the race. He was beaten and left with a broken leg.[48] A mayor who had long been loyal to the PAN in Yucatán was reluctant to become its candidate because he worried about reprisals that would affect his career as a teacher.[49] The local PAN president in yet another municipality recalled the early days of party organizing. "I joined the PAN in 1981, when we fought against the single party. . . . We were attacked, the police pursued us, and people erased the slogans we painted on walls."[50]

The overall story of opposition party emergence in the thirty municipalities was not primarily one of local heroics in the face of repression by the PRI, however. Instead, a much more common story was that the local PRI organization did not provide candidacies for all aspiring office holders; disgruntled members defected to form or join incipient local opposition parties, as soon as it began to be clear that parties other than the PRI stood some chance of winning. In short, many aspiring candidates "shopped" for parties and selected those that they thought would give them the best electoral support and the best relationship with state and national governments.[51] Jockeying for leadership, parties also offered councillorships to members of other parties in exchange for the votes of their followers.[52] These dynamics helped diminish the importance of ideology and party platforms in elections.

Parties under Fire

According to many public officials and citizens, increased competition for political office was important in "forcing the parties to modernize themselves."[53] This was perhaps most true for the PRI. While there continued to be complaints that the PRI had not changed its colors from the old days of its dominance, many more of those interviewed referred to elections in which the PRI won with lower margins of victory as "a wake-up call" for the party.

A PRIista administrator observed that "suddenly, we didn't have the power we had had for decades," and in a staunch PRI municipality, a local party president asserted that in the previous election, it was clear "the people have given a vote of confidence to the PRI for the last time."[54] According to the latter, "I'm an old militant of the PRI and I realize how things have changed. Now you can't trick people. Information is available and now it is important to speak truthfully because people are aware."[55] A former PRI mayor commented that since 1989, "the population has realized that it was possible to participate more actively. Now the PRI is more open, there's more internal competition, and the credentials of its leaders are clearer."[56]

There were certainly pressures on the PRI to clean up its act. But, as other parties became more likely to control the *ayuntamiento*, they also began to face these same risks. Indeed, in the thirty municipalities, the probability of an incumbent party losing control over town hall had risen from .06 in 1990 to .50 by 2004, even though incumbents routinely benefited from municipal funds and logistical support for their campaigns. This sense of threat even encouraged a party in a Yucatecan municipality to hire a political consultant from the United States to manage its local campaign.[57] In several municipalities, unlikely coalitions emerged out of the pressure to win elections—the leftist PRD with the rightist PAN, for example, or the traditional PRI with the new green party (PVEM).

Deep divisions within the party controlling town hall were regularly cited as reasons for election losses. In one traditionally strong PRI municipality, for example, a PAN win was credited more to the "political deterioration" of the PRI than to the expansion of the newer party's membership base.[58] In many cases, intraparty strife resulted in defections to other parties. Where the PRI maintained control in local elections, the failure of opposition parties was often blamed on their internal conflicts, "capitalized on by the PRI, which continues being the party that offers people [at least] a minimum of certainty."[59] The PRD in one Oaxacan municipality, for example, was plagued by the kind of internal divisions that portended electoral disasters. "So, when the mayoral candidate belonged to [one faction], those of the [other faction] would not help out in the elections and [when it worked in reverse, the losing faction] refused to mobilize its people during the campaign."[60] After losing an incumbency, party leaders in all states routinely noted the need for reestablishing unity if the party hoped to win again.

Not surprisingly, then, party unity became significantly more important as competition increased, and parties used diverse strategies to achieve it. For example, important changes in internal procedures were sometimes put in place to limit the divisive effect of jockeying for leadership of the local party list. In contrast to the days of PRI hegemony when the governor or the local *cacique* determined who would stand for election by *dedazo*, more democratic internal party processes evolved within party organizations in many places. In some cases, local party leaders described efforts to make candidate selection processes more open and transparent.[61] Contending leadership candidates might be presented and voted upon by the membership of the party. Winning these internal elections at times meant that an entire list of candidates for council positions was also agreed upon. Frequently, though, losing precandidates were offered positions on the list of candidates for the council.

In some cases, once the candidate for mayor had been decided, a process of negotiation with contending lists of councilor candidates ensued. In such cases, party unity was sought by providing places on the list for various factions. In one municipality in Guanajuato, the leader of each of three lists proposed three candidates for council seats on the final list, and then their order on that list was negotiated.[62] There were times, however, when internal party conflicts could not be resolved locally. The 2003 candidate for the PAN in one locality in Guanajuato, for example, had to be decided by the state level party directorate because competing local factions could not agree.[63] A similar kind of internal dissent elsewhere led the PRI to curtail local voting for precandidates in favor of selection by the governor.[64]

The threat of losing elections encouraged another development in the parties—they began to pay more attention to selecting candidates they hoped would be appealing to local voters. At times, the means for doing so contributed to internal democratic practices. After losing an election in a PRI stronghold in Tamaulipas, for example, that party organized a broad consultation with its voter base to select its next candidate for mayor.[65] In Puebla, a municipal party began conducting voter surveys to determine the popularity of potential candidates.[66] A deeply divided PAN in a Oaxacan municipality sought to overcome its inability to win elections by selecting a candidate who was well respected in the community but not affiliated with any party.[67] In Tamaulipas, the PRI state party council ceded more authority to its local organization in selecting candidates, a change from the old days of the governor's *dedazo*.[68] The PRI in some locations began to rejuvenate itself by drawing new and younger members into local party decision-making councils.

Retail Campaigns, Old Style

Increased competition was an important factor in altering the internal dynamics of the parties and, in many cases, encouraging them to adopt more democratic processes in selecting their candidates for public office. Modernizing the internal workings of the parties did not dramatically affect how campaigns were carried out, however. Instead, campaigning in a multiparty Mexico closely resembled campaigns in the old dominant party Mexico. Continuing practices from the days of PRI hegemony, for example, promising jobs was the most important way to recruit campaign workers.[69] As a consequence, when campaigns were under way, *ayuntamientos* tended to resemble ghost towns, as elected and appointed officials absented themselves to work for their candidates.

As in traditional campaigns of the PRI, party platforms were not important means for generating votes for local offices. Campaign slogans generally focused on vague promises of a better future—among them "Working Shoulder to Shoulder," "A Government that Works for You" and "Working Together for a Better Municipality."[70] Specific promises for attention to very specific problems—a better access road to the community, potable water and electricity, drainage, a new bridge—were the stuff of daily campaigning. Equally important were individual promises of a job, a water hookup, a new roof for a house. Thus, as in the past under the long reign of the PRI, community-level political rallies were complemented by a great deal of one-on-one campaigning and listening to the individual grievances of citizens. In the research municipalities, candidates visited as many homes and localities as possible during a campaign, listening to problems and promising to resolve them when the candidate won. Significant numbers of citizens helped organize rallies and marches, put up signs, and worked to get out the vote for their candidates. Parties also sent their activists out to do surveys and to report back on what local communities were most concerned about. Campaigning in a more electorally competitive Mexico, then, mirrored a long tradition of labor-intensive retailing of promises and candidates.

Beyond promises, candidates brought gifts to potential voters. To demonstrate their sincerity, for example, they might bring paint for the local school and set local party activists to work painting it, or distribute sports equipment to community clubs or schools. Again, individual benefits, such as those distributed in the days of PRI dominance, were important for attracting voters—a chit for medicine from a local pharmacy or food from a local store, cement blocks for housing, free seeds and gasoline, for example. In the case of highly competitive elections, the amount of patronage and clientelistic practices might even have increased.

These preelection gifts led to widespread charges of electoral fraud and vote buying. In one municipality, it was asserted that candidates could buy a vote for about $20; elsewhere votes were reputed to cost between $15 and $25.[71] Frequently, also, incumbent parties were accused of using municipal funds for the campaigns of their candidates; similarly, incumbents were not above hoarding municipal funds so they could be spent on social services and public works just prior to elections.[72] And charges of electoral fraud, common enough during the heyday of PRI ascendance, were also part of the more competitive electoral arena, and included such counterproductive behavior as a losing party seizing ballot boxes in a contested election and burning them, thus destroying the only evidence it had for securing redress.

On a more positive note, this form of campaigning did much to educate candidates about the needs and desires of their constituents. In addition, unconstrained by party platforms, parties could alter their priorities from one election to the next. Thus, for example, "In the last election, the candidates promised a university, more health clinics, school lunches, handouts, and cement blocks. This year, the people are worried about roads, jobs, and seeds for their crops."[73]

Living with Pluralism: The *Cabildo*, the *Ayuntamiento*, and Performance

Common patterns in the research municipalities indicated the emergence of hotly contested local elections, something new in Mexico. The way in which campaigns were carried out, however, closely mimicked the kinds of political campaigns that were characteristic of Mexican politics in the past. The strong tradition of retail campaigning meant that winning parties usually arrived in the *ayuntamiento* without a clear program of office or even a mandate about important issues they should tackle. Programs were typically crafted once newcomers had arrived in municipal offices and, at times, no consistent programs at all were developed. Moreover, once in office, incumbents found that governing often entailed significant conflict within town hall. Such conflict could stand in the way of improved performance even if local leaders were committed to better governance.

Mayors in the thirty research municipalities, citing increased electoral competition, routinely commented that they felt pressured to ensure that the local government performed well during their administrations. The closer the election, it seemed, the more they felt the pressure to do well so the party could win the next election. This concern was particularly interesting when it came from PRI incumbents. Repeatedly, they referred to the "wake-up call" of the previous election; they were clearly looking over their shoulders at the returns of other parties, very aware of the implication of the narrowing gap in votes between winners and losers.

Specific changes in town hall were often credited to this kind of electoral threat—increases in the number of professionals who were part of municipal administrations, greater attention to the concerns of citizens, less corrupt use of public resources, more effort to distribute resources equitably among communities, selection of appointed officials on the basis of merit, and so forth. In several municipalities, mayors introduced measures to select sub-municipal representatives through election rather than the older method of appointment by the chief executive.[74]

Many mayors indicated that the motivation behind introducing better administration and other innovations was a direct response to the need of the party to maintain its electoral edge. In a municipality in Puebla, for example, a process for more equitably allocating public resources among neighborhoods was credited with increasing the vote for the PRI after the government had been in PAN hands for some years.[75] In another municipality in the same state, the mayor introduced changes in how public works were done in order to demonstrate that "The PRI also knows how to work."[76] In yet another site in the same state, the PAN was credited with demonstrating how to bring good governance to the municipality: "Now that we have won," said a councilor, "let's show that we know how to do a good job."[77] There were even cases of a highly unusual decision in Mexican politics—when a different party took control of town hall, the incoming party maintained improvements introduced by the previous government when these had proved popular among citizens.[78]

Nevertheless, statistical tests of electoral competitiveness and government performance failed to produce a significant correlation between these factors in the research municipalities.[79] In fact, some of the most competitive electoral sites were characterized by very low and even dysfunctional performance.[80] There was also little connection between performance and the party controlling the government.[81] This is interesting,

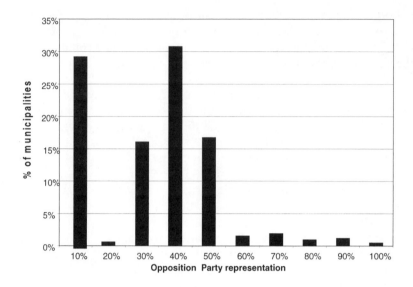

Figure 3.2. Opposition party representation on all municipal councils, 2003. Source: INAFED, Sistema Nacional de Informacion Municipal, available at www.inafed.gob.mx.

given that many have credited the PAN as a party with particular concern about good governance; the empirical assessment suggests that PAN governments were no more likely to be heading up satisfactorily performing governments than were their PRI and PRD counterparts.[82]

A strong sense of pressure to perform well, but little evidence that electoral competition resulted in better performance—what is behind these contradictory findings? Increased contention within the *ayuntamiento* provides part of the answer to this question. More competitive elections often left behind divided councils, partisan bickering over the allocation of municipal resources, and administrators frustrated by gridlocked decision making.

Mexico's electoral system contributed to the fractionalization of the local legislature. As indicated in chapter 2, the 1983 revision of Article 115 of the national constitution mandated proportional representation for seats on municipal councils. As a consequence, pluralism became a more regular feature of these councils. Figure 3.2 indicates the increasing representation of opposition parties in *cabildos* nationally. A third of Mexico's municipal councils had at least 40 percent opposition party representation. Figure 3.3 shows the extent of pluralism on councils in the research municipalities in 2003, showing only six with less than 30 percent representation of opposition parties. By the early 2000s, then, may-

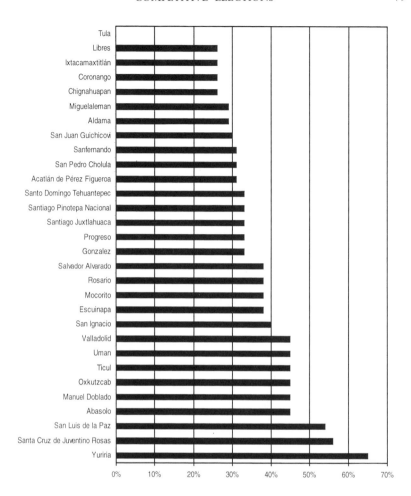

Figure 3.3. Opposition party representation on municipal councils in research municipalities, 2003. Source: INAFED, Sistema Nacional de Informacion Municipal, available at www.inafed.gob.mx.

ors presided over municipal councils that had multiparty representation. For these mayors, it was no longer true that "the PRI and town hall were one and the same."[83]

More pluralist municipal councils resulted in more conflict over the distribution of social and physical infrastructure and the distribution of jobs. Characteristically, mayors and some councilors would disagree about responding to particular local needs or particular communities. Frequently, these disagreements were about whether the municipal seat or other, primarily rural, communities should be favored with public works. Similarly, there were hotly contested processes for appointing officials to local government positions, with opposition parties pressuring mayors for a share of the jobs.

At the center of these conflicts were the mayors, who presided over council meetings. They were the most important decision makers, largely because of their appointive powers within the municipal government and, in most cases, their leadership of the party with the greatest representation on the council. This gave them considerable capacity to affect municipal investments in social services or public works and to pack the municipality with party loyalists. A councilor in Guanajuato, for example, spoke for many of those interviewed when he stated that the mayor responded to all requests for various kinds of works by saying, "I won't support these people because they aren't of my party, or I won't help these people because they offended me during the campaign." Another councilor in the same municipality lamented that "people trust in us, and then, because they didn't vote for the mayor . . . he doesn't approve their petitions [for services and works]."[84]

Depending on the makeup of the councils, however, the councilors also had some capacity to stall or derail mayoral plans. Forming coalitions in which parties aligned in opposition to the mayor's party was one way to do this. "There isn't physical or verbal friction, of course," a municipal secretary said, "but lots of political gaming."[85] Council meetings could be long—in one municipality a meeting dragged on for fourteen hours—as councilors and mayors tussled over their differences. In some cases, conflicts could only be resolved by higher levels of government, as was the case in a Guanajuatan municipality in which the state government had to step in to help negotiate who would secure important administrative positions.[86] Mayors in some localities complained that the system had become ungovernable.

The increase of candidates shopping for party labels prior to elections contributed to difficulties in reaching agreements in the council. In several cases, councilors arrived in the municipal hall under the banner of an adopted party, and then changed their affiliations to other parties. For example, in Tamaulipas, PANista councilors who had been PRIistas before the election defected back to their original party; in Sinaloa, a winning party coalition reverted to individual party blocs once it arrived in town hall.[87] Thus, it was not uncommon for a new mayor to arrive in office with a fractured council. *Cabildazos*, in which councilors voted to oust the incumbent mayor, occurred in a number of the research municipalities. In a locality in Oaxaca, nineteen mayors served between 1984 and 2004: seven finished their full term of office, two were ousted by citizen uprisings, two were administrators sent by the state government as caretakers, two left before their terms were completed to run for higher office, and six were voted out by the *cabildo*.[88]

Such tensions were moderated in some municipalities through negotiation; in others, decision-making gridlock occurred. Where opposition on the *cabildo* was particularly strong, mayors might even join it. For example, a PAN mayor in Oaxaca aligned himself consistently with the PRI in the council, in large part because he was a PRIista who had left that party to find a leadership position in the PAN.[89] In another state, the mayor was willing to work with the opposition party to facilitate agreement in the council.[90] Some mayors sought to defuse partisanship through the introduction of improved management practices, as did the mayor who was able to convince the city council that examinations should be required for aspirants to administrative positions.[91]

Similarly, in the contentious state of Oaxaca, mayors and opposition councilors regularly negotiated over which parties department heads would be selected from and on one occasion, the mayor was pressured into conceding one more seat on the council than required by the election results.[92] Elsewhere, regular meetings among ten councilors representing five different factions and the department heads helped moderate conflict over the allocation of public resources.[93] In yet another municipality, the mayor and the councilors used ties of affinity to overcome political differences among them.[94] In efforts to establish consensus, there were incentives in many councils to commit the municipality to invest in highly visible public works that all councilors could take credit for—remodeling parks, building a new highway into the town—and adding people to the municipal employment rolls. Thus, considerable effort often went into becoming "very good enemies," as one party president said.[95]

Yet in a number of municipalities, partisan conflict affected the ability of the local government to function. A director of public works complained that in a pluralist *cabildo*, each party bloc had a different set of priorities.[96] Holding up the approval of budget resources for particular activities was one way councilors tried to control the administrative aspects of town hall. The relative importance of councilors and administrative directors was another source of friction. Opposition councilors, appointed to oversee particular aspects of municipal government, complained regularly that the appointed officials whose work they were supposed to oversee did not communicate with them, failed to respond to their requests, and did not send them information. Almost as frequently, officials maintained that the councilors did not support their initiatives because they interfered with their constituent relations—traffic tickets that were "fixed" at a town hall that was attempting to provide more consistent service was a classic example of this kind of discord. Whereas administrators always had offices, councilors were often relegated to cubicles or had no place to sit other than the main *cabildo* meeting room.

At times, conflicts threatened the peace of the municipality. In one location in Oaxaca, dissident PRIistas left the party in 1994 to create a "Council of Municipal Collaboration," that was subsequently recognized by the state government as a parallel government—the only way to deal with the depth of local conflict over the control of the *ayuntamiento*. The alternative government—which affiliated itself with the PRD—began receiving funds from the state government, issuing licenses, and managing public works investments at the same time that the "official" government carried out the same functions. The municipality was characterized by extensive conflict, with protests, road blocks, and various "takings" of town hall.[97]

In the same municipality, town hall was again taken over by the PRD in an electoral dispute; the newly elected mayor and his government set up shop in a private home.[98] A citizens' assembly was eventually called and voted to oblige the losing party to abandon its siege; it did so, but not before it had set fire to the *ayuntamiento*. In yet another municipality, the town hall was taken by the opposition in the early summer of 2004 in a demand that the municipal government be audited; the elected government repaired to local offices of a state program.[99] In a municipality in Puebla, one mayor was thrown out of town for six months and another had to leave for a month in related disputes. Three people died in these conflicts.[100]

An even more difficult situation developed in a municipality in which two governments emerged from the elections. In 2001, charging electoral fraud, a coalition of the PAN, the PRD, and the Partido del Trabajo (PT) took over the *ayuntamiento*, with the loss of some life. The state government recognized the PRI electoral victory and the "official" government set up shop in the municipal cultural center, while the "popular" government remained in the town hall. Within months, however, a semblance of order was worked out by distributing activities between the official and the popular governments—the official government responsible for cleaning some streets, the popular government responsible for others, two separate police departments, the official government receiving federal funds, the popular government collecting taxes in the market, and property owners left to decide which government they wished to pay taxes to. Meanwhile, the state government recognized the continuance of this situation as the only way to maintain peace in the municipality.

These kinds of conflicts, and the methods adopted to try to resolve them, were not exclusive to a more electorally competitive Mexico, of course. Some of the most conflict-ridden municipalities had histories of violent politics long before the PRI lost its hegemony. However, electoral competition introduced more pluralism into town hall, and broader participation in municipal decision making contributed to more widespread disagreements in that process of decision making. Not surprisingly, greater political pluralism was sometimes damned for bringing divisions, inability to extract resources from the state governments, and violence. While municipal officials acknowledged greater awareness of the need to perform their activities better because of the threat of losing office in the next election, they were not necessarily able to transfer this concern directly into better governance.

CONCLUSIONS

Countries that moved toward more democratic elections and decision-making processes after 1980 often had high expectations about the problems that more democratic systems could resolve. Citizens in such countries were probably right to anticipate, eventually, greater transparency and accountability from government. No doubt citizens in democratizing countries were also wise to anticipate that their votes would be more assiduously courted and their participation would become more important to political parties. In Mexico, certainly, these were among the clear benefits of more competitive local electoral contests, contests that became more meaningful as a result of the decentralization of responsibilities and resources to the municipal level.

But democratization of elections does not necessarily lead to less conflictive politics, easier decision making, or better functioning governments. In Mexico, multiparty elections brought multiparty decision making in town hall. Although an electoral system based on proportional representation and party lists integrating executive and legislative positions should have minimized the problems of gaining approval for government initiatives and programs, there were many opportunities for failure to achieve just this result. Among them, the often opportunistic emergence of parties in opposition to the PRI encouraged the defection of elected officials from their party blocs on the council. In addition, mayoral control of extensive patronage opportunities furthered the distance between winners and losers in decision making in town hall, increasing incentives of losers to forestall action. For such reasons, the relationship between competitive elections and good governance remained weak.

In a book on federalism and state governments in Mexico, Ward and Rodríguez conclude that "The rise of opposition parties at the state and local level has broken the mold of governmental (PRI) orthodoxy and brought to the foreground new actors, new approaches to government, and new styles of governance."[101] In the thirty medium-sized municipalities in this study, new actors did indeed emerge in political life. On the question of "new approaches to government and new styles of governance," however, the picture was much less clear.

Photo by Xóchitl León.

Chapter 4

AT WORK IN TOWN HALL
Leadership and Performance

In 1993, a chapter of the Junior Chamber of Commerce was inaugurated in Chignahuapan, in the state of Puebla. Soon, the organization had a committed membership of local businesspeople and professionals, and it met regularly to explore topics related to leadership, personal development, organizational management, and communication. Over many years of common experiences, members developed close ties and deep commitment to the ideals of the chamber. They praised the organization for providing them with insights into how they could work toward higher personal and professional goals. In their municipality of 50,000 people, the chamber was a source of inspiration and new ideas.

In 2000, a member of this close-knit group ran in the PRI party primary as a candidate for mayor. This was a logical step for any aspiring politician in Chignahuapan, given that the PRI had long held monopoly power in local politics.[1] But the chamber's candidate did not win the primary. His supporters, charging fraud, took to the streets in protest. Soon after this, the local PAN (Partido Acción Nacional) organization—with twenty-one official members—voted him the top position on its electoral list. Then, in a surprise toppling of the old order in 2001, the PAN triumphed in the local elections; the PRI was left with a mere 20 percent of the seats on the council.

The new mayor quickly selected five members of the chamber for important jobs in the *ayuntamiento*—director of professional training and social communication, chief of personnel, director of urban development, chief of the municipal fair, and municipal legal officer. Inspired by their common experience, the new team quickly committed itself to bring a different style to town hall. "From the beginning of the administration, we decided that this wouldn't be like the previous administration."[2] Instead, the team would work for a professional and service-oriented administration. It wanted the activities of town hall to be transparent and focused on results.[3]

Soon, a local government that was best described as mediocre began to change dramatically. Large signs appeared outside departments within the building to inform citizens about where to go for specific services; a mission statement was placed at the entrance; suggestion boxes appeared in the marketplace and other locations where residents were likely to congregate; employees received extensive training about how to do their jobs better; council meetings were opened to the public; the town budget was made available to citizens so they could monitor expenditures; garbage collection improved. Impressively, within three months of taking office, the civil registry was computerized; to speed service, "customers" obtained a numbered ticket from a machine so they would be assisted in the order of their arrival; the number of the person currently being helped was displayed electronically. Branch offices of the registry were also established. According to officials, the waiting period for obtaining documents from the registry declined from a week or more to as little as twenty minutes, depending on the number of people in line. The need to bribe officials to get service disappeared, they said.

The mission-focused leaders of Chignahuapan were confident of their success in turning town hall into a more efficient and effective place, in improving services, and in reducing corruption. And, at the end of their three years in office, they were proud of the changes they had made. Yet they were equally certain that a PRI administration would succeed them—the municipality had always been a party stronghold in a state with a strong PRI machine. They believed that the 2001 election had been an aberration. Nevertheless, the incumbents hoped that any PRI candidates would have learned the lesson that they needed to be more attuned to public service than had been true in the past. In fact, the PRI backed a reformist candidate reported to be close to the incumbent mayor—who continued to identify himself as a PRIista even though he represented the PAN as mayor. The PAN's candidate also promised to continue its record of good government policies if elected. In November 2004, the PAN was returned to town hall; many were optimistic that the new mayor would continue the work introduced by the previous administration.[4]

Chignahuapan's experience suggests how quickly performance can be altered at local levels of government. Within months of taking office, visible and significant changes had taken place in the way the municipality carried out its business and delivered services. Party ideology and membership did not play a large role in this minor local revolution. After all, those who entered town hall in 2001 had been PRIistas prior to having been courted by the PAN. Although they conformed to much of the stereotype of PAN members—local businesspeople and professionals with strong commitments to providing good service, conservative in social values, believers in the role of professionals in managing public and private affairs—their ideas were formed by membership in the local Junior Chamber of Commerce rather than the party. Moreover, when interviewed, members of this team were clear: leadership, not party affiliation, was the key to understanding what they had been able to accomplish. The fact that Mexico was becoming more electorally competitive opened up an opportunity for them to acquire positions of public influence. But it was their personal values of public service, efficiency, and effectiveness that made the difference, they claimed.

The story of Chignahuapan raises an important question: how central is public leadership to the performance of local governments? Certainly the leadership factor has been found to be important in bringing about policy and institutional changes in many developing countries. Beginning in the 1980s, for example, studies of policy reform consistently demonstrated that economic crisis, abysmal social sector conditions, or mobilization of dissent were not sufficient to explain why new economic or social sector policies were introduced or why some countries introduced changes and others balked at doing so.[5] When new policies were put in place, researchers regularly found that leadership was an important factor. Thus, it became common to read of policy entrepreneurs, policy champions, and change teams acting as strategic players in complex political processes in order to increase opportunities for reform. Increasingly, studies went beyond accolades about impressive and forceful leaders to consider how particular actors worked to promote change.[6] Leadership, in this perspective, was not to be confused with charisma or blind idealism; instead, it was the result of strategic action within particular contexts to make way for the introduction of new policies and practices.

A number of studies of innovation in local government have concurred that leadership matters. In a study of decentralization in Latin America, for example, Tim Campbell observed that "a champion or visionary is found in virtually every experience of innovation."[7] The skills such leaders bring to the reform process are multiple, according to the same study. "A champion—an author, entrepreneur, or leader—was able to 'read' what is possible at a given historical moment, to understand what the public wants and to visualize a new way of doing things. Above all, the champion is able to convert this vision into reality."[8] In another study about municipal innovation, Enrique Cabrero identified important activities undertaken by dynamic local leadership, including improving organizational performance and strengthening intergovernmental relationships.[9]

Was leadership—referred to in the first chapter as state entrepreneurship—an important factor in explaining performance differences across the research municipalities in Mexico? This chapter explores this question. It traces patterns of decision making about resource allocation in town hall, details the activities of local officials, considers the extent to which such officials had room for maneuver, and discusses the competing pressures they experienced. The analysis suggests that mayors and other officials had extraordinary opportunities to introduce change, in large part because of the weak institutional context within which they were working; it also indicates that their ongoing impact was limited by the same institutional context. The story of Chignahuapan can be generalized, it seems, but opportunities for change do not necessarily speak to the sustainability of governance improvements.

Welcome to Town Hall, Your Honor

The scope for introducing change was apparent as newly elected and appointed officials entered town hall for the first time. They encountered a wide range of issues that needed attention. Their first challenge was to address three overriding questions: what was to be done? how would it be done? and, when would it be done? Answering these questions required considerable hard work, given a paucity of guidance from inside town hall.

Almost universally, municipal authorities complained of the conditions they encountered when they assumed office. Typically, they reported that the previous administration left no useful records of expenditures or activities undertaken, no lists of projects or their beneficiaries, no instructions about how various offices were to be run; no information on past activities, no planning documents. Just as frequently, they charged that they found large bills due to suppliers and contractors. They told of garbage trucks and machinery in disrepair or missing and of the municipal treasury empty or deeply in debt. Previous incumbents, even those from the same party, were faulted for corruption and extensive mishandling of public affairs. There were stories of bridges that collapsed as soon as they were built, new roads that disintegrated rapidly, and deliberate bias in the selection of beneficiaries of social services. Officials described the need to "start from zero" when they entered their offices for the first time.

In one municipality in Guanajuato, the chief administrative officer complained about the lack of organization manuals and the absence of policies and pay structures for public officials, as well as the lack of documentation needed to resolve some ongoing conflicts.[10] In Tamaulipas, a councilor complained that the entire tenure of the incumbent government was spent paying off the debts of the previous administration, and in Yucatán, a councilor was incensed that the *ayuntamiento* had been turned over with chronic deficiencies in maintenance and funds.[11] A similar complaint came from a mayor in the same state.[12] A councilor responsible for overseeing the treasury in a Oaxacan municipality claimed that he inherited only a chair and an official stamp from his predecessor.[13] In Puebla, another complained that in the past there had been no way, other than relying on friends, patrons, or bribes, for citizens to get documents from the civil registry.[14] In Sinaloa, a former mayor was heavily criticized for his frequent absences from the office.[15] These complaints were aired regardless of the party affiliation of the predecessors.

Undoubtedly, incumbents look good if they can cast at least initial blame for faltering services and fiscal conditions on their predecessors. Some of the frequently aired complaints might well be attributed to such a motive. Yet, the extensive turnover of officials that occurred with each election, discussed in the last chapter, did reduce the extent to which institutional memory could survive an election. And some of the actions taken by new arrivals in town hall attested to the validity of at least some of the complaints they made.

In Sinaloa, for example, a new administration organized a parade of municipal vehicles immediately after taking office to demonstrate their state of disrepair and signal to citizens that town hall would not be able to respond immediately to demands for service—at least until it had repaired old and purchased new equipment.[16] A mayor in Yucatán reduced his own salary by one-third as a gesture to emphasize the budgetary difficulties facing the municipality.[17] In another municipality, there was no money to pay salaries for several months after a new administration took office.[18] Elsewhere, recently arrived officials were visited by contractors who offered sizeable personal returns on any work that was directed their way; they explained to the newcomers that this was always the way public works were carried out.[19]

The lack of documents, regulations, and plans that might carry over from one administration to another was endemic in the thirty research municipalities. As indicated in chapter 2, many did not have formal documents in place to define the development activities of the locality, its administration, its zoning, its basic governing institutions, and so forth (see table 2.3). Many of the research municipalities were run without clear boundaries on their activities and decision-making processes. Relationships with other levels of government were often ambiguous or poorly understood. A mayor in Yucatán acknowledged this lack of institutional infrastructure when he committed his first year in office to establishing norms and rules; only in the second and third years of his administrations, he told citizens, would any public benefits become apparent.[20] Even in Chignahuapan, "Every [mayor] has his own style of governing and normally there is no continuity. The new [mayor] arrives and says the previous [mayor] didn't do things well; they have to be done differently. So we start learning all over again about the new [mayor's] style of governing."[21]

Clearly, then, many officials entering office found that not much was set in stone in terms of what needed to be done and how it needed to be carried out. This unstructured context provided ample room for hiring new people, redrawing organizational charts, introducing new departments and responsibilities, and setting up new systems to deal with routine business. Similarly, the daily work of the municipality was subject to considerable change as new administrations came into office—how often the council would meet, whether directors of programs had regular access to the mayor, if work was supervised for quality control, how routine activities were undertaken, whether work progress was reviewed or not, the extent to which councilors spent time in the *ayuntamiento*. At the same time, an agenda for municipal action needed to be determined, and this agenda was typically shaped by the campaign that brought newcomers to town hall.

Legacies of the campaign. For most new administrations, the first order of business was to deal with the consequences of campaigns that were organized around retail politics. As described in the previous chapter, candidates characteristically made a series of promises during their campaigns to attend to particular problems—potholes, drainage ditches, basic services such as water and electricity, roads, garbage, a hospital, a bridge—rather than putting forth a more general program of government. The promises were sometimes initiated by the candidates and sometimes by citizens.

A mayor in Sinaloa, for example, arrived in office having promised to construct a hospital so that citizens would not have to travel far to seek medical attention.[22] A new mayor in Yucatán had promised a large number of individuals that he would help them improve their housing if he won the election.[23] In Puebla, a mayor had committed himself to end the need for bribery or friendship in order to obtain documents from the civil registry.[24] In Tamaulipas, a new highway was promised.[25] Sometimes, the promises suggest that the normal state of municipal governance was particularly low. One mayor explained that he "promised the people that the councilors in my administration would come to work [every day] just like any other worker."[26] Some commitments had personal consequences for the mayor, as when one pledged during the campaign that 50 percent of his salary would be used to provide small grants to senior citizens.[27]

Also characteristically, local campaigns included time-honored rituals in which neighborhoods and individual citizens presented petitions and requests for municipal services. Petitions from communities were usually short, written explanations of an ongoing need, presented to the candidate when he or she came to the community to solicit votes. The petitions were for familiar things—that a road be paved, electricity and public lighting be extended to the location, funding be granted for the annual celebration of the local saint, better service be available for a particular need at town hall, jobs be found. Requests came from individuals who had particular needs such as a uniform to enable a child to go to school, a new roof for a house, medicine, a loan.

However humble, these petitions and requests were taken seriously by most incoming administrations; frequently, collections of them were put together in binders for the perusal of the mayor and the council, and they were discussed even before the budget was determined. Inevitably, they presented new incumbents with a long list of options for municipal attention, raising an immediate issue for decision makers—how to set priorities among a vast number of potential uses of resources.

Setting priorities. State and national laws required that each municipality have a municipal development committee (Comité de Desarrollo Municipal, CDM), composed of the mayor, the councilors, officially chosen community representatives, school directors, and representatives of civil society organizations. It was the job of the CDM to review promises, petitions, and requests and to determine what should be done and in what order. Some municipalities did follow this practice, while others did not. Where this procedure was followed, the initial meeting after an election was often prolonged and tense, as members debated priorities and needs and advocated for the projects that benefited them or their communities.

In some cases, the job of setting priorities through the CDM was eased by prior meetings at the community level in which participants were asked to determine their most important needs before sending this list along to the municipal group. Again, however, there were many municipalities that did not follow this practice. In addition, the CDM was supposed to meet at the outset of subsequent years to review progress and assess priorities; at times, only an initial meeting occurred. Whether followed up or not, the first meeting of the council after an election was the most critical in determining the allocation of public works.

Informal decision rules often emerged in the process of setting priorities for public investments. For example, while laws instructed that resources had to be distributed on the basis of measures of community poverty, other decision rules often emerged. Sometimes, for example, the mayor, the municipal council, and/or the CDM would agree informally on principles such as giving priority to projects that benefited the most people, or ones that benefited rural communities over the municipal seat (or vice versa), or ones that allocated public works equally among communities.

In fact, the role of the CDM in determining public investment allocations was significantly affected by the willingness of mayors to encourage its formation and follow its guidance. Even where this council existed, some mayors pursued priorities that were not consistent with its decisions, as when communities known to be in need of basic services were selected for attention by the mayor even when they had not submitted petitions, and the petitions of others were ignored.[28]

In addition to the work of the CDM, municipal council meetings also played a role in decisions about the allocation of public investments. It was not unusual for each councilor to arrive at meetings with a pet project; over time, in many cases, allocations were made on a quid pro quo basis, in which councilors would trade support for each other's petitions. A very common result of this kind of closed decision making was public works that reflected the political and personal commitments of the mayor or deals he was able to strike with recalcitrant councilors.

Where a municipal development committee was not formed, development priorities were determined by the mayor or debated in the council until agreement could be reached.[29] The requirements of the law were well understood, but alternative mechanisms for making choices about public works priorities were justified by public officials on the grounds of efficiency and lack of citizen engagement in local decision making.

Despite various kinds of inputs into investment decision making, the vast majority of activities undertaken at the local level were a result of mayoral preferences. Some mayors were particularly well-known for dominating the decision process, as suggested by the official who complained that "If it isn't the idea of the mayor, it isn't a good idea."[30] Mayoral intervention was routinely important in developing project ideas, overcoming resistance to change, deciding which communities would benefit from municipal programs, establishing new institutional relationships, effectively delegating responsibility, changing attitudes among councilors, providing vision, professionalizing the work of the government, and communicating effectively with constituents.[31]

The early determination of priorities was intended to set a blueprint for an administration's investments and institutional and procedural changes. Yet the blueprint did not ensure smooth sailing. Competing with the plan was an inflow of petitions and requests that arrived at town hall every day. These requests could prove overwhelming for the mayor and local government if they were not closely channeled and monitored. They could mean the difference between a municipal administration that accomplished its established goals and one that did not.

According to a municipal secretary in Yucatán, and the mayor in another site, about 90 percent of those who came to town hall daily were there to make a request for a favor.[32] The director of public works in a municipality in Tamaulipas estimated that about thirty new petitions arrived in town hall every day.[33] However many there were, they routinely ended up on the mayor's desk, reminiscent of a long tradition of personal and centralized decision making in Mexico. A councilor close to a mayor in Sinaloa repeatedly advised him to cease giving money to those who came to town hall with individual petitions in order to save municipal resources for other, more general tasks.[34]

Routinely, then, mayors were at the center of decision-making processes related to allocating public investments and determining how local government business was to be carried out. Indeed, a number of mayors were able to introduce important changes in the administration, service provision, and public works carried out by the administration in relatively short order. Just as easily, however, this official could fail to take charge, determine priorities for public works, or deal with the day-to-day pressures on town hall. In Mexico and perhaps many other decentralized systems in the developing world, the lack of institutionalized routines and systems expanded the centrality of the mayor to the business of local government. This was certainly true in terms of the role of the mayor in acquiring resources for local development initiatives.

Go Get the Money, If You Can

"If you don't knock on the door, you don't know if there is money or not," reflected a former director of public works.[35] In a decentralized Mexico, municipalities had to work hard to find resources for responding to the long list of undertakings that emerged from campaign promises and priority setting in office. Of course, municipalities had more resources in the 2000s than they had in the 1980s and 1990s, and the trajectory was, overall, in an upward direction. Nevertheless, the bulk of the resources came from federal and state levels, not from increased local revenue from taxes or fees. And much of this money was earmarked for specific purposes. For many kinds of expenditures, including many kinds of public works, disbursements were not automatic or necessarily pegged to a distributional formula. They first had to be "liberated" from state and national sources.

Indeed, liberating funds was *the* priority activity of mayors, councilors, and office directors who wished to improve local conditions and governance. Municipalities differed significantly in the extent to which their officials were able to capture new resources. Table 4.1 indicates wide variability in the per capita public income available in the thirty municipalities in 2002. At the extremes, one municipality had only 527 pesos per capita while another could count on more than three times this figure. Performance, however, was independent of per capita resources, suggesting that the use and management of funds was more important than their availability. The level of per capita resources was also independent of the level of poverty of the municipal population.[36]

TABLE 4.1
Performance and Income of Research Municipalities, 2002

State	Municipality	Performance Score	Population (2000)	Municipal Income (2002)	Municipal Income per Capita
Guanajuato	Abasolo	12	79,093	$84,873,899	$1,073.09
	Manuel Doblado	9	38,309	$55,450,366	$1,447.45
	San Luis de la Paz	13	96,729	$122,203,011	$1,263.35
	Santa Cruz de Juventino Rosas	12	65,479	$81,216,659	$1,240.35
	Yuriria	5	73,820	$95,405,835	$1,292.41
Oaxaca	Acatlán de Pérez Figueroa	6	44,579	$44,552,520	$999.41
	San Juan Guichicovi	8	27,399	$4,451,417	$527.44
	Santiago Juxtlahuaca	9	28,118	$25,912,523	$921.56
	Santiago Pinotepa Nacional	7	44,193	$3,831,720	$765.54
	Santo Domingo Tehuantepec	9	53,229	$37,340,420	$701.51
Puebla	Chignahuapan	15	49,266	$71,260,636	$1,446.45
	Coronango	3	27,575	$25,203,561	$914.00
	Ixtacamaxtitlán	4	28,358	$37,411,393	$1,319.25
	Libres	8	25,719	$31,382,263	$1,220.20
	San Pedro Cholula	5	99,794	$109,124,288	$1,093.50
Sinaloa	Escuinapa	8	50,438	$50,919,814	$1,009.55
	Mocorito	15	50,082	$59,833,320	$1,194.71
	Rosario	11	47,934	$54,441,910	$1,135.77
	Salvador Alvarado	18	73,303	$82,745,503	$1,128.81
	San Ignacio	10	26,762	$34,916,016	$1,304.69
Tamaulipas	Aldama	7	27,997	$32,008,831*	$1,143.30
	González	11	41,455	$42,791,675	$1,032.24
	Miguel Alemán	13	25,704	$39,990,624*	$1,555.81
	San Fernando	9	57,412	$63,296,030	$1,102.49
	Tula	6	27,049	$48,313,521	$1,786.15
Yucatán	Oxkutzcab	13	25,483	$28,572,975	$1,121.26
	Progreso	11	48,797	$58,252,590	$1,193.77
	Ticul	11	32,776	$32,233,447	$983.45
	Umán	9	49,145	$49,757,758	$1,012.47
	Valladolid	6	56,776	$63,865,247	$1,124.86

Source: INEGI, Sistema Municipal de Base de Datos, http://www.inegi.gob.mx/prod_serv/contenidos/espanol/simbad/default.asp?c=73.

   * 2001 figures.

Finding the resources. It was no small undertaking to find resources for local development, to convince those who controlled the funds that they should be committed to a particular project, and to ensure that the money was actually made available. The sources of such funds were numerous, as an assistant to the director of economic development in a Tamaulipan municipality explained; part of his job was to scan state level programs to see which offered the fastest and most appropriate response to local needs.[37] Indeed, the national municipal development institute, INAFED,

TABLE 4.2
Federal Programs for Municipal Development, 2004

Organization	Number of Programs	Number of Subprograms
Banobras (public investments)	12	51
National Commission for the Development of Indigenous Communities	7	32
CONACYT (National Science and Technology Council)	3	0
Ministry of Agriculture, Livestock, Rural Development, Fishing, and Food	26	42
Ministry of Communication and Transportation	14	14
Ministry of Social Development	20	76
Ministry of Government (Interior)	2	0
Ministry of Environment and Natural Resources	8	46
Ministry of Public Education	45	25
Ministry of Finance and Public Credit	11	16
Ministry of Agrarian Reform	3	0
Ministry of Health and Assistance	15	0
Ministry of Labor	3	5
Total	169	307

Source: INAFED,   http://www.inafed.gob.mx/wb2/ELOCAL/ELOC_Descentralización,
April 29, 2004.

listed 169 different federal programs with 307 subprograms providing funds for programs and projects to local governments; each was located in a different part of many different kinds of ministries and could be released only upon conclusion of a set of negotiations and commitments on both sides (see table 4.2). States often were organized in similar ways to support local governments—through funds and programs that required considerable local initiative to unlock.[38] Specific municipal government departments were often in charge of managing fifteen or twenty programs whose funding came partially or fully from nonmunicipal sources.

Obtaining funds depended in the first instance on acquiring information about what was available and who had control over it. This was necessary for two reasons: there was little institutional memory in most town halls that could be drawn on to flag important sources of funds; and the number of possibilities for funding was expanding rapidly, making it difficult for municipal leaders to keep up on the availability of different programs and projects.

Multiple sources of information about funding were available, from the Internet to word of mouth. As an example of the former, a director of rural development found the Web site of the national ministry of social development and discovered a program for microcredit for rural areas;

he followed this up with a phone call to his friends in that ministry to learn more about it.[39] In another municipality, the director of social development found an important housing program in the same way and discovered other ideas from a national program on municipal innovation.[40] Regional meetings of officials, such as treasurers and controllers, provided information on the availability of different kinds of projects, particularly those having to do with capacity building. In some cases, state and federal governments had liaison officers who provided information about various programs. National associations of municipal governments also helped spread the word about funding opportunities.

Much more frequently, however, information reached town hall by way of the personal relationships that local officials established with those at other levels of government. In such cases, the ability to obtain knowledge about programs was one of the hallmarks of an activist mayor. A mayor in Yucatán, for example, spoke of knocking on the doors of three federal undersecretaries in an effort to improve housing in his town; he was able to acquire the resources when he could show that he had the support of the state governor for the project.[41] A former mayor in Tamaulipas told of traveling to Mexico City, as well as to the state capital, to find out about a new program that could provide significant funds for social development.[42]

Liberating the resources. Among the most important relationships for obtaining resources was that developed between the local and state governments, given that the latter increasingly acted as a gatekeeper for federal funds and managed a range of its own programs. In a municipality in Tamaulipas, a state government official defined the job of the mayor as that of "negotiating for money from the state government" in order to implement projects; he commented that some mayors had more friends than others.[43] Indeed, when mayors were praised by local officials and citizens, it was usually because of their ability to "bring down" resources from other levels of government, and particularly from the state government. "The center is no longer the federal government but the state government," one municipal official reported.[44]

The relationship between a mayor and a governor was particularly important in this regard, and it was one carefully cultivated by change-oriented local leaders.[45] A councilor in Oaxaca was clear about the importance of the relationship. "The capacity to attract resources is principally a result of two things; (1) principally it is the result of the mayor's great capacity to hustle (*gestionar*), and (2) his personal friendship with the governor and the majority of state secretaries. . . . He has the trust and friendship of the governor."[46] The mayor reinforced this idea. "Thanks to my friendship and political affinity with the governor, we are finishing [public works] projects."[47]

In Tamaulipas, a mayor was deemed to have been very successful in his job, "because of his great capacity to hustle [funds]. He is a great negotiator."[48] In Sinaloa, one mayor's success was credited to his ability to have a good relationship with the governor, as well as a team he could rely on in town hall, giving him time to devote to the search for resources.[49] In Oaxaca, a municipality was able to construct a new hospital because the project, proposed by the mayor, was one close to the priorities of the governor for his period in office.[50] The availability of computers in schools in a municipality in Puebla was also credited to the friendship of the governor and the mayor, and in Sinaloa, local economic development was acknowledged to be a result of the governor's engagement in local affairs.[51] The views of three mayors who dealt with the same governor are revealing.

> I would talk to the governor when he would come to visit Tula about three or four times a year. You have to learn in what way you can get close to the governor and make your project convincing. I knew that [the governor] was a visual person . . . I laid the projects out on a table with pictures for him to decide which one he would approve.[52]

> When the governor first came to Miguel Alemán in May 2002, I already knew the projects I wanted to implement. In the car ride over from the airport, I laid out my plan. That afternoon [the governor] gave a speech to the people of Miguel Alemán and promised that he would support all of our needs. He said that the drive over with me was the most expensive car ride he had ever taken; it had cost him thirty million pesos![53]

> The new highway was a promise I made during my campaign. Every time I go out, people ask for assistance. You have to know which projects match the municipal priorities and are economically feasible. I met with the governor when he came here to inaugurate a bridge, which was started during the past administration. I already had some basic studies done and the project was well laid out.[54]

Accordingly, mayors were constantly traveling to the capital city to meet with the governor and his secretaries; it was important that they know "which doors to knock on."[55] When citizens complained that the mayor was never in his office, officials routinely reported that he or she was in the state capital, trying to bring down resources for a particular project. One former mayor in Sinaloa said that he had been in the habit of visiting the state capital at least twice a week while he was in office, in each case in pursuit of funding for projects and programs.[56]

Courting the governor's attention meant understanding the governor's own political ambitions. The inauguration of a rural electrification project, for example, provided one mayor with an opportunity to mobilize a large number of people so that the governor, arriving by helicopter, would be impressed by the turnout. When asked by the governor why there were so many people, "I just told them that the governor had invited them so of course they came."[57] And, it was certainly always helpful if the governor or any of his secretaries was a native of the municipality in question; such localities were certain to obtain additional funds.

Where the party affiliation of municipal and state leadership coincided, the development of good relationships between governments was more certain. A mayor in Yucatán believed that he was able to receive federal funds because he had the backing of the state governor, who belonged to the same party as the president and the mayor.[58] A PAN official in Tamaulipas blamed the differing availability of funds from one municipal administration to another on the fact that the state government was controlled by the PRI.[59] A former mayor complained that the state accounting office was used to punish his administration because it did not represent the PRI.[60] In Oaxaca, the lack of equipment in a local health clinic was blamed on the state secretary of health, who had party disagreements with the municipal government.[61] In the same state, one reason given for holding gubernatorial elections prior to municipal elections was so that municipalities could see how the partisan wind was blowing in the state capital before they cast their votes for local officials.[62]

The importance of close relationships to the state government was not limited to the mayor. Almost all directors of various municipal offices reported that much of their time was spent getting to know state level officials who could be helpful to them in liberating funds. A director of social development in a municipality in Guanajuato explained that his primary job was not to handle resources, but to secure them from state and federal offices.[63] For the director of public works in another municipality, a good relationship with the governor meant that the state would send resources, sign agreements for public works, and provide training.[64] "Up until now, no one has said no," reported a chief administrative officer who worked hard to find courses, human relations tools, and computer training from the state government.[65] Local representatives to the state legislature were also important actors in liberating funds for local development and public works, although many said they were not as important as they had been during the time of PRI hegemony, when municipalities had many fewer responsibilities.

A director of cultural development was frank about the sources of her success (and failure). "I depend a great deal on my ability to negotiate for resources, although at times, no matter how much ability you have, you can't get anything."[66] A director of sustainable economic development was pleased with the good working relations that his department had established with the federal and state governments, and was hopeful that similar "political wills" would reverberate in increased economic activities in his municipality.[67] In Oaxaca, community representatives gained enough power over local public works that they often went directly to state offices to solicit resources, rather than going through the municipality.[68] A director of rural development in Tamaulipas lamented that, having invested a great deal of effort in developing good relationships with federal officials of the social development ministry, he would not be in office for another three years to bring additional resources to his municipality.[69]

Ensuring the flow of resources. The dependence of local governments on the cultivation of personal relationships with state and federal ones speaks to the lack of well-founded institutions in the context of decentralization. To the degree that efforts were being made to set rules in place for the distribution and use of resources, these were located at state and federal levels, and, as indicated in chapter 2, their purpose was usually more to control than to facilitate the institutional development of the municipalities. Much of this effort was directed at minimizing potential sources of corruption. In many cases, federal and state governments were more concerned about the process of transferring funds than they were about the actual content of the programs being implemented locally.

State level laws that imposed requirements on the receipt of funds were one way these governments sought to oversee the operations of local governments. In all states, there was a basic law for the municipalities, determining their structure, function, and powers. In Sinaloa, a law required that all municipalities develop an official web page for the municipality; another law required local governments to computerize the civil registry; yet another required municipalities to comply with an access to information policy. In Puebla, a series of laws regulated how federal funds could be distributed at the local level.[70] There were also state laws for municipal procurement, planning, and taxation. The states of Puebla and Sinaloa also took responsibility for auditing the use of federal social development funds.

Administrative and technical regulations were other ways that state and federal governments placed constraints on municipal governments, often in the expectation that they would reduce the extent of local ad hoc decision making. Such requirements usually meant significant delays in funding, their purpose being more to regulate the flow and use of funds. In some cases, resources were not released until local governments had appropriate organizational structures in place for receiving the funding.[71]

Rules about what particular funds could and could not be used for were sometimes introduced after a program was under way.[72]

Local officials resented these constraints. They complained loudly about the "meetings, papers, and requirements" involved in bringing down programs and projects.[73] An official in Tamaulipas reported feeling that the state government was "breathing down our necks."[74] And a councilor in Oaxaca related, "It isn't easy to acquire these funds because the officials of the state executive [branch] want technical studies to back up the request for resources. This requires a significant capacity to propose projects that have technical support."[75] In Sinaloa, the secretary of the municipal government complained about the effort necessary to fill out the paperwork for everything, especially as the municipality was short on trained workers. There were numerous programs and different organizations in charge of them; she often found it almost impossible to understand the distinct rules and regulations of each one.[76] But, the cost of not complying with the regulations, stated one director of public works, was delay in acquiring the funds.[77]

The criteria imposed by such requirements encouraged some municipalities to develop technical skills in project preparation. States often encouraged changes in administrative systems, providing assistance for progressively minded mayors to set up regular systems for assessing property; paying taxes; registering births, deaths, and other personal information; and accounting for resources expended.

However, as long as the personal relationships between the governors and the municipal officials remained important to resource allocation, there was a limit to the extent that state and federal governments could also insist on proper administrative systems for transferring funds from one level of government to another. Indeed, although a number of the research municipalities had made progress in institutionalizing fiscal and administrative activities, the quest for resources often continued to be based primarily on noninstitutional relationships.

GOOD MAYORS, BAD MAYORS

Most respondents concurred that the principal job of the mayor was to liberate funds from other levels of government, by whatever means. Table 4.1 hints at the differences in the ability of mayors to acquire such resources. Yet this was not a full job description for a successful mayor. In addition to spending large amounts of energy on resource extraction, it was also important that this official pay attention to the workings of town hall, undertake constituent service, and be an effective conflict manager and problem-solver. These activities placed considerable burdens on the mayors who wished to promote change in their localities. Moreover, the tasks of liberating resources, managing town hall, constituent service, and conflict resolution required distinct skills and often placed contradictory demands on the mayor.

Managing the *ayuntamiento* in the absence of durable institutions required at a minimum a close monitoring of what different departments were doing and how projects were unfolding. In the municipalities that were notable for their better performance, the mayor met weekly with directors and councilors in charge of various functions. The ostensible purpose of the meetings was to learn about accomplishments and problems these officials were encountering and to allow them to interact with each other where cooperation was necessary. For the mayors, in fact, this was a primary means of increasing the accountability of officials for their work. Failing the prodding of the mayor, few such meetings were held and officials often worked without internal oversight; in some cases, municipal officials might be absent from their offices a good portion of the time. Given the need to travel frequently in their resource extraction role, many mayors appointed loyal friends to the position of secretary of the municipality, who would adopt the mayor's priorities as their own and assume his place when he was away.

In addition, mayors often began their administrations by reorganizing the activities of town hall. Often upset by the chaos they encountered on entering office, activist mayors emphasized such activities as inventories of municipal property and audits of its finances. If they were interested in enhanced performance, they created new departments, particularly those for managing human resources. They developed mission statements and job descriptions for various positions. Similarly, many worked hard to recruit professionals into particular roles, sponsored new systems for performance monitoring, and promoted the computerization of basic municipal activities and records. Mayors who were particularly concerned about capacity building in their administrations sought help from state level programs for institutional development, and responded to imported ideas of how things could be done better. Some used the laws that were set in place by state and federal levels as the reason for making such changes, even though monitoring of municipal compliance was usually weak. Thus, mayors who wished to improve efficiency, effectiveness, and responsiveness were often engaged in introducing more objective criteria and systems for organizing work, monitoring officials, and dealing with citizens. A number had been influenced by reading or studying about the New Public Management that had been adopted in some industrialized countries in the 1990s.

Efforts to improve management and efficiency in town hall, however, were often in conflict with an even more onerous part of the mayor's leadership—constituent service. In large part, constituent service meant

responding to individual and group requests for assistance, honoring patron–client ties, and considering party relationships in the distribution of
resources and services. Thus, mayors were being pressured to modernize
the management of town hall while at the same time being pressured to
support a traditional system that linked citizens to office holders through
personal contact and response to particularistic needs. Indeed, in terms of
a mayor's reputation and electability to higher office, constituent service
regularly counted more than efficiency and more general good performance in town hall.

Those familiar with Mexico's government in the past will understand
the importance of particularistic relationships in most government offices,
at whatever level, over a long course of the country's history. However,
as the federal level liberalized the country's economy in the 1980s and
1990s, decentralized social services and other responsibilities, and moved
toward more targeted programs for social assistance, offices of federal
ministers, vice ministers, and directors of important programs were no
longer as congested with petitioners and clients; in many states, the same
occurred as the implementation of specific programs was passed along to
the municipalities. Thus, a traditional social safety net provided by the
PRI government—the use of patron–client ties to government officials at
all levels, but particularly at national levels—weakened significantly in
the decades after 1980. Those in need increasingly congregated in the
mayor's office, appealed to councilors for special favors, or sought out
the directors of important services.[78] Clientelism continued apace, but adjusted to new distributions of power and resources.

The most important local source of help and assistance, of course, was
the mayor's office. "Everyone wants to see the mayor because they believe
that he can solve their problems."[79] In addition, mayors were targets for
requests anywhere they went in their constituency. A mayor in Sinaloa
complained about the extent to which his popularity was determined by
handouts and money, a culture of "now what are you going to give us?" as
he explained the problem.[80] When they visited local communities, mayors
were approached by groups with petitions for various public works or
services, as if the political campaign were still going on. A walk down the
street could be an occasion for other petitioners to argue their case to the
mayor. Elsewhere, a conflict in a neighborhood about filling potholes
could not be solved without the personal intervention of the mayor. So
frequent were these individual requests, group petitions, and conflicts that
it was difficult for many mayors to focus attention on their priorities.

It is important to note that citizens judged mayors harshly with regard
to how well they managed this aspect of their role. Thus, even for those
who were able to liberate significant new resources and organize town hall
to work more effectively, local support could wither if he or she proved to
be a "bad mayor" in terms of interactions with constituents. In particular,

efforts to standardize the administration of town hall business could easily run afoul of the importance of direct contact with constituents.

For example, a mayor who put in a new system of performance by results, who was lauded by some as an important reformer in the town, who was seen as an administrative modernizer by outsiders, was condemned by local citizens for her brusque, businesslike manner with constituents. Her predecessor, who spent a good deal of time being seen and being generous to petitioners, was remembered as a fine mayor, although he did not accomplish much for the municipality.[81] In Tamaulipas, a mayor was faulted for not being warm enough in his treatment of constituents, while his predecessor reportedly hugged everyone and gave out 100 pesos to those who asked.[82] According to a former councilor in this municipality, "My experience with the past and current mayor has taught me that you can pave every road in the municipality, but if you don't treat people with respect, people don't like you."[83] In another municipality in the same state, the mayor was hailed for his motto, "He who asks cannot be mistaken," and for his dealings with constituents.[84] Similar stories were heard in several of the municipalities, and style seemed to count more than substance.

Although many, particularly those from outside the municipalities, were often impressed by the orientation toward efficiency and good governance of some enterprising mayors, this was not enough to win them plaudits at home. Indeed, "good" mayors and "bad" mayors established these reputations on the basis of responses to a multiplex and often contradictory set of criteria. They were expected to be generous and personal in providing benefits to individuals and community groups, they were under increasing pressure from state and federal governments to improve and professionalize the activities of town hall, and they were responsible for using whatever means possible to liberate resources from other levels of government to improve conditions in the municipality. Being an effective mayor, therefore, required significant leadership skills that were both modern and more traditional.

CONCLUSIONS: STRONG LEADERS AND WEAK INSTITUTIONS

Among the thirty research municipalities, state entrepreneurship—the impact of the preferences and activities of high-level officials in town hall (mayors, councilors, directors of various offices), independent of party affiliation—was a critical factor in distinguishing better performing municipalities from those that were less efficient, effective, responsive, or change-oriented. Municipalities that performed well were consistent in being led by those who had a clear vision of a more ideal municipality, a policy agenda that specified priorities, commitment to a mission, and a variety of skills for dealing with multiplex and often contradictory demands. As in Chignahuapan, electoral calendars were important in providing opportunities to introduce new leadership groups, even while party affiliation remained a poor predictor of improved performance.

Also like their counterparts in Chignahuapan, public leaders in other localities could introduce significant changes in a relatively short period of time. The situation that mayors and their teams encountered when they entered the *ayuntamiento* after an election tested their ingenuity—many unsolved problems, few resources, and no clear mandates. These officials had to respond to different and sometimes conflicting expectations—acquire resources, manage town hall, perform constituent service. They also had their own electoral futures to consider.

Nevertheless, they had wide scope for action. The lack of continuous and constraining institutions offered mayors, councilors, and public officials extensive room for introducing new practices, new ideas, and new programs and projects. They also had wide scope for not attending to business and performing their functions poorly. Most municipal officials were not constrained by prior policy- or decision-making outcomes, nor by the routine implementation of well-institutionalized programs. They were not bound by a resistant career bureaucracy; instead, they had extensive capacity to appoint those who shared their values and who would follow their lead. There were few rules of the game that they found binding on their activities.

A major function of local officials was to travel to state capitals, and sometimes as far as Mexico City, to find the spigots to turn on more resources. This activity, known as the capacity of local officials and particularly mayors to negotiate or hustle with other levels of government, was a skill and drive that some possessed and some did not. Effective municipal government officials showed great capacity to manage the complex web of fiscal and political relationships that brought federal, state, and local governments together in uneasy and fluid alliances for the distribution of public goods; there were also governments where such capacity did not exist.

Behind the extensive room to maneuver lurked a serious problem in most of the *ayuntamientos* in the study—the institutional void in which municipal leaders operated. This void made their improvements—and their mistakes, unresponsiveness, and/or venality—subject to change when they were no longer in office. Mayors and other officials had the capacity, then, to introduce significant change, but they had much less capacity to ensure that their perspectives, policies, programs, and projects could transcend the three-year limit on their tenure in office. Weak institutions were the counterpart to the impressive evidence of entrepreneurial leadership.

Photo by Xóchitl León.

Chapter 5

MODERNIZING TOWN HALL

ABUSIVE POLICE OFFICERS, tax agents on the take, lost records, long waits for service, surly and officious personnel, rampant bribery, clientelism, disorder, failure to accomplish even the most basic responsibilities—these are pervasive stereotypes of how local government is carried out in many countries. Around the world, average citizens often relate impressive stories of rudeness, corruption, malingering, and wasted effort when they have requested a service from town hall. They can tell of the ease with which they worked out "arrangements" not to pay a bill or a fine. Indeed, those who resist decentralization generally use lack of local government capacity as a principal reason why it will not work. Even advocates of decentralization willingly admit that significant administrative and institutional changes are essential if municipalities are to live up to its promise.

Thus, the popularity of capacity building as a means of getting better governance is certainly understandable: the solution seems as obvious as the need. It is not difficult to spot inefficiencies in how routine activities are carried out within municipal governments, to discover organizations that spin their wheels in uncertain action, to encounter officials who have little idea of their responsibilities, to see evidence of corruption. With new processes, redesigned organizations, job descriptions and training, better technology, altered incentives for performance, and other investments in capacity building, supporters of decentralization are certain that local governance can improve. Moreover, extensive literature on the New Public Management and private sector organizational change, in addition to beguiling technologies that offer to revolutionize routine activities, add further fuel to the idea that it is possible to deliver on promises for improved performance. Empirical evidence from efforts to "reinvent government" show how it has actually been done in diverse settings.

Capacity building is thus a generalized tonic prescribed for town halls in poor performance health. Decentralization promises better governance, capacity builders assert, but only when local institutions develop the ability to provide good services and attend to citizen demand. After all, they argue, local governments were systematically deterred from developing such abilities during decades of centralized government and local administrative impoverishment. Capacity building is also popular among reformist local officials. Although they are likely to paint the institutional past in somber colors, they like to proclaim a future that is inevitably bright with new procedures, better organizational structures, more transparency, and greater probity from town officials.

Because of promises such as these, governments, NGOs (nongovernmental organizations), and international development agencies annually invest hundreds of millions of dollars in capacity-building initiatives. They fund programs and projects in institution creation and strengthening, organizational engineering, human resource training, computerization, and technical inputs for electronic government. They provide support for process development and monitoring, participatory decision making, and other managerial innovations that are to bring more efficiency, effectiveness, and responsiveness in local government.[1] With such inputs, they anticipate clear improvements in how local governments work. They often argue that capacity building can deal effectively with the scourge of corruption. They warn, however, that building capacity is a complex process that requires time and ongoing effort.

Not surprisingly, then, capacity-building initiatives were very much on the agenda of some mayors and their allies in the Mexican research sites. They wanted to modernize town hall and make it a place where citizens could find responsiveness and assistance. They wanted routine activities to be accomplished with greater speed and efficacy. They wanted to bring order out of what was often chaotic and irresponsible administration. They often found help at the state level, where municipal development institutions offered a variety of services, particularly ones related to training. From computerizing tax records, to developing departments of institutional development, to employing people with professional training, to using citizen surveys for monitoring the performance of municipal departments, to contracting out basic services—modernizing town hall meant a significant range of activities to improve capacity and increase the efficiency and effectiveness of government. In a number of municipalities, new ideas, new incentives, and new organizational structures were priorities for local leaders.

To what extent did the introduction of capacity-building initiatives improve local governance? Indeed, investments in administrative and managerial change appeared to be leading to better governance in some of the research municipalities, lending support to the hypothesis that modernization of the management of town hall could be the key to better performance. In Mexico, reorganization, professionalization of local officials and activities, training and computerization, and the introduction of standards for performance became evident in the late 1990s and continued to gather momentum in the 2000s. In some cases, the ability to transform the activities of municipal government in a relatively short period was arresting. In some cases, also, the sophistication of the initiatives being introduced in medium-sized municipalities was equally surprising.

Yet the research also revealed that the political dynamics behind capacity-building initiatives were crucial to understanding their impact. Those who initiated modernization activities were reformist mayors and officials such as the municipal treasurer, the police commissioner, and the chief administrative officer. These officials made purposive decisions to set capacity-building initiatives in motion and to maintain them in place over the term of their period in office. In purusing this demand-driven strategy, they sought to mobilize resources made available by other levels of government or the private sector. Without local level leadership, however, municipal services did not improve and supply-side resources available for capacity-building initiatives remained untapped.

Thus, state and federal level policies or programs could make ideas, resources, and technical support available to local governments and even mandate change, but it was the goal setting at local levels that opened up opportunities to deploy these factors effectively. In the research municipalities, administrative modernization was a function of leadership preferences, not an independent source of improved performance that could be effective regardless of these preferences. As such, modernization initiatives supported by those outside of the local government were only successful when they met committed champions within those governments.

In addition, the chapter indicates that capacity-building initiatives were significantly affected by electoral cycles. Characteristically, when municipal officials were concerned about performance issues, their actions were framed by a well-defined electoral calendar. At the same time, in Mexico's newly democratic but poorly institutionalized local governments, electoral cycles also undermined capacity as well as encouraged its development. Frequently, elections meant that existing modernization initiatives fell prey to the priorities of the next incumbents in town hall. Thus, to view capacity-building initiatives as a simple key to improved performance is to misunderstand how such activities are embedded in political preferences and electoral rhythms.

INTRODUCING CHANGE

Political calendars in the research sites offered considerable scope for introducing change, as discussed in prior chapters. In particular, when mayors assumed office, there were few formal limits on their ability to appoint officials and reorganize town hall. Some believed that it was important to make use of these powers because of the poor performance of governments that had gone before theirs. In fact, there were significant incentives for new political administrations to differentiate themselves from their predecessors, even when they represented the same political parties. As we have seen, local parties were nonprogrammatic and local elections were fought on the basis of particularistic commitments and the personalities of those in the race. Typically, new administrations introduced new priorities and paid scant attention to those of their predecessors.

Newly arrived officials most commonly claimed that in the past, municipal activities were carried out in pencil and on decades-old typewriters, and they certainly believed that many citizens got service only because they had a proverbial friend in town hall.[2] According to one, "In the past, the records were all kept manually. If you were my friend, it was sufficient for me to tear [up] this card and your tax record would disappear."[3] In the view of a new director of public works in Oaxaca, "It is thought that, ultimately, everything is politically negotiable" in letting contracts and paying for services.[4] Officials complained that their predecessors, in addition to leaving no records or regulations, did not appoint officials with training appropriate to their responsibilities.[5]

Among those most frequently cited for low capacity and corruption were police departments. In many municipalities, the police kept no records of arrests and followed no written policies with regard to imposing fines on citizens or arresting people for misdemeanors and other infractions of the law. Citizens regularly accused them of abusive behavior.[6] They were paid poorly, and often had little or no education. Many supplemented their pay by demanding bribes in exchange for impunity. When police collected fines in some municipalities, they were allowed to keep them as part of their pay.[7]

In this kind of environment, one councilor argued that those concerned about improved performance had little choice other than to "throw oneself into the current and try to navigate against it, to see what could be changed."[8] At a general level, four strategies of modernization were used to navigate against the current—reorganizing town hall, including contracting out some activities formerly performed by the municipality; altering the profile of those appointed to public office; providing training and technical upgrading for carrying out municipal responsibilities; and introducing performance standards to measure the behavior of individuals and organizational units within the municipality. As indicated in table 5.1, almost all municipalities made efforts to introduce training and computers and a significant number of them reorganized their administrations. Professionalization of personnel was put in place in about a third of the cases, and a few tried the introduction of performance standards. There were ten municipalities in which the administration in office at the time of the research had undertaken at least three such serious activities to alter the performance of town hall through capacity-building activities.[9]

TABLE 5.1
Modernization Initiatives in Research Municipalities

Type of Initiative	Number of Municipalities	Percent of Municipalities
Reorganization	16	53
Professionalization	10	33
Training and Technology	27	90
Performance Standards	4	13

Reorganization. New administrations often began their tenure by re-drawing the organizational map of the municipality. At times, this activity was undertaken as a way of expanding the number of jobs that would be available for patronage, such as the decision of the mayor in Yucatán that all councilors should have substitutes. In some places, however, reorgani-zation was undertaken as a way to make sense out of poorly designed or antiquated municipal structures. Thus, in the early days of a new adminis-tration, decisions about policy priorities were often accompanied by new organization charts that reflected what mayors believed to be the most pressing issues. Among the research municipalities, several added depart-ments of human resources, institutional development, professional devel-opment, social communication, and legal affairs, each of which suggested a concern about the performance of town hall.

In addition, departments to stimulate urban or economic development or tourism often appeared in new organigrams. Liaison offices and depart-ments of community affairs were created to help citizens navigate the municipal bureaucracy, to work with non–Spanish-speaking groups in their interactions with town hall, or to improve communication with citi-zens more generally. At the same time, some departments disappeared.[10] These changes were usually justified on the basis of efficiency and better service. Some mayors and other officials spoke of wanting town hall to work like a business, without much bureaucracy, and with good manage-ment of information and responsiveness to "client demand."[11] These offi-cials anticipated that new organizational structures would add consis-tency to the activities of the municipality.

In some municipalities in which mayors were concerned with perfor-mance, legal departments were given responsibility for ensuring that the municipality was up to date in terms of complying with state and federal laws, that it had in place basic legal instruments, and that the actions of the municipality left a paper trail of documents and proof of appropriate actions. In the past, said a director of one such office in Puebla, "there was no legal certainty."[12] In laying a stronger basis for claiming legitimacy for municipal actions, this department sought the approval of the state legislature.

Similarly, reorganizations came in the form of altered procedures, often with the intent of eliminating sources of corruption. Traditional efforts, such as taking officials from the previous administration to court for corrupt practices, were complemented by other changes. In one municipality in Oaxaca, for example, by separating the property tax office from the treasury, town officials hoped that decision making about how much was owed to the local government would become more transparent and discourage decision making on the basis of friendship and political influence.[13] Developing or improving lists of town employees, providing organizational manuals, and inventorying municipal property were widely believed to be important steps toward lessening corruption in town hall.[14]

Actions to ensure that the municipal police had systems for recording fines and accounting for revenues were introduced in several municipalities.[15] Along with this, some local governments supplied the police with new equipment and raised the officers' pay.[16] In a municipality in Tamaulipas, the number of contractors who were eligible for municipal projects was expanded with the hope that this would limit corruption in public works departments.[17] In Guanajuato, councilors in one site formed a procurement committee to oversee municipal purchases, and in another in Yucatán, a new government introduced competitive bidding for municipal purchases.[18]

Some of the changes introduced, and spoken about with pride by local officials, were extraordinarily simple ones. In a Oaxacan municipality, for example, a change in how bills were paid made for a more ordered government—purveyors and contractors would be paid on a set day each week, saving the treasurer and the mayor from having to interrupt their activities on all other days to sign and countersign checks.[19] In Puebla, garbage collection was reorganized into two shifts, allowing for greater efficiency with the same number of people and machines.[20] In another locality, for the first time, the municipality was divided into zones for the purpose of property assessment.[21] In Yucatán, a municipality reorganized its licensing process so that small and medium-size entrepreneurs could take care of all business in an expedited way through a "single window."[22] In several other places, regular council meetings were opened to the public once a month and, in some cases, sessions were televised.[23] Similarly, copies of the budget and transfers from other levels of government appeared at the entrances of some town halls, and several municipalities introduced newsletters and radio programs to inform citizens of local activities.[24]

A few municipalities followed the advice of management specialists and introduced contracting or autonomous units for administering some services. In a Yucatecan municipality, administrative officials debated contracting out garbage collection, having seen such a system at work in the state capital.[25] In the same municipality, the town government contracted with a private firm to collect water fees and property taxes; the tax collectors were students from a local technical institute and received a percentage of what they were able to collect on their rounds; computerization of records was expected to limit corruption.[26] In Sinaloa, management of the annual municipal celebration was reorganized substantially by setting up an autonomous agency to oversee the funding of yearly activities. A major reason for doing so was to cut down on the amount of corruption involved in providing permits and contracts for the annual events.[27]

Professionalization. Along with reorganizations, officials in a number of municipalities were outspoken about the need to hire professionals to provide services and carry out routine business in the municipality. Regularly, they argued that past administrations had relied on "ignorant" and "uneducated" mayors who appointed people with little education to carry out the municipality's business. Some local leaders argued that having professionals in office was a "first" for the municipality in question. The replacement of poorly educated or corrupt or lazy officials with "people with profile"—professional credentials—was frequently considered an important adjunct to reorganization if municipalities were to improve their performance.[28]

Thus, the triennial migration of officials in and out of municipal offices was used by some mayors as an opportunity to bring in administrators with more education or with skills specific to a particular job. In the municipality of Chignahuapan, discussed in the last chapter, professional credentials were considered a *sine qua non* for working in a management position in town hall. The impact of professionals in government was thought to be impressive. Changing personnel in one municipality was credited with a fourfold increase in the income from municipal services and a 40 percent improvement in fiscal accounts.[29]

For those seeking to professionalize administration, personnel recruitment meant matching education with the requirements of a job. It was, therefore, important that the comptroller be an accountant, that the director of public works be an architect or an engineer, that lawyers staff specific offices, and so on. In Sinaloa, the municipality hired a veterinarian to oversee the work of the slaughterhouse.[30] Even in the southern state of Oaxaca, far from the influence of the business-oriented PAN, a former treasurer acknowledged that he was appointed because the mayor believed that someone with private sector experience would be able to do a better job with municipal finances than anyone else.[31]

The professionalization of town hall referred primarily to staffing positions at managerial levels with those who held professional degrees—
in Mexico, this meant a university education. This ordinarily encom-
passed the treasurer, the comptroller, the secretary of the municipality,
directors of departments, and at times the subdirectors. Yet lower level
officials, such as police officers, were not immune from pressures to up-
grade their credentials. The problem was a real one for several municipalities in which some police officers were known to be illiterate. In a
Yucatecan municipality, only eight of thirty-seven transit police knew
how to drive. In Guanajuato, primary education was the norm for police
officers.[32] In Tamaulipas, the mayor and the police commissioner determined that police officers must have a high school degree in order to
work for the municipality.[33]

Electoral office was not excluded from the trend toward professionalization in several municipalities. In Oaxaca, a state with relatively low
levels of educational achievement, a former mayor observed that to be
elected to his former position or to become a councilor, it was now necessary to have a high school degree. It was no longer true that just anyone
could aspire to municipal office, he said.[34] In Yucatán, one town official
boasted that councilors representing the PRD were primarily professionals while those of the opposition were not.[35] In Tamaulipas, a municipal
official described more than thirty years during which "illiterate" mayors
held office, largely because the peasant sector of the PRI held power rather
than the "popular" sector (middle class). When the latter became more
powerful in the mid-1990s, he said, those with more education acquired
electoral office.[36] According to a local party president and former mayor,
"Now we are trying to attract agronomists, doctors, and accountants to
become candidates and to bring better proposals to the population." [37]

In some cases, the flow of new ideas and practices into town hall was
significant. In particular, some municipalities became more aware of the
benefits of planning for their future development, and "strategic plans"
became a common reference point for mayors, directors of public works,
economic development managers, and others. Strategic planning generally included meetings to diagnose issues that needed attention and then
deciding on a focus for short- and medium-term activities.[38] As town halls
became more impressed by the advantages of planning, they began pressing submunicipal representatives to submit clear plans and proposals.[39]

At the same time, however, professionalization in most municipalities
was the result of a simple process of appointment made possible by the
change of administrations. As such, a time-honored tradition of clientelism was pressed into the service of modernizing town hall. As a consequence, new job descriptions, qualification codes, and hiring processes
were made a permanent part of municipal operations in only a few cases;

by and large, merit hiring remained a choice, not a requirement. As with other aspects of municipal governance, the criteria used for selecting personnel remained primarily the prerogative of the mayor.

Training and technology. Closely aligned to activities designed to bring more qualified officials into public offices were activities aimed at upgrading the performance of officials and offices. Again, it was usually the start of a new administration that brought such changes to the table. Municipal officials regularly reported that their initial introduction to their jobs was through training courses on municipal regulations and scopes of authority. Newly elected or appointed officials would then turn their attention to their own departments. A police commissioner in Guanajuato, for example, discovered on taking office that police officers had little or no training when they were hired and began to send his agents off to state level training courses.[40] For departments like the police, where job turnover was often significant when a new administration came into office, ongoing training activities became the norm.[41] In other departments, such as in the treasury and the comptroller's office, training courses were a regular part of the activities undertaken by department heads.

Those who were most active in seeking or delivering training courses were the town treasurer, the chief administrative officer, and the town secretary. Often, the mayor put them in charge of upgrading the capacity of the employees in town hall. Surprisingly, much of the training given to municipal officials was not technical but oriented more toward providing effective service and interacting well with citizens. In Chignahuapan, the former leaders of the Junior Chamber of Commerce worked to pass along what they had learned about service orientation and the need to be responsive to customer demand. In fact, the bulk of the training received in that municipality pertained to time management, motivation, getting along with others, working in teams, and leadership. The director of professional development there spoke of courses called "Only for Champions" and "God Forgives, but Time Does Not."[42] In Tamaulipas, one department head argued that because most of the people working in the town were qualified for their jobs, training needed to focus on motivational and service-oriented courses.[43] In Guanajuato, a training course was concerned with how to shape "empowered organizations."[44] Others focused on human resource management, leadership, and organizational change, at times complemented by the introduction of new management techniques, such as total quality measurement.[45]

Training courses were sometimes offered by the directors of departments at the local level, and at times they were contracted out to consulting firms. In one case, an industrial interest group representing the national construction industry provided training for unskilled workers in municipal public works departments.[46] In another case, the PAN offered municipal officials training courses for different municipal functions.[47] Most common, however, were state-level training programs offered to municipalities that were interested in improving their performance. In Guanajuato, a state level secretariat of public management was put in charge of providing courses as well as introducing programs to improve performance.[48] Puebla's center for municipal development offered twenty-five different training courses free to the municipalities, including such diverse topics as solid waste management, quality service, family planning, participation, and management of the treasury.[49] Guanajuato, Oaxaca, and Yucatán created institutes, centers, or departments for municipal development and posted activities of these organizations on state web pages. In other cases, secretariats for particular sectors, such as financial management, civil registry, and rural development, provided training courses.[50] These courses served a useful purpose of orienting new officials to their responsibilities and alerting them to the kinds of services that the states could offer them.

In addition to a multitude of training courses, computerization was being widely adopted in the research municipalities. Above all, tax and civil registry offices were transformed by the use of computers to manage information and to process documents and payments. In Oaxaca, a councilor spoke approvingly of the reduction of processing time in the civil registry from at least two weeks to only one.[51] When the municipal offices were taken over by the "popular government" in one Oaxacan municipality, this served as an opportunity for the "official government" to invest in new computers for basic activities of the municipality.[52] During a research visit to a municipal office in Sinaloa, two officials were busy monitoring international weather patterns online in order to provide information to local farmers about the arrival of rain and appropriate planting times.[53]

In Tamaulipas, digitized aerial maps provided a more accurate basis for property assessment; local farmers were given GPS (global positioning system) devices to walk their land and establish property lines.[54] An official in another Tamaulipan site explained how easy it was to pay taxes now that all the relevant information was on a computer.[55] In another municipality in the same state, the director of public works expressed his satisfaction with having introduced computers to the project designers in his department, who had formerly used pencils to develop their plans.[56] In Sinaloa, property tax receipts could be reported daily.[57]

Several municipal officials acknowledged that the trend toward computerization had begun in the late 1990s and had been expanded under more recent administrations. Officials were proud of the number of computers that had been introduced during their tenure, regularly making boasts such as, "When I arrived there was only one computer, now there are thirty-five."[58] In a municipality in Yucatán, bringing computers to town hall was a campaign promise.

State governments were again the most important facilitators for providing computers, software, and training. Secretariats of finance, the civil registry institute, and municipal fiscal coordinators in some states were particularly important for providing these kinds of services, with municipal treasurers and comptrollers often acting as the liaisons in requesting such services and planning the implementation of new systems. Some state level governments had introduced new systems in their own offices and then made their expertise and assistance available to municipalities that were interested in change. When local governments implemented some state or national programs, they received computerized lists of beneficiaries from those sources and were able to track their clients more accurately.[59]

For a few municipalities, computerization was a step along the way toward visions of e-government. The use of municipal web pages for providing information and services to local residents was most advanced in Sinaloa. One municipality had won an award for online government, in which information was provided about how to obtain municipal services and what kinds of documentation were required for them. In the same municipality, the government introduced a feature on its web page to link local producers with potential buyers and investors.[60] Computers were available for citizen use not only in town hall, but at community centers scattered around the municipalities. "Virtual Fridays" allowed citizens to have direct Internet contact with municipal officials who would answer questions and respond to problems.[61] Municipalities in other states also introduced computer centers for citizens to use.[62] Some municipalities were paying their employees directly through their bank accounts by using software provided by local banks.[63] A municipal treasurer in Tamaulipas spoke of the effort to become a paperless office with the use of technology.[64]

Standards for performance. The fourth way in which some municipalities were working to improve their performance was through the introduction of new systems for measuring performance. Even though only a few of the research sites were implementing such systems, what they were doing was impressive. In Guanajuato, a municipal secretary explained that on taking office, the administration had set out objectives and measures for a plan of work—for example, reducing petty crimes, better management of the informal sector, and avoiding clandestine business activities. Every departmental director was expected to produce a plan and weekly meetings were called to evaluate how each was doing. In the same municipality, citizen surveys measured results, which were then tabulated and presented to the directors of various departments for action.[65] Surveys were also used internally in another municipality to assess the morale of public workers.[66]

Two municipalities adopted international standards to plan and implement quality management systems. When appropriate processes were in place for measuring performance and customer needs and satisfaction, the municipality would receive certification by the International Organization for Standardization, which provided software for achieving better performance results.[67] The idea for introducing this change had come from the state government, which implemented the system for its own administration and then offered it to the municipalities and followed up with assessment and implementation support. For one municipality, this was an avenue of effort that led to a new organigram, definition of responsibilities, elimination of duplication, and a new schedule that made it possible to save electricity. In the other municipality, the system was first implemented in the police department, and then expanded to the treasury, public works, and municipal services.[68]

Police commissioners were among those most concerned about performance measuring systems, and, as one indicated, "I was given the instruction to make sure the system worked."[69] In the language of efficiency and effectiveness, such officials spoke of developing measures of response time, the number of urgent calls, and the number of arrests and fines that were made over the course of a day, week, or month. With better measures in place, they stated, the municipality would be able to cross-reference crimes with other municipalities and with state and federal agencies and would also be able to know which areas needed work and where there were success stories.[70]

Much ado about modernization. The extent to which municipalities took up public sector modernization was often surprising. Even poorly performing and highly politicized municipalities made attempts to adopt new organizational forms, new procedures, and new technologies. Indeed, the amount and kind of changes introduced could be impressive, as when a councilor in a Yucatán municipality spoke of carrying out cost-benefit-reliability comparisons before purchasing parts for police motorcycles.[71]

As indicated, of course, the sophistication of new initiatives ranged from very basic to quite complex, and there were clear differences among municipalities with regard to what they were taking on in terms of mechanisms to improve performance. Moreover, that change initiatives were undertaken does not necessarily mean that change occurred. Although many municipal officials spoke in glowing terms of the changes they had introduced, only some of them were able to demonstrate that reorganization had led to greater efficiency or effectiveness; few could provide evidence that new systems worked, or reduced corruption, or left durable marks on the behavior of public officials through training or performance monitoring. New computers and computer systems did not necessarily signal work actually being accomplished in new ways.

Yet, given the extent to which the capacity- and institution-building literature emphasizes the long-term and difficult nature of the task, the extent of efforts in this direction was surprising. Why was there so much ado about modernizing town hall?

THE DYNAMICS OF CHANGE

Almost universally, the initiative to improve the capacity of local governments was a demand-driven phenomenon, set in motion by municipal leaders as part of "taking charge" of municipal government. New ideas arrived with new administrations. And, because of constraints on immediate reelection, the time frame for achieving results was shortened to three years—performance-oriented leaders needed to work fast if they expected to make any impact. They believed that the longer new initiatives were in place, the more likely it was that they would be sustained beyond a three-year incumbency. The first few months of a new administration were therefore a critical time for the reform-oriented to act. At times, changes in organization, technology, and professionalization built upon the work of past administrations, although few municipalities began introducing significant changes before the late 1990s or early 2000s. When such initiatives did become more frequent, they were often accomplished quite rapidly.

That this was possible is the result of three factors that were discussed in previous chapters. New administrations brought changes in personnel, which helped overcome the resistance to change that is characteristic of entrenched bureaucracies. Similar to a large number of other countries, Mexico had no civil service or administrative cadre to staff town halls independently from electoral cycles. As we have seen, jobs in local government were important to party support building, and extensive rotation of personnel after elections was universal. When a reform-oriented mayor assumed office, then, there were few formal limits on the ability to appoint officials—department heads, the chief administrative officer, the secretary of the government, subdepartmental officials, secretaries, office workers, laborers, police officers, and others. This provided considerable opportunity to bring people with shared perspectives into positions of authority; in turn, appointees usually had the capacity to select their own teams.

In addition, as discussed in the previous chapter, the degree of institutionalization of municipal activities was often weak; when capacity-building initiatives were undertaken, they were replacing relatively weak structures and rules that did not stand firmly in the way of change, as more embedded institutions might do. Finally, capacity building and technological changes were often welcomed by local officials as evidence that the municipal leadership cared about their functions and was ready to invest in training people and providing them with better tools for carrying out their activities.

Mayors generally set the agenda for modernizing town hall, and determined what was to be done and when. This is not surprising, given the importance of the leadership factor explored in the previous chapter. A few examples suffice: in Oaxaca, a new mayor worked hard to make municipal fiscal transfers to sublocal governments more transparent; in Sinaloa, it was the mayor's idea to create an autonomous body to manage the funds for the annual town celebrations and by doing so, to limit corruption surrounding the use of the funds; another mayor in that state worked the deals to bring the Internet to the public; it was also mayors who took the lead in developing a regional development plan in the north of Tamaulipas; electronic government was promoted by a mayor in Sinaloa who had studied e-government and decided it was a first priority for his administration; and so on.[72] Even in cases in which state governments set standards and timetables for municipalities, some mayors decided to comply, and others ignored such mandates.[73]

Although initiative was strongly invested in municipal politicians, the sources of ideas and support often came from the state level. Frequently, officials learned about programs and projects from regular meetings held in the state capital or from friendships with those who knew the state level well. The digitization of property taxes in Tamaulipas was put in motion after the municipality bought equipment and the state sent technical assistance to start up the program and train the officials who would use it. According to the treasurer, the office continued to be in frequent communication with those in the state capital when "glitches" occurred in their work.[74] In Tamaulipas, a rural development director learned of new ideas from the state level planning organization, in its weekly broadcast about public administration.[75] As indicated, capacity-building workshops and seminars were frequently sponsored by state government secretariats. In Sinaloa, a state that was more successful than others in establishing requirements for local governments, one municipality used a new freedom of information law to launch a Web site that held significant amounts of useful information about the municipality.[76]

Despite the relative ease with which capacity-building initiatives were introduced, however, there were darker realities underlying this success. Possibilities for capacity development were built upon an institutional base that rewarded change initiatives but worked against their institutionalization. Thus, the larger problem many of the initiatives faced was that of their sustainability. In this regard, the very flexibility that allowed for significant change—the nonprogrammatic nature of political parties, the impact of the personal preferences of those in leadership positions, the extensive opportunity to appoint officials and initiate new activities—raised barriers to its institutionalization over time. Administrations with new priorities and new appointments in town hall would come and go, and what they left behind could not be ensured, even if it provided a reasonable solution to a problem.

Moreover, too often in the research sites, new capacity initiatives were introduced informally; they were based primarily on exhortation or the commitment of a person or small group; it was difficult to hold officials accountable for their correct functioning; a culture of service was limited by personnel changes every three years; and citizens did not have sufficient information to be able to insist on their rights to appropriate service. Moreover, modernization initiatives in several municipalities were derailed by partisan politics, by informal institutions and norms, and by proponents who lost sight of capacity building as a priority. For those who propose capacity building as a tonic for poorly performing organizations, then, the research municipalities indicate the importance of political contexts to the introduction—and demise—of reform initiatives.

Well-embedded past behavior could also cast a shadow on new initiatives. Thus, for example, new efforts to collect taxes often made little impact when there was widespread belief that citizens didn't have to pay taxes or that there was no reason to pay taxes because the municipality was accused of stealing or misusing them, or that it was possible to appeal to the mayor for tax forgiveness, as was the case in several municipalities. There were also municipalities in which positions continued to be awarded on the basis of political criteria, usually a distribution of awards to factious political parties resisting the leadership of the mayor on the council. Officials appointed in these circumstances felt little obligation to improve their performance. Similarly, where municipal government was under siege from "alternative governments," as in the two cases in Oaxaca, the combination of divided resources, lost records, and efforts to woo voters with tax holidays and free services meant that reform initiatives faced considerable obstacles.

In addition, despite considerable hype from leaders about changes put into effect, these might often have been more window dressing than anything else. In a vaunted administrative reform in one municipality in Sinaloa, for example, a number of public officials and well-informed citizens claimed to know nothing about it.[77] In this municipality, the reform was not implemented as it was planned, and so many of its components, including performance measurement, were not effective.[78] In Tamaulipas, a mayor began as a firm supporter of change, but then withdrew his support, and change initiatives faltered.[79] In Yucatán, despite a promise from the state-level president of the PAN that municipalities won by his party would not engage in nepotism, one of the research municipalities, governed by the PAN, made headlines in its use of this time-honored way to enhance the fortunes of the families of the powerful.[80] Thus, some initiatives were more successfully implemented than others, and new policies, programs, projects, and procedures did not necessarily pay off in terms of improved performance. Yet in some cases they did, and Mexican citizens reaped the benefit of more efficient, effective, and responsive town halls—at least for a while.

CONCLUSIONS: NOT BY MODERNIZATION ALONE

Capacity-building initiatives were ubiquitous in many of Mexico's municipalities in 2004. The actions undertaken spanned organizational and personnel changes, technical and managerial upgrading, the introduction of more "client-friendly" modes of operation, and new incentives for officials. These initiatives, however, were a result of leadership, not a substitute for it. This chapter, then, has added to the story of local government performance that has been developed in the previous two chapters. First, electoral competition is important to improved performance because it opens up more opportunities for change-oriented leaders to assume power at the local level. Second, it is not party competition per se, but leadership values and initiatives that are primarily responsible for improved performance. Third, capacity-building activities are dependent upon the promotion and support of local officials. They are tools of effective leadership, not independent sources of change.

Capacity-building initiatives were undertaken by local officials who represented a range of political parties; contrary to much popular belief, at least in the research municipalities, the business-oriented PAN did not have a monopoly on concern about good governance. Yet, it was clear that, although not necessarily partisan, capacity-building initiatives were political in the sense that they responded to the preferences of political leaders, they were dependent on electoral cycles for their timing and rationale, and they were facilitated and constrained by political rules of the game about the scope of action available to municipal leaders.

The political context in Mexico was a two-edged sword in promoting change in how local governments performed. On the one hand, it encouraged change, providing incentives to incumbents to introduce it and reducing the incidence of bureaucratic inertia and resistance at the same time. Thus, the political context meant significant room to maneuver. On the other hand, it also set constraints on the ability to institutionalize performance improvements in local government, thus undermining the relevance of reforms for addressing problems over the longer term.

An important lesson from this evidence is that municipalities attempt to modernize when politicians are ready to promote it. How officials in Mexican municipalities became ready was a result of many different factors influencing their priorities—some had previous experience that taught them to value administrative and managerial efficiency and effectiveness; some were influenced by their belief systems; some learned serendipitously of new ideas and decided to pursue them; some gained insight from courses and workshops; some came by it casually, in conversations with colleagues from other municipalities or state level officials; some searched for it on the Internet. It is important to note that the research municipalities produced little evidence of local government being reorganized, professionalized, computerized, or incentivized by citizen groups demanding such changes or simply because state or federal levels of government mandated it.

For those who propose capacity building as a tonic to poorly performing organizations, then, the lesson from the research municipalities bears an important message: these activities can make a difference in how organizations operate, but they cannot do so without the help of organizational and political leadership. The help is needed to introduce change, and also to sustain it. Modernization initiatives in several municipalities were derailed by partisan politics, by informal institutions and norms, and by proponents who lost sight of capacity building as a priority. In introducing capacity-building activities, then, mayors and other officials need to pay considerable attention to maintaining them during their tenure and finding ways of sustaining them beyond the short period of incumbency.

Photo by Sergio Cárdenas-Denham.

Chapter 6

CIVIL SOCIETY
Extracting Benefits and Demanding Accountability

IN HIS TOWN, a municipal treasurer complained, the people "aren't moti-vated when they are offered an opportunity to work together to improve things."[1] Advocates of decentralization do not generally anticipate this kind of complaint. With decentralization, they argue, citizen participation in public life, and the regulation of public life, should actually increase. Indeed, they contend, citizens in a decentralized system of government can expect enhanced opportunities to demand public attention for their needs, monitor how government responds to these demands, hold local officials accountable for the performance of services, and punish those who fall short on such measures. Felicitously, decentralization is widely expected to improve the potential for government "by the people."

And, in fact, it may be easier for citizens to organize around common governance concerns at local levels than at other levels of government, where issues of collective action are more complex and common objec-tives more difficult to identify and act upon. Under the best of conditions, organizations that mediate between government and individual citizens at the local level can be relatively efficient in identifying common interests, selecting effective leadership for organizational and advocacy tasks, ac-quiring information, devising strategies to influence local officials, and taking advantage of mechanisms to discipline those who do not perform their responsibilities effectively. They may also have opportunities to cre-ate alliances with other organizations to increase their influence in local public affairs.

This chapter addresses such expectations: how well does the mobiliza-tion of civil society explain the quality of local government performance? It explores the ways in which citizen groups in the research municipalities sought to influence local government and how they interacted with au-thorities over the content and implementation of local government re-sponsibilities. Here, I am interested in the connection between organized group activities and good governance and so, for the purposes of this chapter, I confine the analysis to groups organized at the local level around local public purposes.[2]

Despite widespread grousing about the apathy of citizens in political and policy arenas in Mexico, the research revealed a surprising amount of citizen engagement with local government. Indeed, there was evidence of considerable local initiative in the interest of enhanced public welfare. It was also clear that efforts to influence government—identifying common interests, deciding on leadership roles, generating strategies for action, and undertaking those actions—did not seem to pose insurmountable obstacles for citizens, even those in relatively poor communities. Further, groups followed very similar strategies in interacting with government, regardless of municipality, and seemed quite well informed about how to go about achieving their public purposes. Moreover, there were few systematic differences among municipalities in terms of how local citizens were mobilized for public purposes.

There were, however, noticeable gaps in the kind of citizen mobilization that occurred at the municipal level, gaps that revealed shortcomings in how local groups interacted with public officials and agencies and whether good governance could be anticipated as an outcome of these interactions. More specifically, organized civic activity was almost exclusively focused on extracting tangible benefits from government; there was little evidence that citizens were concerned more generally about holding public officials and agencies accountable for the performance of their responsibilities, although elections increasingly served this purpose.

These findings suggest that civil society organizations in democratic settings have at least two ways of influencing the performance of local government, one that relates to the capacity to demand responsiveness to social and economic needs—extracting benefits from government—and one that relates to the more general capacity to hold public officials accountable for their actions and inactions in ways that encourage them to perform their responsibilities consistently and well. After more than two decades of decentralization, civil society in Mexico was well able to perform the first role, while falling short in the second, and perhaps more difficult, role. I argue that differential performance of these roles was a consequence of the problem that plagued most of the municipalities in the study—the weakness of ongoing institutions capable of effectively constraining official action. Thus, in settings in which institutions were weak, the links between government performance and mechanisms of local accountability were not particularly strong.

CITIZEN ACTIVISM IN PRACTICE

Despite a lively history of revolution, insurrection, and political mobilization, Mexico's twentieth-century political system discouraged the emergence of a vibrant and independent civil society. For most of this period, the dominant theme in national politics and administration was centralization of authority and decision making in a national government that was held tightly together by a dominant national political party. Citizen demands were routinely met with clientelistic responses channeled through the PRI—in the case of peasant, worker, and middle-class concerns—and with accommodation and mutual interest between government and economic elites. Important decisions were made at national levels, usually by the powerful executive branch, in ways that increased the importance of the national leaders of organized interests and, in many cases, encouraged an alignment of their interests with the strength and persistence of a centralized and authoritarian government and a party machinery based on patronage and clientelism. Similarly, paternalism characterized many policies of government toward issues of social welfare and poverty.

At local levels, where organization around common interests for civic purposes might be easier to accomplish, Mexican politics generally provided little incentive for such action. Local officials and governments controlled few resources and did not have significant decision-making power; local elites and ubiquitous *caciques* used their ties to the PRI or organized interests to extract personal benefits from government and maintained control of local populations through clientelist networks that originated at the national level. There were not, in fact, many policies or actions of local government that local citizens could influence locally.

Of course, there were events in Mexico's history that attested to greater potential for effective citizen action. Certainly the Mexican Revolution of 1910 demonstrated a significant capacity of a very wide range of groups to mobilize for political and military purposes. After the consolidation of the PRI-dominated system, strikes, marches, and protests of various kinds were not unusual, despite the degree to which this system maintained a long-lasting, if inequitable, political peace. A student uprising in the late 1960s became emblematic of protest against the strictures of party government and authoritarian decision making.

In addition, in some regions of the country, indigenous groups were able to maintain traditions of local decision making and action, although this too was frequently denatured through clientelistic relationships with political bosses. Then, after 1980, middle-class groups began to demand more local control and resources for dealing with issues of development and the environment; indigenous groups pressed for recognition of traditional rights and greater autonomy; other groups organized around demands for security, jobs, and human rights; and many increasingly demanded an end to the dominance of the PRI.[3] At the same time, government programs began more consistently to include opportunities for local participation in programs and projects targeted for local areas.[4]

Nevertheless, the general pattern for state–society interaction in the twentieth century was one in which the state was dominant and civil society groups were dealt with in corporatist, clientelistic, and nondemocratic ways, and in which overt repression was always available as a last resort. As a result, and in contrast to countries where a very vibrant civil society emerged during the latter part of the twentieth century—the Philippines, for example—civil society was neither strong nor very independent at the outset of the twenty-first century in Mexico. A generalized expectation of a weak and often disorganized civil society often pervaded public discussion of state–society relations, even after the country's politics had become more democratic.

Certainly this was a perspective widely held in the research municipalities. With some exceptions, government officials did not credit local citizens with much interest in politics or in the activities of town hall. They referred often to the history of paternalism that characterized much of the relationship between state and society. One municipal councilor, for example, observed that "one gets very disillusioned with the apathy of the people—they just want everything given to them."[5] A local PAN president noted the lack of political engagement that meant his party was unable to form a municipal organization, even though it was required by the party statutes.[6]

Similarly, a former mayor indicated that during his three-year term, there were no social groups that demanded anything in particular of him or his administration.[7] A municipal secretary complained about the lack of citizen participation, based, he believed, on the assumption that it was the responsibility of government to resolve all their problems.[8] "Citizens . . . expect that the municipality will do everything . . . and that all works should be free, which isn't true because with participation, everything would be done better," stated the president of a local development committee in Guanajuato.[9] Another official blamed the state of apathy on a lack of local employment opportunities, a high rate of out-migration, and the failure of municipal authorities to provide a model of citizen participation or opportunities for it.[10]

These perspectives, however, did not capture the full reality of citizen engagement in the research municipalities. A councilor in Guanajuato believed that since the mid-1990s there had actually been a gradual awakening of a spirit of interest-based politics, encouraging more people to become active in public affairs.[11] In fact, many of the municipalities boasted local community groups such as Lions Clubs, Rotary Clubs, and women's clubs, professional associations of lawyers and doctors, producers' associations, and a variety of cultural organizations. In many, groups of citizens had joined together to establish and maintain a local history museum. Community improvement committees were ubiquitous. These were organized at the neighborhood or village level to increase the availability of public amenities such as roads, potable water, sewerage, and electricity. Indeed, in all of the thirty municipalities, there were organizations formed explicitly for the purposes of proposing, assisting in, and monitoring local investment projects.

Interestingly, the origin of these organizations varied significantly. Many of them were mobilized from the top down, at the initiative of public officials. Others showed that, at times, citizens had a keen capacity for bottom-up organization. Whether from the top down or bottom up, however, the purpose of these organizations was to extract benefits from government.

From the top down. Among the most common patterns of local organization was that resulting from official requisites for acquiring benefits from other levels of government.[12] As we have seen, national and state laws required each municipality to have a municipal development committee (CDM) whose purpose was to establish priorities for investments and to monitor their execution. In many places, the meetings of the CDM were preceded by community level meetings in which residents drew up petitions for public investments in their neighborhoods or villages. Creating a municipal development plan was a major formal requisite for acquiring various project funds from state and national level agencies.

As indicated in a previous chapter, these committees, whose membership was formed of elected and appointed municipal officials and representatives from each community, usually met seriously during the first year of an administration when public works agendas were being set; after that, meetings were more perfunctory and at times did not occur at all. In most municipalities, their purpose was to formalize the promises made to different communities by the winning candidate during a political campaign and, at times, to discuss the priorities of the administration.

Investments made in particular kinds of activities—a new health clinic, for example, or a school rehabilitation project—also required the formation of citizen groups if funds were to be released by public agencies. In many cases, such committees were formed by municipal directors of various offices, such as public health or public works, and often served as participatory "window dressing" for decisions made elsewhere. In a municipality in Sinaloa, for example, an important local citizen remembered being asked to serve on a committee for public security.

> After the committee was composed, we did an extensive analysis of the needs of the municipality and I developed plans for constructing police kiosks, we

figured out routes for patrol cars, and we laid out needs for capacity building among the police officers. Well then, when we presented our report to the mayor, he told us it wouldn't be possible to carry out any of them because there wasn't any money. And so he told all the groups. As a consequence, the people who make up the committees get discouraged because they see that the mayors already have their security plan . . . Many times, when these committees are formed, an official photograph is taken, and then they never meet again.[13]

There were, however, some examples in which municipal development committees became more authentic drivers of collective action. In a municipality in Oaxaca, for example, the CDM met one Sunday a month from 10:00 A.M. until 4:00 in the afternoon and reported average attendances of two to three hundred people.[14] In a municipality in Tamaulipas, sixty to seventy people met as the municipal development committee every six months; after the initial priority-setting meeting, subsequent gatherings were dedicated to follow-up and review of progress. In another Oaxacan site, the legally required formation of a social development council was credited with the democratization of information about the budget—how much money the government had and how it was being spent.[15] In one community in Sinaloa, a committee regularly coordinated activities for local development with municipal authorities—dances, rodeos, and raffles to raise money; materials to connect households with piped water; a police kiosk, and other such works.[16]

At times, the commitment of a particularly dedicated public official, often the director of social development, could also result in useful citizen input. These officials were assigned responsibility for organizing the groups necessary for benefiting from specific public programs. In one municipality in Guanajuato, for example, the director of rural development was committed to organizing rural development committees in each community, at times in the face of considerable apathy by local residents. Eventually, he argued, people would see the benefit of participating when they saw that it got results, the delivery of benefits. "Attendance [at meetings] can improve, because in fact people didn't anticipate that they would be listened to."[17] In Tamaulipas, a director of social development began by recruiting local participatory committees with radio announcements, written invitation, and cars with bullhorns. When only a few people showed up to initial meetings, others were scheduled to demonstrate to people the benefits of participating in local decision making.[18]

A good example of an effort to establish a participatory decision-making process for public investments comes from Santo Domingo Tehuantepec, a municipality in the state of Oaxaca, where public officials had set in place an annual planning process. As soon as the local budget for public works was approved by the state government, the department of public works requested that each community convene an improvement committee to fill out a form it sent them.[19] The form asked each committee to list and assign priorities to the public investments needed in its community. Then, a municipal level meeting was called, attended by the mayor, the councilors, a representative of the governor, the principals of local schools, reporters, heads of civil society organizations, and representatives from each community.

In this meeting, characteristically held in a large auditorium due to the extensive public interest in its outcome, local public works officials, in concert with the municipal treasurer and the council member responsible for the budget, used a blackboard to create a matrix of investments requested. For example, under the rubric of potable water, all communities that selected such an investment as a priority were asked to report and each community was duly registered on the blackboard. When it became clear that there were not enough resources for all the requests, community representatives were pressed to establish their most important priorities, and at times to make trade-offs of investments this year against promises for investments in the following year. In addition, communities were encouraged to contribute land, labor, or money to extend the reach of public funds.[20] At the same meeting, a social auditor was elected. It was the job of this person to monitor the implementation of the investment plan and to make sure that every community received benefits.

With a list of priorities in hand, then, Tehuantepec's public works department could begin a detailed assessment of the economic and technical feasibility of the proposals. When an investment was approved by the municipal council, the department sent the community committee the planned budget and technical specifications for the project. It was then the responsibility of the committee to monitor expenditures and the quality of the work being performed. According to one observer of this process, "the positive aspect of the creation of this municipal social council is that it has democratized information about the budget . . . currently, the population—especially those in rural communities—knows what the budget is and can participate, even if indirectly, in the decisions taken by the municipality about works financed by the budget in any given year."[21] A local councilor indicated that the process had helped the municipality obtain more resources from the state government and, as a result, the municipality "was able to finish 120 of the 193 projects that had been prioritized . . . although it is always impossible to meet all of the demands."[22]

From the bottom up. Beyond top-down initiatives, some of which were more effective and democratically motivated than others, all of the research municipalities demonstrated citizen activism at the submunicipal

or community level. Organized by local residents, community improvement committees of various kinds reflected an apt understanding of effective ways to influence decisions about public investment.

These organizations functioned with remarkably similar dynamics.
First, they organized around a specific common interest. This was almost
always an investment project and represented a significant local need—a
road, potable water, or drainage ditches, for example. At times, the problem to be solved was one that had been identified by a community as a
priority over a significant period of time. In one community, for example,
the rainy season regularly brought flooding; in another, annual rains created an impassable stream that separated some residents from the main
road to town; in yet another, residents had to travel long distances for
emergency medical care and people had been known to die while being
transported to the nearest hospital. In some cases, a very specific common
interest brought a group together, as in the case of handicapped people in
a Oaxacan municipality who organized to obtain a government-financed
rehabilitation center.[23]

In some of the poorest regions of the country, where indigenous roots
were strongest, a tradition of *usos y costumbres* encouraged open assem-
blies and the election of community leaders as a matter of course for local-
level problem solving. As with other communities, this tradition often
included the pooling of financial resources that could be used to lobby
municipal officials for investments.[24] In a number of municipalities, a tradition of *tequío*, or community labor obligation, was a way of encouraging projects by lowering the overall cost to the municipality.[25]

In its initial meeting, the committee would elect a president, secretary,
and treasurer. Usually, those who emerged as leaders of an initiative were
well recognized for their prior work on behalf of the community and were
often those who had taken the initiative to mobilize the group at the outset. Those elected were also often those known to have a good reputation
or good connections in the *ayuntamiento*—people who had acquired benefits for the community in the past or those who had stood firmly with a
successful candidate during an election.[26] It was the leadership's responsibility to represent the community to the municipality, and at times, to
higher levels of government.

Community level committees selected similar strategies for approaching the municipality with their needs. The main focus of action
was initially to draw up a petition that laid out the difficulties created by
the problem and that asked the municipality for help in resolving it
through a particular investment. The petition was signed by as many
members of the community as possible. Very frequently, the committee
would assess each member a small fee—usually from one to five dollars—
to be used for transportation costs to send the leaders to the municipal
seat to present the petition and then to follow up on a weekly basis to see

what had become of it. Usually, they would take the petition directly to the mayor's office. While often this involved waiting for long periods of time in the mayor's anteroom before being granted an audience, this official would usually accept the petition, promise to give it priority, and then refer the group to the appropriate department for follow-up.

Follow-up with the director of the department or the councilor who oversaw that department was an important part of the committee's subsequent strategy. This often meant repeated visits by the committee leadership to check on whether action had been taken by this person or when action was scheduled. Such follow-up activities were often sustained for weeks, months, and even years, and typically were financed by contributions from committee members. Persistence was essential, and met ruefully by some public officials. According to one, "It is impossible to escape from them. They always come to the town to investigate [what's happening] and demand attention for their projects."[27] Some successful efforts to influence the allocation of investments were credited to the capacity of a local group to go public with its demands or otherwise be obstreperous.[28] Making waves sometimes paid off in terms of getting a speedier response from government officials eager to keep the political peace.

From a strategic perspective, it was well understood that local contributions might mean a positive response from the government. As the principal of a school noted, "If you have money in your hand, the municipality is more likely to help. It shows you are committed and willing to work with the municipality."[29] In the same municipality, the legal affairs officer noted that if "you arrive with your petition—for a street, for example—and you have a good budget and 50,000 pesos, we see that you are willing to meet the municipality halfway. We can spend [the saved] money elsewhere."[30] At times, acquiring funds meant tapping into a variety of sources. In a municipality in Sinaloa, a group of migrants in the United States signed an agreement with the government to provide scholarships for local children.[31] Some projects came with explicit agreements that local residents would have to put up some of the money, as was the case with a health center approved for a community in Tamaulipas that required $15,000 to be collected locally before construction could begin.[32]

A good example of the combination of local initiative and a facilitative municipality was the construction of a small bridge to join two parts of a community in Sinaloa. This community had long been divided by a gulch that could not be crossed by foot or motor traffic during the rainy season. For many years, community members had petitioned the municipality to put up a bridge, but had never been successful in their quest. Then, in 2002, community members elected a new committee to take on the task of advocating for the bridge.

Led by their president, the committee acted shortly after a new municipal government came into office. Having decided that the bridge could be made of the kind of drainage pipes that were currently being used to build a sewage plant in the municipality, the committee petitioned the local agency in charge of constructing this plant. The agency agreed to donate two pipes, and then later two additional pipes when it was determined that two was not enough. The municipality was then asked to provide equipment to do the heavy work of shifting soil and laying the pipes. The committee sponsored dances and horse races and collected a 5 percent tax on beer sold in the community after certain hours to buy cement and other material and to pay for labor. Committee members also helped out in the construction and, reportedly, when others saw their leaders doing this work, they joined in. Within a short time, the community was connected in good weather and bad. The municipal director of public works held up this community as an example of what could be accomplished when people worked together on local problems.[33]

A Focus on Extracting Benefits

Underpinning all of the strategic choices made by community improvement committees was the use of formal and informal networks to tap into the "right connection" for acquiring technical studies, approval, funding, equipment, and labor for the actual implementation of an investment.[34] Thus, those who knew the mayor or who had been important in mobilizing people and votes for an election campaign or who were related in some way to influential public figures were often chosen to take the petition to town hall and follow up on it. Committees that were successful in gaining their objectives often did not stop at the municipal level but worked with contacts at the state level, at times even circumventing a local government that was distrusted or considered unresponsive. Indeed, as the following cases demonstrate, the mobilization of connections was the basis of most strategies for influencing the allocation of public investments.

A preschool for Aldama. Aldama was a pleasant town.[35] Nestled at the foot of the Maratines mountains of Tamaulipas, it was surrounded by a landscape of green hills. Most of its roads were paved, and the town boasted a hospital and a sports arena. It also had an active population of teachers who joined together to find a way to provide day care for their children. After several years of work, they were able to find a way to answer this need, largely through a consistent strategy of using networks at local and state levels that enabled them to acquire land, personnel, and eventually, a building.

In 1998, fifteen teachers, concerned that their children needed better care while they were working, formed a committee, elected a president, and drew up a petition to establish a preschool in the municipal center. The leader of the group was the municipal coordinator of the teachers' union, but when the committee sent the initial petition to the regional teachers' union headquarters, it received no answer. In the following year, the committee's president, who had long been active in local politics, as well as in the teachers' union, was elected to the municipal council. Under her guidance, a new petition, this one signed by the mayor, was taken to a state level agency responsible for preschools, known as CENDIs (Centro de Desarrollo Infantil), by five committee members. Again, the petition was refused—the municipality did not meet the size requirements for a preschool.

After this rebuff, two committee members asked the municipal council to donate land for the preschool project; that the committee president was on the council helped ensure a positive vote. Then, committee members contacted all the teachers in the municipality, enlisting their support if they were interested, and obtaining copies of birth certificates of the children who would be eligible to attend the preschool. Next, they identified unoccupied buildings in the municipal seat, located their owners, and discussed possibilities for the loan of a house while they pursued possibilities for a building on the land they had acquired from the town. Eventually, a building owner living in the state capital and well known to many of the teachers agreed to sign a contract with the municipality, the regional teachers' union local, and the committee for an indefinite loan of the house.

Now, having acquired land, a temporary location, and evidence of demand (the birth certificates), the committee returned to the state capital to reopen discussions with the state agency responsible for CENDIs. Urged along by phone calls from the mayor and the head of the teachers' union local, state officials agreed to assist in finding staff for the new preschool. Eventually, a number of staff with ties to Aldama were recruited, and, with the strong support of the head of the union—also originally from the municipality—the state level agency agreed to pay their salaries.

Several bake sales and raffles later, the committee had raised enough money to clean and remodel the building that had been loaned to them. The group convinced the municipality to pay for installing electricity and improving the plumbing. In 2002, with an enrollment of eighteen children, the preschool opened. Soon, however, the owner of the house demanded its return. The committee then had to return to the municipality for help in constructing its own building. Again, with friends on the council, the group was allocated funds for building materials. It then set about raising money to pay for the construction. By the fall of 2004, the preschool had a home, sixty-eight children enrolled, thirteen teachers, a doctor, a psychologist, a social worker, and a cook.

Drinking water for San Francisco Ocotlán. The road into the municipality of Coronango was pitted with potholes and those who drove into the center did so by zig-zagging around them.[36] A mere twenty minutes from the capital of the state of Puebla, a city of two million people, the municipality was in disrepair, its green painted town hall a monument of broken benches, unhealthy smells, and idle workers. Efforts to bring drinking water to San Francisco Ocotlán, a community of 17,000 people within Coronango, indicated that the physical appearance of the municipality was symbolic of its history of poor performance.

An agricultural community in which many traveled to factory jobs in the state capital, Ocotlán had a church and a secondary school, but no direct access to the municipal seat. It was a poor community, with an obvious lack of public services. In late 2003, after six years of sustained effort, Ocotlán finally began construction of a potable water system for the community, an accomplishment that was achieved without the assistance of the municipal government, but by following networks of relationships to the state capital. The history of how this happened indicates the importance of persistence.

During a gubernatorial campaign in the early 1990s, the PRI candidate, sensing increasing demands for democratization of the political system, created citizen support groups in many communities, forswearing the usual practice of simply relying on mayors to mobilize votes. After winning the election, this governor visited Ocotlán in the summer of 1997. Setting up shop in the local school, he began receiving local community leaders. First on the list was the newly elected head of the community, formerly the local organizer of the committee to elect the governor. As they discussed the most important problems facing the community, its leader focused on water, formerly abundant but now severely threatened by a project that tapped the local aquifer to supply Puebla's capital city.

The governor offered to help the community resolve this problem and encouraged its leader to get in touch with the state level secretary of the interior. This secretary then directed the community to the state water agency, and provided support for its appeal to this organization. A few months later, the state government and Ocotlán signed an agreement in which the government committed itself to paving three streets and installing potable water and drainage systems. In exchange, the community would provide land for the project and allow the government to continue to use the local aquifer for water for the capital city.

The project got off to a good start; the streets were paved as agreed and the drainage system installed. The potable water system, however, languished, and no further action was taken until 2001, when a native of Ocotlán was elected mayor of Coronango. The election of a native son raised hopes that, with a friend in town hall, the water issue would be quickly resolved. The new president was as good as his campaign promise; he offered the system to Ocotlán for $200 per household hookup.

But community residents were shocked by the price tag and felt that they had been betrayed by their erstwhile friend and neighbor. They convened a community meeting to discuss how to respond to the municipality's offer and decided they needed to establish a committee to review options and revive the agreement with the state water agency. This committee, which counted among its members engineers, architects, and other university graduates, sought the technical advice of the water agency about how to save costs in individual hookups. After meeting on several occasions, the committee and the agency agreed to move forward with the potable water system on condition that residents pay for their own hookups. The committee again looked to Coronango's government to help defray the costs, and was again refused.

At this point, the committee took matters into its own hands, agreed to the project as designed by the state agency, and proceeded without assistance from the municipality. In 2003, the project began, assessing each household $120 per hookup; eighteen months later, 45 percent of the community was being supplied with potable water.[37] When all houses were connected, the community would elect another committee to manage the water system. From government failure at the municipal level, then, came an initiative that linked the local community with a state level agency, bypassing an obstructionist local government.

A rehabilitation center for the disabled of Acatlán de Pérez Figueroa. Acatlán was located in a sugar-producing region in the north of Oaxaca.[38] Physically, the municipal seat resembled a movie version of a wild west town, its streets dusty and its central plaza seemingly abandoned. It was not a municipality that functioned particularly well. Yet, some important programs came to Acatlán by way of citizen engagement.

This was the case with a new rehabilitation center for disabled people that was supported by the municipal level branch of DIF (Desarrollo Integral de la Familia), a social welfare agency traditionally headed by first ladies at local, state, and national levels. In 2002, a representative of the Disabled People's Association of Acatlán, himself a paraplegic, called on the president of the local DIF. This association leader had spent many years trying to encourage the government to build a center for those with disabilities and he explained the many difficulties experienced by such people in the municipality. Many of these people's lives could be improved, he argued, if only there were a rehabilitation center where they could get the necessary physical therapy and other attention.

"He opened our eyes to the reality that disabled people were living in our municipality," recalled a DIF administrator some two years later.[39] She determined that there would be a rehabilitation center for people like the association's president. In fact, she asked him to take the role of coordinator of the project and to be in contact with the families that most needed the help of such a center. Then, with the association's assistance, a census of disabled people in the municipality revealed some seven hundred people with different kinds of disabilities, and together, the association and the DIF president set to work to make the center a reality.

First, they contacted the local PAN state representative, a doctor who had previously worked in the Instituto Mexicano de Seguridad Social (IMSS). She lobbied with IMSS to acquire a room in its local clinic. Meanwhile, the DIF president went to the members of the municipal council to ask for $13,000 for the acquisition of therapeutic equipment. With this money in hand, a therapist was hired who would come three times a week to the center. Soon, the new center was providing a range of therapies and, in the opinion of the therapist, "This center is helping [patients] regain their hope of being able to live a normal life."[40]

Drainage for Praxedis Balboa and César López de Lara. The municipality of González in Tamaulipas was built on a flat agricultural plain, and boasted a pretty plaza with a gazebo and a statue of Mexico's founding father, Benito Juárez.[41] It had a lively town center. Traditionally, however, parts of the town were subject to flooding during the rainy season. Almost since the founding of the municipality in 1922, residents of the communities of Praxedis Balboa and César López de Lara complained about their vulnerability to annual weather cycles.

In 1992, residents of the communities met and drew up a petition, signed by as many people as possible, asking the municipality to resolve the problem. They presented the petition to the mayor, who immediately contacted the state level office of the national ministry of urban development and environment. Under a temporary work program, the agency agreed to provide the municipality with resources for a project in the affected communities. It sent engineers to carry out a study of options for resolving the problem; their recommendation, however, was outside the norms established by the temporary work program.

So, the mayor and the director of public works decided that the only way to carry on with the project was to modify the engineers' expensive plans. Rather than build a canal to divert the water, they simply cleared some existing drainage pipes and hoped water would not so readily back up into the streets and houses of the neighborhoods. The communities set up a committee, duly electing a president, secretary, and treasurer, to monitor the project. In time, however, the drainage pipes silted up and could no longer handle all the runoff. Two years after its formation, the committee again went to the municipality, but was told that funding was no longer available.

Elections brought a new mayor to town hall who promised that he would find some way to help the communities affected by the floods. Another committee was created and the municipality paid for a bridge over a culvert that was the source of much of the problem. This did nothing to deal with the flooding, however, and local citizens became angry at the failure of the municipality to deal directly with it.

In 2001, another newly elected mayor received a petition from yet another committee of residents affected by floods. They spoke directly to the mayor and then visited the office of the director of public works. The mayor had developed a good relationship with the governor, someone who had witnessed the devastation caused by the flooding during a visit to González in 1997. He convinced the governor to send engineers to do another study of the problem and to recommend a solution. In time, the technical study indicated that the best way to deal with the problem was an open canal that would channel the runoff water away from the streets and homes in the communities. The mayor visited the state capital to press the governor to approve the project, which he did. A new citizens' committee was formed to oversee the project.

Strategies for benefits . . . These histories of local citizen action to improve public welfare share several traits. First, in all of the cases, citizens met formally to create organizations whose purpose was to influence the allocation of public resources. They elected leadership, they drew up petitions, and they directed their leaders to lobby officials at various levels of government. These organizations were formed around very specific common interests and were regularly re-formed as the nature of the task at hand changed. Organizational and leadership tasks seemed well understood across a variety of communities.

Second, each of these histories of citizen activism indicated the importance of mobilizing networks of influential people to resolve local problems. Committee members used their networks to meet with mayors and councilors, to call on their state representatives, to make connections to other groups—such as the teachers' union—and to seek out the agencies responsible for particular issues. Talking, negotiating, and invoking political support, the groups demonstrated good knowledge of how to find the right connections that would eventually result in their success. They formed alliances with officials willing to commit themselves to solutions, they worked around obstructionist local officials and appealed directly to state level officials, and they contributed from their own pockets to make something happen.

Third, each of the citizen groups persisted in making their demands, at times over the course of several years and several different municipal administrations. It sometimes took a number of initiatives to get to a solution, and early efforts often resulted in refusals or failures. When efforts to work with one level of government failed, they solicited help from another. Although their persistence paid off, their activities suggest the ways in which government priorities, promises, and responsiveness changed as incumbents in office changed; there was little institutional infrastructure that could be relied upon over time to take responsibility for delivering a particular benefit—initiatives often had to be restarted as governments at state and local levels changed hands.

Finally, each of these histories was about extracting benefits from government. Indeed, citizen groups showed considerable sophistication in how to acquire responses to basic infrastructural needs. Their objectives were to obtain tangible benefits that could be provided in the short term; not surprisingly, they often found politicians ready to respond to their requests for these types of projects—these investments provided concrete evidence of actions that were bringing benefits to the communities.

. . . But not for accountability. At the same time, in these and many other municipalities, there was scant evidence of citizens organizing around demands to improve the overall quality of government performance. Thus, while many communities mobilized around the need for potable water, a new road, a bridge, or drainage, they did not identify the quality of education delivered by the local school, the helpfulness of nurses and doctors at the local clinic, or the right to efficient service in the civil registry as issues around which to organize. How they were treated at town hall was a matter for complaints, but not for organization. Waiting in line, having to pay bribes, being refused service were conditions to be endured, even while many citizens expected that organizing around investment petitions would eventually pay off. Groups were primarily concerned about particular benefits, not about the more abstract idea of "good governance" as a right that could be demanded by citizens.

This does not mean that there were no initiatives to improve the quality of governance through citizen participation in the research municipalities. There were. But interestingly, these initiatives almost always originated in town hall, not in the demands, ideas, or actions of citizen groups. In Chignahuapan and several other municipalities, for example, officials placed suggestion boxes in town hall and other localities so citizens could complain about services; these were often used to denounce particular officials who were judged not to be doing their jobs correctly.[42] In a municipality in Yucatán, the local government created an office of citizen response, where residents could report water leaks, broken or burned out streetlights, problems with the police, and other such local concerns.[43]

In several municipalities, public departments carried out surveys to learn which services were working well, which ones were experiencing problems, and how the municipal government's activities were viewed by its citizens. In many, "Citizen Wednesdays," "Citizen Mondays," "Itinerant Government," or "Saturdays in Your Neighborhood" took municipal officials outside of town hall to meet directly with constituents who had problems or complaints. When these kinds of accountability measures worked well, they did so because there were mechanisms in place to follow up and ensure that problems had been dealt with. Open sessions of the municipal council provided opportunities for greater transparency in some localities. As with other such innovations, these emerged at the initiative of public officials and agencies.

As indicated in chapter 3, of course, there were instances in which citizens sought to hold officials accountable for their actions in ad hoc and sometimes violent ways. Thus, for example, the Citizen Movement of Ixtacamaxtitlán was formed in order to sack several mayors for poor performance, one after only six months in office.[44] In the 1980s and 1990s, political movements ousted authoritarian political bosses in some municipalities.[45] That chapter also indicated that voting was used as an accountability mechanism in some municipalities and significant citizen mobilization accompanied election campaigns. In this way, some mayors and councilors felt pressured by political society to improve the performance of local government. Absent the sanction of elections, however, the right to good governance was not one that was clearly articulated or acted upon by citizens in the research sites. Moreover, where nonelectoral mechanisms of accountability did exist, they were much more likely to have been introduced by public officials than by citizen action.

CONCLUSIONS: TWO ROLES FOR CIVIL SOCIETY

Citizen organizations can be important in demanding good public sector performance in at least two ways—by extracting benefits from government and by holding government accountable. In the case of the municipalities in Mexico, citizen groups showed considerable sophistication and knowledge about how to extract benefits from government—especially how to get government to deliver on promises to provide public works. Using a fairly universal set of tools to influence public decision making, many were relatively successful in affecting the allocation of resources for particular projects and communities. The means they used were familiar ones, petitioning and invoking networks of influentials, often through time-tested forms of clientelism.

At the same time, there was a paucity of effective citizen mobilization around accountability issues. In the municipalities studied, most citizens had an extractive relationship with government rather than one based on their rights as citizens to demand good performance. Parent groups were not active in demanding that schools perform effectively or that teachers show up for work regularly; committees formed to plan municipal investments or to oversee the construction of a clinic or a road did not subsequently oversee the management of the clinic or the maintenance of the road. When garbage collection services failed, there was little evidence that citizens organized to demand their improvement. Moreover, even with investment projects, when local officials were unresponsive, citizen groups went elsewhere rather than demand more accountability locally.

Of course, demanding accountability is a more elusive task than demanding public investments in infrastructure. The performance of teachers and schools, for example, was responsive to state level secretariats; nurses and doctors were hired and managed by state and national level institutions; road maintenance required expertise not always available to local citizens; garbage collection was a service that many were used to doing without. In addition, elected officials, barred from succeeding themselves, could not necessarily be directly punished at election time for poor performance, although their parties could be. Moreover, organizing for accountability entailed more ambiguous and ongoing scrutiny than did mobilizing around interest in a particular infrastructure investment. It was clear when potable water was made newly available, but how could citizens identify "good governance"?

This distinction in terms of civil society activism in local government is an important one in the design of development policies, programs, and projects and in understanding the impact of decentralization. Currently popular forms of encouraging participation in local decision making— such as organizing groups to help plan municipal investments—may help to restrict citizen input to tasks of petitioning, making connections, lobbying, and finding ad hoc methods to influence government, rather than encouraging the development of a culture of accountability, of a sense that citizens have a right to demand effective government. In the research municipalities, good performance of ongoing administrative and service delivery tasks often remained solely the responsibility of public officials, who at times may have been motivated to improve conditions, but who were usually not spurred on by an active and engaged civil society.

Two forms of citizen engagement—extracting benefits and holding officials and agencies accountable for their actions—are strengthened when there are ongoing institutions for the delivery of services and administration. In both cases, the effectiveness of local civic action in Mexico was limited by the weakness of such institutions. In the case of extracting benefits, the response to petitions from local communities depended primarily on the decisions of mayors, councilors, and public works officials rather than on enforceable institutional commitments over time. When administrations changed, community improvement committees often had to start all over again to gain support from the local government—a paper trail of commitments from the past was not an effective way to ensure that projects could be sustained across administrations. In the case of accountability, mechanisms for ensuring it—with the exceptions of triannual elections—depended on the willingness of public officials to create and maintain them. Although the loose institutional context that has been noted in other chapters often provided municipal officials with ample room to maneuver and bring about change, it was a significant constraint on citizen engagement in monitoring government performance.

To what extent is the quality of government a response to civil society activism in Mexico? The research suggests several ways of answering this question. First, municipalities that scored differently on the performance index discussed in chapter 2 could not be clearly differentiated on the basis of civic activism or apathy. All of the municipalities, even ones that performed very poorly, could boast a range of civic associations, many of them focused on extracting benefits from government. All of the municipalities, even those that performed quite well, were notable for the paucity of accountability initiatives that originated in civil society. Thus, across the thirty municipalities, civil society activism did not clearly correlate with the quality of government.

Nevertheless, the extent to which civic organizations became mobilized and pressured government to deliver on promises for public works and social infrastructure undoubtedly contributed to the delivery of these services in all the municipalities. The ongoing petitioning, lobbying, and reminders of commitments made to specific communities kept public officials from ignoring their responsibilities and promises. These activities also kept municipal leaders from assuming total control of resource allocation decisions. Although there were few institutional constraints on decisions about the distribution of public investments, the mobilization of community groups acted to shape these allocations in ways that would have been different, absent these organizations.

Moreover, the increased importance of competitive elections in Mexico's municipalities also enabled citizens to call public officials and agencies to account and provided opportunities for new leadership groups to reach public office. Some of them, as we saw in previous chapters, had good ideas for introducing more participatory and responsive forms of governance. Many citizens did participate actively in political campaigns, and election time in many of the municipalities was a period of intense discussion and action around the candidates. That accountability was not an important focus of (nonparty) civic organizations does not imply that citizens were not exercising demands for accountability through their votes and their political party activities. As experience with more democratic elections increases, it may well be that ideas about the right to accountability will become more prominent in other types of organizations as well. Additionally, the accountability mechanisms introduced in a number of municipalities from the top down may become more institutionalized over time and thus provide more focus on good performance as an everyday expectation.

Photo by Sergio Cárdenas-Denham.

Chapter 7

WHAT'S NEW?

Patterns of Municipal Innovation

IN ABASOLO, the municipal government introduced new technology to reduce the air pollution caused by the region's brick-making industry. In San Juan Guichicovi, a local health service was organized around the needs of an indigenous population. A sewage treatment plant was opened in Salvador Alvarado, and in Rosario, the municipality undertook a major mission review to improve government administration. Citizens in Coronango began to receive regular information about the municipal budget and in Miguel Alemán, the treasurer's office introduced digital mapping to modernize the property tax base. In Progreso, the government contracted out its tax collection process and significantly increased its revenues.

In each of these examples, the municipal government initiated and implemented something new—a policy, a process, a program, a project—for the first time in the municipality. Sometimes, the innovation was an idea borrowed from elsewhere, at other times it was the result of research and analysis by local officials, and on some occasions it emerged as the "inspiration" of an individual or small group of people. Despite distinct origins, an interest in promoting change and in demonstrating the relevance of local government to the solution of collective problems was common to these initiatives. Importantly, these innovations interrupted the normal functioning—or malfunctioning—of an ongoing system and introduced new dynamics into the relationships between elected and appointed officials, between various levels of government, and between government and citizens.

Most of the municipalities in this study had introduced significant changes in how local responsibilities were carried out. Behind the stories of what was done in thirty local governments in Mexico lie important political dynamics and relationships that suggest the opportunities for and limits of improved local governance in the aftermath of decentralization. This chapter focuses on sixty-four instances of innovation to explore their origins and fates. The generalizations that emerge from this exploration echo much of what has already been encountered—significant activities promoted by local public officials, introducing interesting changes with uncertain life expectancies.

The origins of governance innovations were diverse, but the most common pattern by far was that of changes introduced by local officials, who sought to achieve their objectives by finding resources and allies within local communities and among networks of officials and agencies at other levels of government. At times they were motivated by their own ideas about what constituted better governance; at times they were responding to long-existing problems. They were often very successful in introducing change; the sustainability of their reforms, however, was much more open to question.

INNOVATIONS AND THEIR AGENTS

In each of the municipalities studied in this project, researchers identified innovations in governance, selected initiatives they thought were particularly interesting, and then, through interviews and documentary evidence, recreated the process through which they were developed and implemented.

Initially, the concept of innovation proved to be a challenge.[1] How restrictive should the definition be? Was it important that an innovation be something entirely new and surprising, something not seen elsewhere or anticipated as an action of government? Might innovation instead be understood as something that was being done in a particular place that had not been done there before? What if a municipality successfully undertook an activity mandated by a higher level of government in the past, but which had been ignored until then by the local government? What if a change were imposed by another level of government?

These questions were resolved through the adoption of a generous—but bounded—definition. It identifies as an innovation actions of government that have not been undertaken before in a given place and whose promotion is a result of local action.[2] This might include something quite novel, such as the introduction of digital mapping for property tax assessments, or something quite pedestrian, such as regular garbage collection or street lighting, if this was an activity introduced for the first time in a given municipality. Indeed, many of the changes documented were of this second, more mundane kind, as municipalities struggled with ways to increase the efficiency of basic administrative tasks and the public services for which they were responsible. These kinds of innovations are as instructive as more unusual ones, however, given that the concern here is with how governance improves—rather than with the originality of the solution to a given problem. From this perspective, introducing effective regulation of the municipal slaughterhouse or market is as important for understanding the dynamics of local governance improvement as more novel achievements such as investing in new solid waste technology, contracting out tax collection, introducing performance measurement, or creating an autonomous agency for water management.

In interviews with present and past municipal officials and with other observers of local affairs, researchers systematically and repeatedly asked about things that had changed in local governance in the decade between 1994 and 2004. In particular, they were interested in finding those innovations that originated within the municipality. Although some of the changes documented utilized funding from other levels of government or introduced programs that were available at state and national levels, it was important that the *initiative* for deciding upon, adopting, and implementing the change come from within the municipality. Over the course of numerous interviews, researchers developed lists of changes that local officials and others considered to be something new in the way the municipal government was working. For each municipality, they chose two to four of these changes to explore in greater detail.[3] For these, additional interviews, site visits, and documentary research reconstructed the history of how the innovation emerged, and was introduced and implemented.

Of course, municipalities varied in terms of how many innovations could be identified—indeed, in two, local officials and others were unable to identify a single improvement in local government during the ten years under consideration. In twenty-eight cases, however, researchers reported in detail on sixty-four, for an average of 2.3 innovations for each municipality. These data do not reflect the overall incidence or distribution of innovation, and most of the experiences documented activities of the administration in power at the time of the interview. Nevertheless, they suggest that innovations emerged in all important areas of municipal governance:

- *Administration:* Improvements in the efficiency, transparency, accountability, and management of municipal departments, such as the civil registry, tax administration, licenses and permits, budgeting, and planning, including the introduction of computers and other technology; anticorruption measures and the creation of new departments. Among the activities documented, for example, were ways to improve the efficiency with which citizens asked for and received registrations, permits, and licenses; initiatives to reduce the town's electricity budget; and a zero-tolerance policy to deal with in-house corruption.
- *Municipal services:* Additions to or improvements in the delivery of basic services to citizens, such as water, sewerage, health programs, public health and education infrastructure, police, roads, and markets, including the introduction of potable water, garbage collection, new clinics, police training, and regulation of public markets and slaughterhouses. Among the innovations discovered in the municipalities, for example, were an

TABLE 7.1
Innovation Initiatives in Research Municipalities (N = 64)

Category	Number	%	Number of States	Number of Municipalities
Municipal services	23	36	6	17
Administration	20	31	6	16
Economic development	9	14	4	9
Social development	8	13	6	7
Environment	4	6	3	4

TABLE 7.2
Origin of Innovations in Research Municipalities (N = 64)

Initiating Actor	Number	%
Mayor	29	45
Appointed municipal officials	12	19
Mayor + appointed municipal officials	7	11
Citizen organization	7	11
Mayor + elected officials	3	5
Elected officials	1	2
Unknown	5	8

incentive system for teacher performance, a mobile health initiative, and a program for upgrading the education of local police officers.

- *Economic development:* Initiatives to create jobs and attract investment, including the development of tourist sites and facilities, industrial parks, agriculture, and job creation programs. Among the experiences documented, for example, were an irrigation system for small farmers, an archeological dig to draw tourism, and a job registration and placement service.
- *Social development:* Efforts to increase citizen participation in decision making, improved information flow, and cultural activities, such as electronic government projects, citizen consultation, community improvement associations, and arts activities. Among the activities documented under this rubric were the creation of a folklore ballet company and an extensive system for citizen input into allocative decision making.
- *Environment:* Programs to improve environmental conditions, such as reforestation and pollution abatement for air and water. In the municipalities, such activities involved the development of tree nurseries, new technology for brick making, and the rehabilitation of lakes and rivers.

As indicated in table 7.1, most of the sixty-four innovations chosen for analysis fall into the categories of administration and municipal services.[4] Table 7.2 presents data on the "agency" behind each of the sixty-four innovations—the identity of the individual, organization, or group that came up with the idea and pushed for its adoption by the municipal government. Mayors introduced almost half of the innovations. When mayors acted in concert with other public officials, elected or appointed, the proportion of innovations originating with them reached 66 percent. Separately, appointed officials were agents of innovation in 20 percent of the cases and, when public officials of all kinds are compared with initiatives that originated outside of town hall, they accounted for all but 12 percent of the innovations. This remaining 12 percent was accounted for by citizen activism, such as that described in chapter 6. Innovations also occurred across municipalities with different parties at the helm of local government.[5]

Again, these data are not representative, but they are consistent with patterns described in previous chapters. The strong agency of the mayor, for example, could be anticipated, given what was learned in chapter 4. The mayor was the dominant figure in local government, the one around whom elections were organized and whose perspectives significantly affected what was decided in council meetings and among departments. Moreover, the relative activism of appointed officials compared with councilors can be explained by the fact that those with operational responsibilities had direct access to resources to carry out their ideas. It was emblematic of the relationship between appointed and elected officials (excluding mayors) that department heads had offices, staffs, and vehicles, while councilors often worked only part time, often had only cubicles or nothing more than a joint conference room in which to work when they came to town hall, and could not be immediately reelected.

In the chapter on modernization of municipal government, there was also evidence of the professionalization of appointed officials, at times giving them education and expertise beyond the capacities of elected officials. In addition, as suggested in the last chapter, civil society groups often appeared as petitioners for municipal attention rather than as organizations whose primary purpose was to lobby for improved government. If these conditions of executive and administrative dominance and legislative and citizen quiescence were characteristic of many of the municipalities, then it is not surprising to find mayors and appointed officials initiating most of what's new in governance at the local level.

The Motivation for Innovation

In a classic article on policymaking in Latin America, Albert Hirschman makes a distinction between problems that are "chosen" for solution by decision makers and those that are "pressing" in the sense that decision makers believe they have no alternative but to take them up.[6] Of course, all innovations are "chosen" at some level—agents make decisions to address them, while they choose not to address other problems. And, at some level, all innovations are "pressing"—they usually would not be introduced unless they provided solutions to some observed problem or constraint. Nevertheless, following Hirschman, in some cases agents have greater autonomy in selecting among possible problems for solution than in other cases, where problems seem more inescapable or inevitable.

This distinction is useful for understanding the motivations that agents had for taking up particular innovations. Some—chosen issues—were selected by agents among a variety of issues of importance that vied for their attention. In such cases, their choices responded to a particular personal commitment, a particular orientation derived from professional expertise, or a selected campaign issue. There were others, however, that responded to a particularly severe or obvious ongoing problem or constraint—a pressing issue. In these cases, an innovation might respond to a repeated crisis or be at the forefront of citizen and group complaints that demanded attention.

Chosen problems. Fifty-eight percent of the innovations were initiated primarily because they were chosen relatively autonomously by the innovator. Good examples of chosen problems were those that responded to the personal commitment or professional expertise of a mayor or department head, or were campaign promises of a winning candidate for office.

ADMINISTRATION: SANTA CRUZ DE JUVENTINO ROSAS, GUANAJUATO. The mayor, who had been in office previously as an independent and then won election on the PVEM (green party) ticket, was personally committed to introducing greater efficiency into local governance—it was the motivation that drew him into politics. Shortly after entering office on both occasions (1995 and 2003), he focused on this issue, introducing systems and processes to accomplish routine activities with greater speed and more transparency. In his second administration, he worked through the department of organizational development to introduce a strategic planning process in which local officials developed a mission for the municipality, a vision for its future, and a diagnostic tool to anticipate the actions that needed to be taken to reach that vision. The two mayors who took office after the first administration of the reformist mayor undermined the changes he had introduced.[7]

ADMINISTRATION: CHIGNAHUAPAN, PUEBLA. The personal commitment of a group of individuals, formed through many years of activity in the local Junior Chamber of Commerce, was responsible for the subsequent introduction of transparency in the municipal budget, the greater efficiency of the civil registry, and the opening of council meetings to the public. When their adopted political party (the PAN) won the next local elections, however, many of the changes they introduced were abandoned, including the effort to streamline the civil registry and to make budgets more transparent. Citizens strongly opposed an effort to close council meetings to the public and, as a result, the meetings remained open.[8]

ADMINISTRATION: ESCUINAPA, SINALOA. The annual municipal festival, which attracted local residents and many tourists to this coastal area, had long been a source of personal enrichment for the officials who granted permits and organized events. In particular, the mayor had traditionally enjoyed both bribes and kickbacks from the businesses and events involved in the celebrations. Although important as an event for the town, these corrupt practices meant that it did not generate much revenue, and the quality of local infrastructure important to the celebrations was declining. In 2002, the mayor proposed—and the council approved—an autonomous agency for managing the celebrations. The initial endowment of the agency came from renting out beach huts that families moved into for the three to four days of the celebrations. With a focus on transparent mechanisms for procurement, contracts, and auditing, the new agency earned about $40,000 in its initial two years of operation, funds that were used to improve the infrastructure important to the celebrations. The agency survived a change of administration.

ADMINISTRATION: SALVADOR ALVARADO, SINALOA. When the state-level PAN organization sent him a brochure about Citizen Wednesdays in 1996, the mayor decided that it was a good idea and introduced it.[9] His successors, from the PRI, introduced a similar but renamed practice, with the added dimension of public officials traveling to specific communities on a regular basis. When the PAN again won the mayor's office in 2002, Citizen Wednesdays were reintroduced, but with the dimension of "itinerant government" now included.

ADMINISTRATION: MANUEL DOBLADO, GUANAJUATO. The mayor introduced a program of zero tolerance for bribe-taking, kickbacks, and other forms of corruption in the *ayuntamiento*. Personally committed to cleaner government, as well as a member of a party long identified with it, he provided mechanisms for citizens and officials to report corrupt activities and to institute investigations and proceedings against those accused. At the time of the research, it was a priority of the mayor, yet was not written policy and had not been approved by the council. As such, it was unlikely to survive the next change of administration.

ADMINISTRATION: MIGUEL ALEMAN, TAMAULIPAS. When the newly appointed treasurer of Miguel Alemán moved into his office, he found a diskette with digital images of properties in the urban area of the municipality in his desk. The diskette had been left behind by the departing administration, and was the product of a state program for improving property tax systems that was never implemented locally. After discussing the system with the mayor, the treasurer sought technical assistance and funding from the state government for equipment; he hired a computer expert and set about implementing a computerized tax collection system and expanding its reach to rural areas. Municipal revenues improved significantly as more residents were assessed correctly, notified about the taxes they owed, and monitored for their payments. It was anticipated that the technology infrastructure and positive results of this innovation would help it transcend political changes in the control of the *ayuntamiento*.

MUNICIPAL SERVICES: MIGUEL ALEMAN, TAMAULIPAS. The mayor and the director of the education department designed and implemented an Adopt-a-School program in which public officials, teachers, principals, and parents spent a day once a month in selected communities painting, repairing, and improving local schools. The department of education coordinated these events with the public works and public health departments, and teachers spread the word about when events were to be held in the community. In this way, the education department was able to deal with numerous problems of individual schools at the same time, rather than attend to them one by one. Politically, this was an interesting choice, as it allowed the mayor and councilors to become familiar with individual communities and their schools, while citizens saw them in action, helping out with community improvements. Nevertheless, because it was so closely identified with the incumbent mayor, it would be difficult for this initiative to survive a change in administration.

MUNICIPAL SERVICES: SAN FERNANDO, TAMAULIPAS. When the director of public security took up his responsibilities after an election, he was shocked to discover that many municipal police were illiterate or semiliterate, or had dropped out of school before finishing primary or secondary schooling. Believing that education was an important prerequisite for a more professionalized police service, he set up a program for his officers to complete primary and secondary school while they were employed in the department. Because of the extensive patronage opportunities offered by police work, and the consequent turnover of officers every three years, however, this innovation would survive only with difficulty.

MUNICIPAL SERVICES: SANTO DOMINGO DE TEHUANTEPEC AND SAN JUAN GUICHICOVI, OAXACA. In both of these municipalities, the mayors were medical doctors; both put great emphasis on health services in their administrations. In the first, the candidate promised a hospital during his campaign and set about delivering it during his administration. The new hospital became the hub of an improved network of cooperation among health centers and medical dispensaries in the municipality. In the second locality, the mayor introduced a new department of municipal health that provided a range of services for residents. These improvements were closely linked to the lifelong professional aspirations of the two mayors, but the bricks and mortar of them would survive over time; the service improvements, however, were more subject to failure, unless citizens also learned to be more demanding of good quality.

SOCIAL DEVELOPMENT: SANTO DOMINGO DE TEHUANTEPEC, OAXACA. The participatory system for developing priorities for municipal investments, described in chapter 6, was the result of the actions of the mayor. Its introduction was linked by many observers to the increased electoral threat felt by the PRI, and a desire on the part of the mayor to take actions to improve the flagging legitimacy of that party in local opinion. Its future was uncertain because of this.

SOCIAL DEVELOPMENT: SAN JUAN GUICHICOVI, OAXACA. During his campaign, a candidate for mayor hoped to mobilize votes among the indigenous population by promising to "save" their culture. On assuming office, he set up a department of culture and sports as a new initiative of the municipality and encouraged activities that promoted knowledge about and pride in local indigenous roots. These activities were organized through local schools and sought to bring indigenous and mestizo communities together in greater understanding of each other. Again, however, the close identification of the innovation with the incumbent threatened its continuance once he was no longer mayor.

SOCIAL DEVELOPMENT: MOCORITO, SINALOA. The mayor, who had a master's degree in electronic government, decided to introduce a municipal Web site—whose basics were mandated by state law—that included creative ways in which citizens could find out about municipal events and obtain answers to questions, file for permits and licenses, and advertise locally produced goods and services. In addition, the municipality built and equipped a series of "community plazas" where residents could have access to the Internet. The future of these innovations would undoubtedly depend on the preferences of the next administration.

ENVIRONMENT: SANTIAGO JUXTLAHUACA, OAXACA AND LIBRES, PUEBLA. The mayor and the head of the municipal tree nursery in Santiago Juxtlahuaca applied to a state agency for funding and technical assistance to introduce

a high productivity nursery to produce plants that could be used in a
badly deforested area. Within a year of its creation, the nursery was sup-
plying trees for a significant reforestation effort that was also creating
jobs for rural workers. A similar program was undertaken in Libres, at
the initiative of the mayor. In both cases, however, reliance on external
funding threatened the future of these programs.

Pressing problems. By contrast to the kind of problems described above,
pressing problems were taken up because they constituted an ongoing
nuisance, annoyance, or constraint on the local community or government. Budget crises, for example, could spur efficiency-oriented innovations. At times, these kinds of problems demanded attention, as when
periodic flooding caused by lack of proper drainage wrecked hardship on
some communities.

ADMINISTRATION: PROGRESO, YUCATÁN. Faced with a large municipal debt
that meant that municipal jobs could not be filled and new programs and
projects undertaken, the mayor proposed contracting out the collection
of local taxes. A business solutions company undertook the project, employing local university students to be ambulatory tax collectors and giving them incentives to perform well. This initiative significantly increased
local revenues, permitting the municipality to move ahead with other activities. Given the positive benefits for the municipality's budget, this innovation was likely to transcend an administration change.

ADMINISTRATION: ALDAMA, TAMAULIPAS AND VALLADOLID, YUCATÁN. High municipal debts and very tight budgets caused two mayors to consider how
to save on high energy costs. They directed research and experimented
with new technologies to reduce the costs of public lighting, in both cases
producing significant savings for the municipality. The changes made to
physical infrastructure encouraged the survival of these changes.

ADMINISTRATION: SAN IGNACIO, SINALOA. Even though the municipality
boasted a new abattoir, animals continued to be slaughtered in the streets
and in the old facility, in ways that did not meet basic sanitary standards.
Residents complained of the smell. But by using the old facility or the
streets, livestock owners avoided paying municipal fees. Moreover, the
new slaughterhouse was poorly managed, further encouraging the use of
alternatives. The mayor, the municipal legal director, and a newly appointed slaughterhouse director decided that the problem had to be dealt
with, despite opposition from those who did not want to use the site or
pay the fees. These officials developed a set of regulations for the operation of the new slaughterhouse and significantly improved its operation.

Enforcing its use became easier as management improved; the slaughter-house began to capture significant amounts of revenue for the municipal-ity. Given the importance of ongoing management effectiveness, however, its future was uncertain.

ADMINISTRATION: ROSARIO, SINALOA. The municipality was so poorly man-aged that the state government refused some of its regularly programmed resources; the municipality was heavily in debt. During her campaign, the PRI candidate for mayor heard many complaints and made many prom-ises to attend to them if she should win the election. When she entered office, she took up the issue, relying on the municipal secretary to spear-head a reform initiative; in turn, he was assisted by the state level planning and development secretariat. Municipal officials met regularly to devise a mission statement, generate a vision for the future, and identify strategic objectives. Following this, the municipal officials set about developing, for the first time, organizational manuals and a number of basic regula-tions for how public business was to be carried out. Each job was defined and its responsibilities detailed. Then, performance measures were identi-fied for assessing the work of all officials. Although the performance mea-surement program was not put into effect, the rehabilitation of a badly functioning municipal government proceeded apace. Its future would de-pend on the orientation and support of future mayors.

MUNICIPAL SERVICES: MANUEL DOBLADO, GUANAJUATO. The town market had long been located in the central plaza of town, despite increasing threats to public health and strong and unpleasant odors. In addition, many citi-zens wanted to see their central plaza like that of other towns—green and leafy, a pleasant place to gather, a picturesque reminder of Spanish tradition, a site for a bandstand and a statue of a local or national hero. Moving the market to new facilities, however, was a source of consider-able conflict—market vendors and their allies fighting relocation and local citizen groups and businesses demanding that it be done. For years, the issue had been in negotiation and its resolution was plagued by reports of double-dealing and corruption. Over the years, many politicians prom-ised to do something about the market if elected, but on taking office proved unable or unwilling to resolve this inflammatory issue. Eventually, the municipality built a new market a few blocks from the plaza. How-ever, only some of the market vendors were willing to relocate there. Fi-nally, a mayor, acting on the basis of a judicial order that had never been enforced, mounted an early morning surprise assault on the market stalls remaining in the plaza and destroyed them. The demolition was followed by a program to indemnify the market vendors for their losses, in ex-change for their relocation to the new market. The mayor acted without the knowledge of the council; he reaped considerable public gratitude, however, for making it possible to establish a central meeting place for town residents. Harsh action as well as bricks and mortar helped ensure the plaza's more pleasant future.

MUNICIPAL SERVICES: TULA, TAMAULIPAS AND VALLADOLID, YUCATÁN. The mayor and council of Tula heard many complaints about the state of traffic in the municipal seat; traffic was often in gridlock on the streets near the central plaza. One of their early activities after taking office was to alter the direction of streets and to regulate the flow of traffic with signals. In Valladolid, a similarly grave problem of public transport was dealt with when the director of public security reorganized the police department to create a separate office of transit police and to employ them to move traffic along more swiftly. While the physical changes made in Tula were likely to endure, the future effectiveness of the transit police in Valladolid would depend on the commitment of its future leadership.

ENVIRONMENT: ABASOLO, GUANAJUATO. Owners of local tourist establishments complained repeatedly and over time about the increasing air pollution that local brick-making factories were causing. The 350 ovens used in this industry—which employed some 3,000 people—regularly burned tires, wood, chemical wastes, and by-products of the local shoe industry to make the bricks. The resulting pollution was creating economic problems for the tourist industry as visitors complained about the acrid smells. In the 1990s, federal environmental officials visited the region and promised to send a model oven that would reduce the fumes; the promise was never fulfilled. In 1994, the state health department, in response to complaints by local businesses, began a process to change the technology, but did nothing to penalize those who were polluting. In 1997, the state environmental institute created a regulatory department that closed five of the ovens for air pollution infractions; nevertheless, this action did nothing to alter the practices of the remaining oven owners. In 1999, conflicts reemerged between citizens and tourist businesses on the one hand and associations of brick makers on the other, and the debate became a classic one about saving jobs or saving the environment. The municipal government became involved in trying to mediate this conflict. As a consequence, and after studying the problem, municipal officials commissioned the design of low-contamination ovens and began experiments with them, eventually finding a model that was both economical and efficient. The mayor called a series of meetings with the brick makers to negotiate an end to the conflict and to inform them about the new ovens. The municipality offered the ovens at half price to the brick makers and also provided a 50 percent loan for the remainder of their purchase. In the succeeding years, the new ovens were widely adopted, air pollution significantly abated, and brickmaking continued as an important part of the local economy. Its sustainability was linked to this win-win situation.

ENVIRONMENT: IXTACAMAXTITLÁN, PUEBLA. The river that passes through this rural and mountainous municipality was increasingly polluted; it was where residents threw their garbage. Eventually, the river became so poisonous that livestock could no longer drink the water without becoming ill. In the dry months, the whole town smelled of rotten garbage. Citizens complained as the problem mounted, but it was not until 2001 that a new mayor took up the problem. A new sanitary garbage dump was established on the outskirts of the municipal seat and the river cleared of years of accumulated garbage and trash. This innovation, like the one above, was likely to endure.

Strategic choices. Almost all of these innovations, whether responses to chosen or pressing problems, involved the mobilization of resources from other levels of government. This was particularly the case of innovations involving expertise or new resources. A good example of this was the digital mapping of property taxation in Tamaulipas. This innovation was possible because a state government program offered its services for aerial photography to a previous administration. In the next administration, the treasurer was able to count on the assistance of a state program for technical assistance in putting it in operation, including buying new computers and hiring an expert to manage the system.

In Tamaulipas, a tourism development program involved linkages to the state university (to carry out a feasibility study), the state planning agency (to provide technical assistance), and the National Institute of Anthropology and History (INAH) (to help the municipality obtain funding from UNESCO for the preservation of historic sites, and to find additional resources from federal and state governments). Part of the project involved the rehabilitation of a lake that required participation by the national environmental secretariat (SEMARNAP) and the social development secretariat, as well as other federal agencies. Similarly, in Guanajuato, the development of an archeological zone that was expected to attract tourism involved the National Institute of Anthropology and History, a research institute from another state, and the state level council on culture.

Intergovernmental cooperation was itself often based on personal ties and networks. In chapter 6, the history of the CENDI preschool provided a good example of the use of such networks, as did the example of how the residents of San Francisco Ocotlán were able to get potable water for their community. In Oaxaca, the development of a new hospital and attendant health services was helped along by the interest of the governor in promoting such services during his administration and the connections that mayors had with him. Relying on other kinds of relationships, municipal officials in Sinaloa made contact with a successful musical group originally from the municipality and encouraged them to donate money for a new school transportation program.

A microcredit program in the same state was also promoted through extra-municipal agencies. The local director of rural development regularly attended training sessions in the state capital and elsewhere to find out about new initiatives. When he heard about a program called Social Credit, he found out more about it on the web page of the social development secretariat, and then followed up with a phone call to a contact in that agency. Shortly, his proposal for a pilot project in one of the municipality's poorest communities was approved and funded by the national agency; initial successes led to a larger and more long-term project for lending money to rural livestock producers that was undertaken between the municipality and the federal government. The first initiative helped create important linkages within the social development secretariat and built trust between central and local level officials.

Thus, once a change had been decided upon, municipal officials looked to other levels of government for assistance, and used whatever contacts they had to facilitate the release of funds and technical assistance. In doing so, they were consistent with what has been learned in previous chapters about the management style in Mexico's local governments.

CONSIDERING SUSTAINABILITY

Throughout previous chapters, change in local government was a constant theme—in political parties that govern Mexico's municipalities, in leadership styles, in technology and management capacities, and in the sources of pressure to improve local governance. In this chapter, the focus has been on change also—the dynamics of policy, process, program, or project innovation. The evidence suggests that innovation—introducing something new in a particular context—is not uncommon in Mexico's local governments. There was evidence of considerable variety and ingenuity in designing and introducing innovative ways to resolve some ongoing problems of local governance.

It is also important to question the extent to which these changes were institutionalized and sustained. As suggested in other chapters, when institutions are weak, opportunities for change are considerable. At the same time, the very weakness of the institutions can undermine the relevance of reforms to address problems over the longer term—what has been introduced is subject to considerable opportunities for reversal or rejection. This dilemma is also relevant to the innovations that were introduced in the research municipalities. Mayors and other officials were often aware of this problem and sought ways to increase the probability that their changes would live on after their administrations.[10]

Of course, lack of sustainability is always a problem when change is introduced. Some innovations do not deal effectively with the problems they were expected to solve and are abandoned or superseded by other changes. Moreover, it is common that many new procedures, rules, and regulations are not observed after being introduced. After all, Latin America is famous for the reply of its colonial officials to mandates from Spain: "*Obedezco pero no cumplo.*"[11] But the region is not alone in recognizing the difference between announcing a policy and actually putting it into practice. Similarly, infrastructure may be poorly maintained and fall into disuse, a recurrent problem where resources are limited and priorities are subject to considerable change. Faulty construction standards and their abuse by corrupt officials and contractors often add to the problem of sustaining infrastructure.

In Mexico, in a context of increasing political competition with rules against political succession, it might be expected that many changes would fail in the first test of sustainability—would they survive from one administration to the next? Characteristically, new political administrations seek to differentiate themselves from their predecessors, even when they represent the same political parties. They do this by introducing new policies, processes, programs, and projects and curtailing, renaming, or ending those of their predecessors.

Some of the innovations produced good results and were based on changes that were difficult to undo. The clean-burning ovens for brick-making in Guanajuato, for example, responded to tourist business concerns by reducing air pollution while at the same time lowering costs for the brick producers, creating a win-win situation that was likely to be sustained in the future. Moreover, some innovations were important in generating more consistent revenues for municipalities, something that should recommend them for sustainability. Indeed, this was the case in contracting out tax collection in Progreso—revenues increased and public officials in a new administration saw the system as one that should be continued. In Libres, the creation of an autonomous water agency might anticipate the same healthy future.

There were other kinds of innovations that were not a source of significant opposition. Introducing new signage on public streets and more efficient traffic flow can solve problems, resulting in their easy acceptance. Similarly, a hospital, a sewage treatment plant, or a new garbage dump might have longer time horizons than, say, efforts to introduce more friendly service in town hall. From this perspective, physical infrastructure, although it can be allowed to deteriorate over time, may be more durable than changes in services. There were also innovations that suggested the potential to become financially self-sustaining.

On the other hand, among the most vulnerable innovations were those that were closely identified with a particular administration, that did not at the same time have either construction or a well-embedded system for keeping them going, and that relied substantially on outside funding for continuation. One mayor introduced a program of cash transfers financed out of his own salary, for example, a change unlikely to be sustained over time. Similarly, the introduction of new processes such as Citizen Wednesdays or Adopt-a-School programs were those that tended to be identified closely with a particular administration and were put in place through ad hoc mechanisms.

Indeed, significant improvements in the efficiency of municipal administration were introduced in 1994 in Santa Cruz de Juventino Rosas, only to be abandoned by the next two administrations and then reintroduced when the original innovators returned to office. A similar fate befell a budget transparency initiative in Coronango. Several of the innovations in Chignahuapan were undermined by the subsequent administration, even though it represented the same political party. One might anticipate a similar fate for the zero-tolerance anti-corruption initiative in Manuel Doblado, unless some well-embedded structures and procedures were put in place to keep it going. The extensive process of mission development and administrative reform in Rosario was vulnerable to the same kind of loss of interest or commitment of its initiators and their successors.

Several municipalities invested time and effort in organizing participatory mechanisms for municipal planning and resource allocation. Such mechanisms might be sustained across time as political parties vie for popular support or as citizens develop the expectation that they will be consulted. Nevertheless, given that such processes do not directly solve particular problems—instead, they democratize the process of problem solving—these initiatives may be more vulnerable than other kinds of innovations.

Finally, ongoing projects that depend significantly on funding from outside sources—state and national governments, for example—can be subject not only to political changes at the local level but also changes that occur at other levels of government. This calls into question the reforestation programs in Oaxaca and Puebla, for example, as well as the training of police officers in Tamaulipas, funded by a state adult education program, and the municipality's new microcredit program for rural producers.

CONCLUSIONS

Innovating, introducing something new as a policy, process, program, or project, was not unusual in Mexico's medium-sized municipalities at the time of the research. In all but two of the research sites, local officials and residents were able to identify initiatives that they believed had made improvements in the way local government was working. Indeed, the opportunity structure for innovating in local governance was fairly open. New administrations, in particular, seem to have had a relatively free hand in introducing change. Their agendas were set in part by selecting among a variety of possible changes and in part by the need to deal with particularly pressing problems. The histories of these innovations showed the importance of networks and contacts for funding new initiatives, but they did not regularly refer to resistant bureaucracies or systematic resistance to change that had to be overcome in order for the changes to be put into effect.

The larger problem many of the initiatives faced was that of their sustainability. In this regard, the very flexibility that allowed for significant change raised barriers to its institutionalization over time. Administrations with new priorities and new appointments in town hall would come and go, and what they left behind could not always be ensured, even if it provided a reasonable solution to a problem. Thus, the innovations that were probably most durable were those that involved bricks and mortar and those that made it particularly difficult or unreasonable to return to old ways of doing things—computerizing basic municipal functions, for example, or changing the direction of traffic flow.

Those that may have been least durable were those that involved behavioral changes in the way public officials interacted with citizens—customer-oriented procedures and participatory forms of decision making—and those that required ongoing funding from external sources. This suggests that local governments will continue to find it easier to build roads and bridges on a regular basis than to institutionalize democratic procedures and responsive administration in local affairs. This hypothesis corresponds to the findings about the ease with which local citizens extracted resources from government, but were much less engaged in efforts to hold government more generally accountable.

In such cases, municipal governments might be able to go farther in institutionalizing administrative and participatory reforms by paying more attention to the mechanisms by which rules and processes become formal. They need to be written down, of course, but they also need to be reflected in the incentives that affect the performance of public officials, there need to be formal mechanisms to deal with those who ignore or shirk their responsibilities, organizational cultures need to be created and nurtured over long periods of time, and citizens need to have information on what to expect in their encounters with local authorities. Too often in the cases of municipal innovation reviewed here, their introduction was informal, they were based primarily on exhortation or the commitment of a person or small group, it was difficult to hold officials accountable for their correct functioning, a culture of service was limited by personnel changes every three years, and citizens did not have sufficient information to understand their rights and obligations. Alternatively, innovators considered the production of a formal rule, regulation, or law as the end goal of their activities, rather than attending also to the kinds of incentives and changes that transcend the gap between formal policy and its implementation.

Photo by Sergio Cárdenas-Denham.

Chapter 8

THE PROMISE OF GOOD GOVERNANCE

THE QUALITY of local governance became newly relevant to millions of people around the world in the early twenty-first century. Whereas municipal governments had long had some role in the management of local affairs, in the final decades of the twentieth century they were given many new responsibilities, provided with considerably more resources, and allowed greater autonomy than had been true in the past. In developing countries, these new powers stood in contrast to decades of centralized management of public affairs. Now, the decentralization of fiscal, administrative, and political responsibilities challenged local governments to become more effective at carrying out the public's business and more democratic in their decision-making processes.

The new context of responsibilities and resources for local government was a dynamic one; to study it was to fix on a moving target. In this book, research carried out in thirty municipalities in Mexico caught all of them in the midst of changing expectations and new pressures for responsiveness and accountability. New expectations came from above—by way of new rules of the game determined by national and state level authorities—and from below—through pressures from citizens and civic organizations. Electoral calendars and the changing face of internal municipal operations also had an impact on how municipal governments experienced decentralization.

FROM TOP DOWN, BOTTOM UP, THE PAST, AND INSIDE

Decentralization came first to Mexico's municipalities through changes in the rules established by central and state level governments over a period of twenty-five years. New responsibilities and a variety of revenue-sharing mechanisms, grant-making arrangements, special funding sources, and specific agreements provided them with new opportunities to make decisions about investment projects and priorities for local development. Particularly after 1997, when the PRI lost control of the national congress, the amount of resources flowing to local government increased significantly, in part because of actions to ensure more resources for non-

PRI governors and mayors. At the same time, new responsibilities and funds often came with strictures about their use and requirements for reporting on them. Thus, along with new opportunities to decide on the use of resources, local governments became more accountable upward for how such funds were used; bureaucracy accompanied funding, often in ways that local officials found burdensome and intrusive. In the case of Mexico, federal officials concerned with fiscal stability were particularly vigilant about the ways local governments were using money, and were especially concerned to ensure that they did not contribute to the national debt burden.

Thus, new and changing expectations from other levels of government were an important part of the dynamic that local governments had to adjust to as decentralization moved forward. Similarly, these dynamics changed in terms of citizen expectations about what municipalities could achieve. In the past, political bosses and state and federal patrons had been expected to mobilize resources from higher levels of government to respond to local needs, strengthening clientelist ties to the dominant party as they did so. In the aftermath of decentralization, pressure from below to resolve problems was refocused on municipal officials. As a result, the pressures from above were often matched by organized and individual demands from below—demands that had principally to do with the allocation of public investments to community level priorities or to the specific needs of individual citizens. Help me! Help us! were refrains that local officials heard increasingly as decentralization advanced. In some cases, town governments introduced new forms of participation in decision making and fora that allowed citizens direct access to public officials when they had complaints or problems.

The dynamics of decentralization responded not only to pressures from above and below, but also to the normal rhythms of political life. In Mexico, this meant the three-year cycles of municipal elections and, to a lesser extent, the six-year cycles of elections at state and federal levels. Increasing competition among political parties meant that elections were more significant in terms of the changes that they might bring to town hall. Equally important, because mayors and councilors could not seek immediate reelection, each election automatically brought new faces and new priorities to town hall, whether or not the party in power changed. Given that the underlying institutional structure of local government remained weak, changes in political administrations brought significant changes in policies, processes, programs, and projects at regular intervals. Each new administration could, to a considerable extent, recreate local government and redetermine its priorities and purposes.

Personnel changes were not exclusive to elected officials. Mayors, or mayors and councilors together, had considerable opportunities to change the faces of the local bureaucracy. With extensive appointive and organizational powers, they could introduce new people, new departments, new procedures, and new forms of dealing with the public. One of the more significant and consistent changes was the increase of professionals appointed to head up departments and important activities for the municipality. Yet even professional managers came and went as the electoral calendar advanced.

The tools of the trade showed impressive change with the advent of efforts to decentralize. In a transition away from handwritten tax rolls and ancient typewriters used to peck out reports and regulations, many medium-sized municipalities in Mexico adopted electronic systems that significantly altered management practices. In some cases, administration became more accurate, less subject to corruption, and more efficient. Some municipal officials became more adept at using the Internet to provide local services and at times sought to provide such access to citizens. Local council meetings were at times televised, municipalities operated info-radio programs, and e-mail became, in some cases, one additional way to reach the mayor with a petition or a complaint.

These dimensions of change—new expectations from above, from below, and from within—drove a moving target of municipal response to decentralization. The chapters in the book indicate that a great deal was happening below the surface of local government in Mexico in the early twenty-first century, as cities, towns, and communities faced up to new demands and expectations in a context of increased autonomy and public resources. Not all of this activity was benign; among examples of improved performance and responsiveness to local needs were numerous stories of corruption and institutional failure. Local governments were still plagued by the legacies of a century of centralization—inefficiencies, ineffectiveness, unresponsiveness, clientelism, graft. Indeed, among the thirty research sites, there was wide variability in the extent to which local governments were responding to new opportunities and constraints and dealing with the legacies of the past. Some proved to be dysfunctional, while others were able to make significant headway in providing better administration, services, and responses to development opportunities. There were stereotypically corrupt, bumbling, unresponsive local governments side by side with municipalities surprisingly adept at introducing better governance.

Four hypotheses introduced in chapter 1 set out alternative explanations for this variability. To what extent is local government performance systematically affected by *competitive elections, entrepreneurial leadership, public sector modernization,* or *pressures from civil society*? In subsequent chapters committed to exploring each of the hypotheses in turn, empirical work revealed a surprising dynamic—the four separate hypotheses actually existed in dynamic interaction with each other. While the leadership of public officials—elected and appointed—emerged as the most important factor in explaining how municipalities were adjusting to new responsibilities and resources, this was given meaning through competitive elections, it drove the dynamics of public sector modernization, and it was challenged to some extent by the mobilization of local civil society.

Empirical work also revealed how legacies of the past continued to characterize many aspects of local governance, even in the context of great change. In particular, the way in which public officials and citizens sought to resolve resource constraints echoed long-existing ways in which levels of government interacted with each other and the forms through which citizens interacted with the state. Centralization continued to affect the behavior of municipal officials and citizens, while problem-solving mechanisms continued to reflect a more authoritarian past. Yet, the promise of better governance also continued to be a real one and decentralized local government may yet prove to be a good school for democracy.

Four Propositions Revisited

Local government as an inspiration for innovation and participation or as a locus of sloth and corruption—these are contrasting images of the performance of local government as it responds to new responsibilities and resources concomitant with decentralization. Yet theories from economics, political science, and public management anticipate that good will emerge from restructuring government through decentralization—greater efficiency and fiscal responsibility, more democratic accountability and opportunities for participation, and better quality services that respond to local needs. As indicated in the first chapter, however, empirical results have not always been as robust as theory would predict, drawing into question theoretical linkages that lead from decentralization to good governance. In this book, the tension between the theory and practice of decentralization is central to exploring how, why, and when better local governance emerges—or doesn't—and the implications of decentralization for achieving the public good. It goes inside town hall to do so.

In Mexico, the official sequence of decentralization ran from political, to administrative, to fiscal. The popular election of local officials in the "free municipalities" enshrined in the Constitution of 1917 reached back to the consolidation of the political regime in the aftermath of the Revolution of 1910—and replicated traditions in effect in some communities from colonial times. In the 1980s, administrative decentralization became the focus of federal efforts to give greater responsibilities to local governments. Then, in the 1990s, a cautious form of fiscal decentralization was increasingly emphasized. Nevertheless, the authoritarian system in place during most of the twentieth century imposed great constraints on the reality of political decentralization. De facto, administrative decentralization was an artifact of the 1980s, and political and fiscal decentralization became much more present realities in the 1990s. Efforts to decentralize responsibilities to state and local governments preceded the clear decline of the dominant party, but initiatives to promote it gathered strength as the PRI became less powerful as a contender in national and local politics.

By the early 2000s, decentralization had proceeded far enough to say that federalism was a new reality in Mexico, as it was in a large number of other countries around the world. Over the course of twenty-five years, three levels of government redefined their relationships to each other and a new research focus emerged—the performance of local government in the wake of decentralization. In the new dynamic of administrative, political, and fiscal decentralization, large cities were in the forefront in terms of insisting on greater autonomy, increasing local capacity to manage fiscal resources and public services, increasing the level of local taxation, and challenging the central government for additional responsibilities and resources.

But questions remained about smaller municipalities—those that were not state or national capitals, for example. Were they blundering in the wake of decentralization, bereft of capacity to handle new activities, too corrupt to manage finances effectively, and too politicized to demand greater autonomy? Or were they, like larger cities, getting better governance? Thus, the 2000s seemed an appropriate moment to consider how local administrative systems in smaller municipalities were adjusting to new responsibilities, how service delivery functions were faring, whether economic development activities were undertaken, and how processes of decision making in local government were changing. Alternative hypotheses responded to these concerns.

Competitive elections. Competitive elections should stimulate local office holders to improve government performance. This is the first of the hypotheses explored in this book, the link between performance and electability. In Mexico, the rationale behind the hypothesis rests on the assertion that politicians in office will try to perform well because they prefer to have their parties win subsequent elections rather than other parties— they cannot succeed themselves, after all—or they want to do well in office because they hope to run for higher level office on the basis of their record of good performance. If these expectations are realized, there will be fewer incentives for elected public officials to perform well while in office where elections are less competitive.

Exploring this hypothesis in the context of thirty medium-sized municipalities in Mexico indicated that there is indeed a link between competitive elections and performance, but it is not a direct one. Greater electoral competition set in motion a number of important changes in local politics.

First, winning positions in local government became more attractive in the wake of serious efforts to decentralize responsibilities and resources. Control over those resources and the jobs and opportunities—for good or ill—that they created increased interest in running for office as mayor and councilor. In particular, becoming a mayor was an increasingly attractive goal for the politically ambitious. It provided access to important resources to distribute to constituents and clienteles and an opportunity to use local office as a "trampoline" to higher office.

As a consequence, competition increased for public office in all of the research municipalities, even where the dominant party had long been unquestioned. Often, the competition began within that party, the PRI. Traditionally in the hands of local political bosses, contestation to be chosen as a candidate gave rise to initiatives to debunk old *caciques* and to introduce new groups into political relevance. In the wake of increased competition for office within the PRI, new local political parties emerged and provided, often for the first time, alternatives for citizen choice in elections.

Second, at least at the local level, the party identities and labels of candidates were often more "shopped" than they were reflective of ideologies, positions, or platforms. Time after time, our fieldwork indicated that new parties emerged when aspiring candidates were rejected by the locally dominant party and defected in order to run for office. Thus, greater competition among parties was more often a result of a changing opportunity structure than it was of the mobilization of particular perspectives and commitments, or even the diligence of party activists in recruiting and organizing new members. When locally ambitious politicians began to believe that it was possible for alternative parties to win elections, competitive parties sprang up in many localities.

Increasing competition was often reflected in the turnover of power from one party to another—at times on several occasions. But even in municipalities that continued to bring PRI candidates to office, the threat of losing elections heightened. Increasingly, there were fewer "safe boroughs" for the party that had dominated political life in Mexico for so long. It was difficult, therefore, to distinguish between more or less competitive political contexts; all parties and candidates were under increased pressure to perform in ways that would win them votes in subsequent elections. Moreover, parties began to pay more attention to internal mechanisms for selecting candidates, to becoming more open and transparent in terms of how they selected candidates, and to finding candidates who were popular locally. Again, this affected all parties, and was not limited to the most competitive areas.

Third, when voters had real alternatives among candidates, electoral campaigns increased in meaning. They were the vehicles for bringing alternative leadership to local government. This leadership was not consistently better than the old leadership—scoundrels were elected as well as reformers—but opportunities were opened up for the election of public officials committed to improving the performance of local government.

Fourth, as competitiveness increased, divided and contentious municipal councils became more likely. Under the principle of proportional representation, most mayors were able to count on a party majority in the council, but the vagaries of close elections, shifting party identities after elections, and negotiations for support in the absence of strong party platforms meant that some mayors found it more difficult to act on their preferences, and some even faced gridlock. Resource allocation decisions at times became more subject to contention and negotiation as the amount of resources increased and as municipal councils became increasingly pluralist.

Thus, while improved municipal performance was not a necessary outcome of increased political competition, this competition was an important condition that facilitated opportunities for introducing change in how municipal business was done. Clearly, it was a dynamic underlying the second hypothesis—that state entrepreneurship is an important driver of local government performance.

State entrepreneurship. Mayors and other elected and appointed officials are the most important source of change in local governments; they have the greatest opportunities to set public agendas and use public resources to achieve their objectives—so goes the second hypothesis. In the research municipalities, this hypothesis found consistent support. Mayors and others in leadership positions were expected to find resources for projects, manage the daily business of town hall, attend to constituent needs, and resolve conflict. Mayors were almost always the primary movers and shakers of local government and they differed significantly in terms of their commitments and abilities. This was reflected in differences among municipalities in how well they operated.

Some of the impact of leadership on local government was explained by the extent to which local electoral campaigns avoided party platforms or programs. Instead, politicians retailed promises to fix this or that at the community level and gathered petitions from individuals and communities about things they wanted. To a remarkable degree, campaigns in a more democratic Mexico were patterned on campaigns when Mexico had a one-party dominant system; it was about promises to fix specific problems in exchange for votes. A consequence of this style of campaigning was that when new administrations came to power, they often had no program of government, no clear priorities, and no consistent goals they were committed to. In many cases, programs, priorities, and goals were selected in the aftermath of elections, in contexts in which new mayors had a major say in what was to be pursued and in which their priorities or perspectives held considerable sway.

As it turned out, mayors were particularly important because many of the resources needed to pursue public goals had to be liberated from other levels of government. Indeed, as resources available to local governments increased, so did the time needed to "bring down" these resources from other levels of government. Thus, the commitments, personality, persistence, and political networks that mayors brought to the office were important factors in determining how much could be done in any three-year period, as were the relationships they cultivated while in office. Indeed, in some of the research municipalities, differences in the party affiliations of mayors and governors were overcome by the creation of close personal relationships. If mayors generally set public agendas for their terms in office, it was their connections to governors, ministers, and administrators at other levels of government that helped determine whether they could carry them out.

In addition, elected leaders had great discretion in appointing officials to public positions in the municipalities. They used this discretion variously—some to appoint cronies, some to solidify coalitions of support on the council, some to bring new purpose to town hall. In making use of this power, they had considerable capacity to change the orientation and performance of the government. Those they appointed could introduce new policies, procedures, programs, and projects. Newly appointed officials usually did not have to deal with embedded administrative routines that constrained their activities; instead, they could create and recreate administrative processes. They directly controlled financial resources and staff, and, often, they were part of the entrepreneurial apparatus that brought new resources to the municipality. Their connections, as well as those of the mayor, were critical factors brought into play in change initiatives. Indeed, liberating resources and managing a large number of projects and programs funded by other levels of government was a principal responsibility of department heads in Mexico's municipalities.

Municipal councils tended to be less important players in local government, although in a few instances individuals on the council helped initiatives get funding and support. Councils approved plans, programs, and budgets, and individual members were usually assigned to oversee some particular function in town hall. In the former role, they usually did little to hinder the mayor and his appointees, although a significantly divided council could bring local government to a standstill. In the latter role, councils were primarily active when they picked up a particular initiative and mobilized their networks at other levels of government to promote or support it. Compared to the mayor and appointed officials, however, councilors were not usually key to promoting changes in the municipalities.

State entrepreneurship, encouraged by the opening of the electoral system to increased competition, was particularly important because of the weakness of institutional structures that could act as a constraint on what leaders were able to do. Party platforms were weak or nonexistent, so leaders were not bound to a particular program once in office. Campaigns often left them considerable discretion to determine a program of government after they were elected. In most municipalities there was no entrenched bureaucracy to resist change—mayors could re-create the administrative structure and replenish its human resources when they came into office. State and federal level laws, rules, and regulations were burdensome and constraining, but it was possible to honor them in the breach.

But the very lack of institutional constraints that helped explain how much things could change in the course of three years also systematically undermined the sustainability of change. Thus, the extensive room to maneuver that local public officials had was matched by possibilities that their initiatives would be undermined by their successors and that institutional memory would be weak. In a relatively open institutional context, then, leadership success and subsequent failure were both relatively easy.

Public sector modernization. New ideas, new technologies, and training provide a stimulus for change in government performance, according to a third hypothesis. In particular, by introducing modern techniques of management and improving the administrative and technical capacities of elected and appointed officials, the efficiency and effectiveness of local administration and service provision could be expected to improve. Moreover, this hypothesis projects that public sector modernization will be an important factor in reducing systematic corruption in town hall.

In the thirty research municipalities, public sector modernization was much in evidence. Reorganizations were common, as was improving the "profile" of those selected to hold appointive office and the extent to which new technologies were used in routine activities. Performance standards were introduced in some municipalities and computers were functioning in all sites, although they were being put to more sophisticated use in some than in others. Indeed, the extent to which computerization was being adopted for administrative and service provision tasks was often surprising, given that some of the municipalities were significantly rural, had declining economies, and were found in regions that were poorly served by higher education and whose electric and transport networks were subject to interruption.

There was certainly no paucity of training courses offered for local public officials and there seemed to be resources in almost all municipalities to allow at least some to benefit from training activities. Many officials were conversant with the principles of the New Public Management and with private sector organizational and management techniques. In some cases, capacity building in order to improve performance took on added importance as a way to improve the legitimacy of the long-dominant PRI.

The professionalization of appointed officials was an important aspect of public sector modernization in many municipalities—accountants in the comptroller's office, architects and civil engineers in charge of public works, doctors and nurses handling responsibilities in the health office. Often, it was these officials who were behind the introduction of new organizational schemes and technologies for accomplishing the work of town hall. They had ideas, contacts, and staff to solve problems. And, although capacity building is often viewed as a difficult initiative that requires ongoing commitment over many years, the experience of Mexico's municipalities suggests that significant changes in the capacities of local officials and the programs they managed could be made relatively quickly. The ability to appoint and dismiss administrators certainly added to the potential for relatively rapid changes in capacity.

Yet the research indicated that public sector modernization was largely demand- rather than supply-driven. That is, while many capacity-building initiatives and programs were available for local governments, it was the agency of local officials that was responsible for their introduction. Municipalities introduced modernization when their leaders promoted it, not simply because it was on offer from other levels of government or required from above by administrative fiat. In this way, the hypothesis that improvements in capacity drive changes in local performance was not a stand-alone hypothesis, but rather one closely aligned to the first two hypotheses. Elections provided opportunities for new leadership to emerge in local governments, their commitments and activities were paramount in explaining how local government fared—at least for three years at a time—and they were the ones to decide how much emphasis to put on public sector modernization during their tenure. Thus, capacity-building initiatives were a tool of effective leadership, not an independent source of change for municipalities.

Civil society. When citizens are organized to demand good performance from government, they are likely to get it, according to a fourth hypothesis set out at the beginning of this book. Indeed, proponents of decentralization place great emphasis on the fact that when government is closer to people, it is easier for citizens to know what is happening, to have input into decision making and management, and to hold officials accountable for their actions. More than any other factor, it is the altered relationship between citizens and the state in decentralized settings that promotes better government, or so economists, political scientists, and management specialists argue.

In the research municipalities, there was considerable evidence of organized citizen interaction with public officials, particularly for a country often viewed as having a weak or incipient civil society. Across communities, groups identified common interests, organized themselves, and adopted common strategies for finding solutions to collective problems. They were not shy in approaching public officials and they seemed to have good knowledge about whom they needed to contact in order to acquire resources—both financial and technical—to achieve their objectives. They wrote petitions and, impressively, persisted in pressing government officials to attend to local problems. Frequently, these groups committed not only their time and energy to community problem solving, they also collected money, donated land, and took on financial commitments in order to "partner" with local government. Collective action was a fact of life in many of the municipalities in the study.

It was clear that groups in civil society were best able to organize around activities that involved extracting benefits from government. The needs they identified were largely tangible and related to works that could be accomplished in relatively short time periods. Participation initiated from the bottom up, then, focused primarily on petitioning for resources and attention. In a country that had, through many years of authoritarian government, encouraged clientelism in the distribution of public benefits, it is perhaps not surprising that much citizen activity under more democratic conditions mimicked previous mechanisms of making connections and presenting petitions.

Extracting benefits, however, was only part of full participation in public life. Citizens also needed to be actively engaged in decision making and able to hold public officials accountable for their actions. There were, in fact, several initiatives to increase the extent to which citizens and citizen groups were involved in local decision making. Particularly in the initial year of a new administration, many municipal governments encouraged community level processes of consultation and priority setting, seeking to establish plans for municipal works for the three-year period in office. Citizens were also invited to attend council meetings in some municipalities, and local opinions were sought on a variety of services through surveys and suggestion boxes. There were also initiatives to take government to the people through mechanisms such as Citizen Wednesdays, when officials made themselves publicly available to receive requests, complaints, and suggestions. In the reorganizations put in place in a number of municipalities, new positions were created for departments of social development or social communication, and part of their responsibilities was to stimulate citizen engagement with the municipality.

These initiatives, however, were far more likely to have been initiated by government than by citizens. Thus, although citizens seemed well able to petition government and to extract resources, it was usually government that led the way in introducing mechanisms of participation and accountability. In time, of course, citizens might become more ready or able to initiate participatory and accountability-related tasks, but at least at the time of the research, the links among decentralization, democratization, and public accountability, so often promoted as one of its clear advantages, was primarily in evidence only at election time, and then only in some locations.

Of the four hypotheses, that dealing with the role of civil society proved to be the most loosely connected to the interactive dynamic of electoral competition, leadership, and capacity building. The constraints on reelection limited the extent to which public officials could be directly punished or rewarded for doing a good job, and leaders, although they had some activities pressed upon them by citizen groups, most frequently set public agendas relatively autonomously. Petitioning rather than participation was the objective of most citizen action. Although the research suggests that changes in the dynamics of elections, in town government, and in management practices can be introduced over relatively short periods of time, it may take longer to take on the full habits of citizenship and opportunities for public debate promised by decentralization in democratic contexts.

WHAT'S NEW? WHAT'S OLD?

More competitive elections, new opportunities for leadership, the introduction of new technologies, new spaces for citizen engagement—these were clearly factors that characterized changes in local governance in Mexico by the mid-2000s. These were the result of a dual process of ongoing decentralization and democratization—both processes slow and halting at times, both demonstrating the potential for reversal, and both needing to be bolstered. Nevertheless, after twenty-five years of initiatives to decentralize and a decade and a half of experiences with a more open political system, Mexico's municipalities were changing.

We have seen how national policies opened opportunities for local governments to have more responsibilities and resources and set constraints within which they would operate. Once the federal government had opened the door to a larger local role in governance, state governments adopted policies and procedures that likewise set opportunities and constraints. Across the world, national and state level rules differ, and thus it can be expected that there will be differences in the opportunities for introducing change and the kinds of changes that might occur. Place is important, and Mexico provides but one example of how new opportunities were taken up and constraints adjusted to in a process of decentralization.

Yet there are important lessons to be drawn from the case of Mexico. If we assume that most populations include politicians and political parties with aspirations to win power, we can no doubt anticipate at a general level that decentralization will serve as a stimulus to more competition for office and opportunities for more alternation of leadership groups and parties in local positions of authority. If we assume that those who win public office are variously motivated in terms of their commitments and objectives, we can expect to see considerable variability in other contexts in the projects brought to local affairs by incumbent leaders. This expectation would be increased in situations in which incumbents have a relatively free hand in appointing officials to fill managerial and administrative positions and where parties are nonprogrammatic and relatively undisciplined.

Moreover, if it is true that modernizing the administration of town hall is not an overwhelming task, given a modicum of resources, then we can anticipate that the trajectory of increasing capacity—seen in many if not all of Mexico's local governments—will take hold in a variety of contexts. If we believe that citizens in many countries have the capacity to observe and understand efficient ways of meeting their needs through the actions of local government, we can anticipate, over time, their improved capacity to organize and extract benefits from local government in countries other than Mexico.

Countries will differ in the policies and processes that surround decentralization initiatives. They may also differ in terms of how new policies and processes interact with the historical and cultural legacies left behind by prior governments or regimes. Mexico, for example, continued to reflect some of the weight of seven decades of authoritarian government and an even longer tradition of centralization. These legacies were particularly evident in the choices that officials and citizens made about how to solve problems.

First, local governments in Mexico were acquiring more responsibilities, resources, and autonomy in a system that was still characterized by considerable centralization. This legacy was most apparent in terms of the fiscal strictures on local governments, in which both federal and state governments looked with some skepticism on local control over resources and hedged their resource-sharing mechanisms. In addition, the spigots that made resources available for specific needs continued to be located in state and national capital cities and in ministries and agencies belonging to governments at those levels. Public officials spent considerable time "bringing down" resources for local initiatives. When citizens found no response to their petitions in town hall, they likewise looked to other levels of government to provide resources and assistance.

Of course, local governments could have done more to free themselves from the legacy of dependence on other levels of government. They had the right to collect property and other taxes and were no longer required to send those revenues to higher levels of government. In some municipalities, public officials took advantage of this opportunity to improve revenue collection for municipal improvements. At the same time, however, the characteristic reluctance of politicians to impose taxes on citizens was very much in evidence in many municipalities. It was not uncommon to hear local officials claim that their municipality was simply too poor, or that citizens would not comply if they levied more local taxes or increased the efficiency with which existing taxes were collected. "We don't have the culture of paying taxes," was a refrain that encouraged many officials to look to other levels of government for salvation rather than to their own citizens.

Moreover, to the extent that local governments continued to be dependent on other levels of government for resources, the success of local officials in gaining access to those resources continued to lie with their knowledge of higher level government and their familiarity with public officials at those levels. The "myth of the right connection," so typical of Mexican politics under the authoritarian regime, seemed to be as much a result of centralization as of authoritarian decision making.[1] This was also true of citizen groups seeking assistance from government—the right connection was as integral to the strategy as it often was to the solution of a particular problem. Clientelism remained an embedded aspect of Mexican local politics.

Similarly, the ways in which citizens related to government continued to reflect the legacies of the past. Citizens had good opportunities to organize and were even encouraged to do so by local government on many occasions. Nevertheless, as indicated above, the dominant form of interacting with government was to petition for relief and to extract resources rather than to make demands for the observance of rights. To some extent, then, local problem solving remained embedded in the clientelist practices of the predemocratic past.

From the same perspective, knowledge about how to make local government responsive proceeded at a faster pace than knowledge about how to hold government more responsible for its actions. Citizens had good ideas for how to get problems solved, but they were limited in terms of what seemed appropriate for demanding performance from government. On the whole, the research suggests that important dynamics were encouraging municipalities to work somewhat better; it was less clear that local accountability was flourishing. A civic culture of accountability remained weak.

INCREASING THE PROMISE OF GOOD GOVERNANCE

Decentralization can contribute to improved performance of local government; it can provide new opportunities for responsiveness to local needs; it can mean that governance improves; it can mean that citizens hold public officials and agencies more accountable. But this book indicates clearly that it does not necessarily achieve these ends. Decentralization is not a linear or consistent process, and it can suffer reverses as often as advances in terms of how local governments and citizens take up its challenges. Clearly, decentralization in Mexico set in motion significant changes. But local governments continued to vary in terms of their performance and in terms of the extent to which they took advantage of the opportunities offered by decentralization. Legacies of the past also continued to mark how public problems were addressed. Thus, the benefits predicted by economists, political scientists, and management specialists as consequences of decentralization provide a palette of possibilities, not of realities. Are there ways of making these possibilities more likely?

Diminishing dependence. A response to this question might begin with some additional reflections on what it is that local government officials spend their time doing. In particular, this book has indicated how much time and effort local officials put into "bringing down" resources from other levels of government. They did so for a variety of reasons—following up on campaign promises, meeting local demand, working toward their own visions of good governance. At times they did so for personal enrichment, and they were often motivated by the desire to advance their own political careers. Some spent this time and effort because they wanted to create jobs, build social and physical infrastructure, and improve conditions of life for citizens in their localities.

Whatever their motivations, bringing down resources was a complex and time-consuming job. Discovering what programs were available, who controlled resources for them, how the resources could be used, what needed to be done to get them released, how they were to be accounted for—these were among the steps that were the routine of daily life for many mayors and department heads in the thirty research municipalities. They also invested considerable time in developing the contacts and friendships that would make it more possible for them to gain access to these resources. They invested more time in preparing proposals and writing reports. This, then, was a major focus of official municipal life, and one that needn't have been as difficult and time-consuming as it was.

Certainly federal and state authorities could consider ways to make resources more readily available to local governments, loosening the purse strings and finding ways to improve fiscal accountability other than through stringent processes of application and oversight. At the time of the research, fiscal mechanisms put in place by federal and state governments were often more focused on control than on facilitating development. Making future resources conditional on the use of initial funds would be one way of altering accountability mechanisms from up-front controls to evaluative ones. Similarly, by better informing citizens about the contents and budgets for municipal improvements and encouraging expectations about what government must and must not do, as well as providing mechanisms for taking citizen feedback seriously, central and state administrators could off-load some of the responsibilities of accountability to local citizens.[2] These levels of government, of course, might prefer to keep local governments more directly dependent on them, but by doing so, they are limiting the extent to which decentralization can achieve the benefits so often ascribed to it.

Obviously, an important way to lessen the dependence on other levels of government and to increase local autonomy would be for local governments to get better at taxing citizens. Only a few of the municipalities in the research sample had incentives to undertake improvements in this activity—those that were better off received less federal funding, thus increasing their interest in local sources of revenue. For most municipalities, though, it was easier to plead poverty and look to the state and federal governments than to take politically unpopular measures to enforce local taxation powers. Changes in federal and state legislation to provide more opportunities to local governments to collect taxes, incentives based on the success of broadening the tax base, and technical assistance in improving collection are all possibilities that could be expanded to good effect. If, as many scholars argue, the shortest route to civil society mobilization and effectiveness in holding government accountable for its actions is taxation, then this is an area in which effective governance and democratic goals can be pursued at the same time.[3] Nevertheless, the incentives for politicians to undertake this approach are ambiguous at best.

A third improvement deals with strengthening the technical capacities of local officials to oversee project design and monitoring. At the time of the research, much was changing in terms of bringing more professionals into public office—architects, engineers, accountants, communications specialists. Often, their training and orientation were important steps toward improving the daily conduct of public business and service delivery. At the same time, there was a clear need for more managerial training and the development of greater expertise for designing and implementing public investments. One of the factors that often made local governments dependent on state and federal level officials, and that led to many delays in program and project initiation, was the need for technical feasibility and approval studies to be done by officials at these levels. An alternative would be to have enhanced technical capacity for these activities at local levels. As we have seen, whether this is possible or not depends primarily on local leadership demand for it.

Improving accountability. Good governance is, to some extent, a function of accountability. Whereas in Mexico federal and state governments insisted, perhaps overmuch, on the accountability of local governments, local civil society was not a vital force for the same end. In particular, citizens were primarily concerned with local government as a source of physical infrastructure and responses to individual needs. They were less engaged in expecting administration and services that were of good quality and responsive. Certainly it was helpful that several local governments initiated their own mechanisms for listening to citizen needs and complaints. More competitive elections allowed citizens to punish parties they believed had performed poorly. With time, such mechanisms could encourage more of a "culture of accountability" at local levels. As we saw, however, these were mechanisms that were likely to suffer considerably as administrations changed. The prohibition on immediate reelection limited the sting of rejection at the polls.

Future improvements in governance might, then, focus more on strengthening the linkages between citizen satisfaction and local accountability. Allowing for the reelection of local public officials is perhaps the most important way in which this could be encouraged. In Mexico, public officials were stimulated to pay more attention to performance if they were concerned about the future of their political parties or if they sought higher-level office. Good performance in office did not allow them to continue in office, however, and citizens were not directly able to endorse or reject their leadership for the future. Reelection could strengthen the incentives to search out mechanisms for improving governance.

In addition, making information more available on the rights and obligations of citizens and on expectations they should have for specific services, institutionalizing feedback mechanisms, providing more opportunities for shared and deliberative decision making, and putting resources in the hands of citizen oversight boards are among some mechanisms that could help shorten the link between action and accountability.[4] Stressing the rights of citizens to have safe and productive lives could help overcome the bias toward a narrowly extractive relationship with government. In Mexico, some local governments were opening up spaces for greater participation in decision making; for this to be an important factor in strengthening civil society, however, these spaces would have to be maintained over more than three-year periods. They would also have to become part of the expectations of citizens about their relationship to government.

Institutionalizing change. Throughout this volume, a recurring theme has been the extent to which change is possible in the performance of local governments. Although local governments were seen to be the site of many important changes and were, overall, vibrant places where new experiments with governance were being carried out, it was also repeatedly stressed that changes—whether for good or ill—were extremely vulnerable. Weakly institutionalized governments had considerable room to innovate and improve; they also had considerable room to regress and fail. The policies, processes, programs, and projects that municipal governments in Mexico put into effect were regularly subservient to the next election and to the priorities and capabilities of newly elected administrations. Formal institutions, embedded rules of the game for how things got done, were often insubstantial, even while informal institutions continued to shape political and administrative interactions. Although innovations might bring improvement to the performance of administration and services in town hall, there was no certainty that they would outlive the tenure of those who introduced them.

The problem, then, was not change, but the durability of new ideas and systems that improved local government performance. For the future of local governments challenged with the tasks of taking on new resources and responsibilities, the larger issue is how to institutionalize measures that demonstrate the capacity to improve local well-being or increase the efficiency and effectiveness of local government.

Characteristically, the response of those concerned about institutionalization has been to put in place a set of rules and procedures that must be followed by local governments. A series of laws and regulations determined that they must have municipal development plans, municipal development committees, a framework for local government, a set of rules for internal structures and another for internal procedures, a set of specified actions to acquire resources, and so on. The dominant focus of efforts to institutionalize local government, then, has been to legislate and regulate it. Yet, throughout this book, we have seen that legislation and regulations are often honored in the breach.

Legislating and regulating institutions, particularly from above, may not be enough to ensure that they are put in place and then serve useful purposes. Sustaining change may require more engaged civil societies that are able to insist on the continuity of structures and processes that provide good results. Particularly with the changes that are most difficult to sustain—those related to the behavior and attitudes of public officials as they carry out their work and those related to the equity and efficiency with which citizens are treated—the role of civil societies informed of rights, observant of local government operations, and armed with mechanisms to insist on responsiveness and probity is important. Several municipal governments in Mexico had introduced mechanisms for citizen engagement that moved in this direction. A federal program of putting citizen councils in place was also an important new effort to encourage more engaged local communities. Ultimately, however, what government can do in this direction is limited by the responsiveness of civil society itself.

In the future, then, those concerned about the weakness of local institutions of governance might usefully focus efforts on the organization and education of local citizens about what their governments are supposed to accomplish, what interactions with citizens are supposed to be like, what rights citizens have to appropriate attention and redress when they don't get it, and what mechanisms exist to call local officials and organizations to account. Surely the introduction of reelection can facilitate this, as can the development of more widespread local media activities and the consequences of more emphasis on local taxation. The challenges ahead may focus less on building institutions from the top down than on sustaining them from the bottom up.

Encouraging economic development. Over the longer term, good governance cannot thrive in decentralized contexts that are in economic and social decline. Many of the research municipalities were bereft of productive sources of employment, and were losing population to other regions of the country and to international migration. Some local governments were responding with efforts to develop local industries around tourism and to attract investment for assembly plants and industrial parks. Some were attempting to increase the potential of local farm economies by investing in irrigation, environmental rehabilitation, and more remunerative crops and livestock. Some worked at the micro level with home industries and local credit associations. Some engaged local universities in applied economic research and the development of new technologies. Some sought to use remittance income for productive purposes.

These were noble efforts, but at least for the middle-sized municipalities in this study, the capacity of local governments to address the economic and technical complexities of creating productive sources of employment in a rapidly globalizing economy was often low. Assessing feasibility, discovering niches for local products, establishing marketing channels, dealing with issues of quality assurance, joining in regional development arrangements—these are difficult and complex problems, requiring expertise beyond the abilities of many town halls. This, then, may be an area in which state and federal governments, international agencies, and NGOs can play a larger role. Thinking through local and regional opportunities for economic development needed considerably more attention than it was getting in the thirty municipalities studied.

Lessening dependence, promoting accountability, institutionalizing change, and opening up opportunities for local economic development—these are some possibilities for improving governance in Mexico and elsewhere. While the specific forms of dependence, the relationship between state and civil society, the shape of formal institutions, and the constraints on economic development are unique to Mexico, the broader issues of local independence, balancing the relationship between government and citizens, mobilizing an informed citizenry, and promoting development in the context of rapid globalization are not. Thus, this study, which focused on a single country, should hold lessons for many others; the accomplishments and constraints witnessed by Mexico's local governments may well resonate in the stories that are experienced in many other places.

A School for Democrats?

Throughout this book, serious shortcomings were noted in the functioning of local government in Mexico. Yet, in assessing their accomplishments over the past twenty-five years, there was scope for optimism. Some innovations were sustained, some functions of government were improved, and some services became more efficient or effective. Particularly where changes became embedded in routine activities and expectation, as well as in bricks and mortar, it could be expected that they would endure beyond the scope of particular administrations. Moreover, it might be anticipated that experiences with better governance could leave behind a legacy of expectations about the functioning of basic administration and services.

The good news from town plazas around Mexico was that elections had come to play a more important and democratizing role in local government. There was clearly greater circulation of elites—one of the classical attributes of democracy—and citizens were increasingly aware that they had options when they went to the polls. Although it did not seem that parties were easily distinguishable from each other in terms of their purposes for local government, they offered alternative lists of candidates and, increasingly, competition characterized election campaigns as well as internal party decision-making processes. From the back rooms of party headquarters and the back pockets of governors and presidents in state and federal capitals, competition increasingly became a public opportunity for choice.

Similar good news about increases in political competition was encouraging leaders in municipal governments to pay more attention to their constituents. Most were aware that the rules of the game had changed and that what had formerly been a system in which layers of political bosses controlled political power had become one in which voters had more importance and citizen satisfaction with leadership was an important way to enhance a political career. While some public officials were more sensitive to this than others, and the chance of losing public confidence was greater in some local contexts than in others, even politicians in traditionally entrenched PRI enclaves spent more time looking over their shoulders at the competition and worrying about the reactions of constituents.

Many town plazas also resonated with more information on the doings of government and on opportunities for citizens to become involved in their decision making and operation. Consistently, information about the workings of government, its funding, and the destination of its resources had been elusive for generations of Mexicans. This legacy was dying slowly in some municipalities, but the trend toward greater openness and more sources of information about what was going on, who was benefiting from local decisions and who was not, and where resources were going was increasing. To the extent that information is a vital component of a vibrant democracy, this was good news. Eventually, it might be expected that the availability of more information could strengthen the extent to which there was public debate about issues of local importance in those same town plazas.

It was also good news that increasing numbers of officials—because of alternation in power—and citizens—because of more opportunities to participate—were developing experience with local level problem solving. In particular, some municipalities introduced new mechanisms whereby citizens had to build consensus around what were the most important local needs that government should respond to and they had to discuss priorities for public investments and attention. Around such mechanisms, it is possible that more democratic communities and more democratic debate could be built.

It is important that expectations about greater democracy be matched with understanding that democratic processes imply conflict and continuing struggles of excluded groups and interests to be included in processes of decision making and resource allocation. Too often, those who have lived without democratic processes in public life anticipate that decision making will be easier, that public purposes will be clearer, and that consensus will be a natural outcome of public discussion. In Mexico, these misperceptions were very common, as citizens continued to voice skepticism about local government and what it could achieve. There and elsewhere, governments and citizens need to work harder to reach inclusive processes of decision making, identify the public purpose of government, and develop adherence to the rules that make it possible to resolve conflicts.

There were some positive signs that decentralization in some of Mexico's municipalities was serving as a school for democracy. Learning was not always positive and not always consistent, and complaints and cynicism were commonplace throughout the municipalities studied. Yet, trends toward greater engagement and possibly greater accountability were in a positive direction. If this is so more broadly, the future of democracy in Mexico should be a hopeful one. In this country and elsewhere, then, experiments with decentralization and its potential for democratic engagement could even redound in strengthened democracy at other levels of government.

NOTES

CHAPTER I
GOING LOCAL

1. Information on the events reported in this paragraph was taken from http://www.terra.com/actualidad/articulo/html/act175268.htm (Peru); http://news.bbc.co.uk/low/spanish/latin_america/newsid_3810000/3810747.stm (Bolivia); http://www-personal.engin.umich.edu/~parv/harbury/archive/cerigua/cwb33_97.html (Guatemala); http://www.manilatimes.net/national/2004/may/27/yehey/prov/20040527pro8.html (Philippines); http://www.deccanherald.com/deccanherald/july 262004/dl.asp (India); http://www.greatreporter.com/modules.php?name=News&Files=article+sid=374 (Malawi).

2. Information on activities reported in this paragraph was taken from Abers (1998); Baiocchi (2001); Straface (2003); IDD (2004) (Kenya and India); http://www.sacities.net (South Africa); http://www.naga.gov.ph/cityhall/nagagovernancemodel.html (Philippines).

3. Campbell (2005) refers to this trend as the "quiet revolution." The literature on decentralization from 1980 to 2005 is voluminous. For good overviews of its promise and consequences, see, in addition to Campbell: Angell, Lowden, and Thorp (2001); Burki, Perry, and Dillinger (1999); Crook and Manor (1998); Eaton (2004); Gibson (2004); Manor (1999); Montero and Samuels (2004); Oxhorn, Tulchin, and Selee (2004); Rondinelli, Nellis, and Cheema (1984).

4. See, for example, Jones (2000); Fox (1994). I use a broad definition of governance in this book. It means "the distribution of power among institutions of government; the legitimacy and authority of state institutions; the rules and norms that determine who holds power and how decisions are made about the exercise of authority; relationships of accountability among state officials/agencies and between these officials/agencies and citizens; the ability of government to make policy, manage the administrative and fiscal affairs of the state, and deliver goods and services; and the impact of institutions and policies on public welfare" (Grindle 2004b:545). For a discussion, see Olowu (2002:4–5); Hyden and Court (2002); Pierre (2000).

5. See Rondinelli, Nellis, and Cheema (1984) for a review of these distinctions.

6. See Oxhorn (2004).

7. See Eaton (2004).

8. See, for example, the essays in Earle (2000); see also Angell, Lowden, and Thorp (2001); de la Cruz and Barrios (1994); Grindle (2000).

9. See, in particular, Escobar-Lemmon (2001); Grindle (2000); Manor (1999); Montero and Samuels (2004); O'Neill (2003); Willis, Garman, and Haggard (1999).

10. See Eaton (2001); Grindle (2004a).

11. See Guigale and Webb (2000); Montero and Samuels (2004).

12. Faletti (2003).

13. Beer (2004); Montero (2001).

14. See, for example, Weingast (1995).

15. See, for examples, Huntington (1968); McConnell (1966); in addition, see Riker (1964).

16. See, in particular, Wunsch and Olowu (1990); Rondinelli, McCullough, and Johnson (1989). Many such discussions cite the work of Alexis de Toqueville.

17. See Fung (2004).

18. NGO type advocates of decentralization for human rights and democracy.

19. See, for example, Rondinelli (1989).

20. National treasury officials and international financial institutions led in this questioning of the positive fiscal consequences of decentralization. See Burki, Perry, and Dillinger (1999); Campbell (2005); Dillinger and Webb (1999); Fukusaku and Hausmann (1998); Peterson (1997); Wiesner (2003).

21. Burki, Perry, and Dillinger (1999); Dillinger and Webb (1999); Guigale and Webb (2000); Prud'homme (1995); Weingast (1995); Wibbels (2004).

22. See, for examples, Cornelius (1999); Diamond (1999); Fox (1994); Hutchcroft (2001).

23. See, for example, Guillén López (1994).

24. Heller (2001:12); Hiskey and Seligson (2003); Schönwälder (1997).

25. Blair (2000); Cabrero Mendoza (2000); Fox and Aranda (1996); Goldfrank (2002); Montero and Samuels (2004); Oxhorn (2004).

26. Crook and Manor (1998).

27. Angell, Lowden, and Thorp (2001); King, Orazem, and Wohlgemuth (1998).

28. Cornelius (1999); Eaton (2001, 2004); Grindle (2004); Montero (2001); Peterson (1997).

29. See, for example, Beer (2004).

30. Responses to citizen surveys in Latin America showed that citizens with "much" or "some" trust in municipalities rose from 31 percent in 2001 to 34 percent in 2004. This was above trust in the police, the judiciary, government in general, congress, and political parties. Latinobarómetro (2005).

31. Recentralization is never out of the question, however, as the recentralizing dynamic of Russia in the mid-2000s suggests. See also Eaton (2004).

32. See Eaton (2004).

33. See especially Rodríguez (1997); Rodríguez and Ward (1994); Ward and Rodríguez (1999); Ward (1998). See also Moreno (2005).

34. See particularly Wallis (1999); see also Abers (1998); Altshuler and Zegans (1997:78); Campbell (1997); González-Rosetti (2001); Grindle (2004); Stoner-Weiss (1997).

35. In the case of Mexico, I found considerable evidence for this explanation in the national level education reform of 1992 (Grindle 2004a).

36. Cabrero Mendoza (2000).

37. The New Public Management refers to a movement in public administration theory and practice that focuses on the role of incentives and accountability in service delivery and champions the use of compectititon among service providers, results-based performance measurement, customer service orientation, and mar-

ket-like systems for the delivery of public goods. See Barzelay (2001); Kamarck (2000).

38. See Campbell (1997); Kamarck (2000); Rondinelli and Cheema (2003).

39. For a critique of this view, see Portes and Landolt (1996). For an empirical test, see Seligson (2006).

40. A series of World Bank research papers make similar points. See Binswanger and Aiyar (2003); Grandvoinnet, Romani, and Das Gupta (2000, 2003); Lall, Deichmann, Lundberg, and Chaudhury (2002).

41. See, for examples, Davis (1989); Rodríguez and Ward (1994); and Ward (1995). Angell, Lowden, and Thorpe (2001) is an exception to this focus on large cities, as it explicitly focuses on medium-sized municipalities.

42. See Stoner-Weiss (1997) and Snyder (2001).

43. In Latin America, municipalities are the equivalent of U.S. counties. They typically include a *cabecera*, or county seat, and numerous other smaller localities.

44. INEGI (2000).

CHAPTER 2
DECENTRALIZING MEXICO

1. Fagen and Touhy (1972:20).

2. I am grateful to Professor Wayne Cornelius, then of MIT and currently of the University of California at San Diego, for this story.

3. The term is variously attributed to Octavio Paz and Mario Vargas Llosa.

4. Presidents and governors in Mexico may not be reelected at all; other elected officials are prohibited from holding the same office for one term.

5. Recent scholarship suggests that, with the exception of a couple of revolts, the large number of uprisings and rebellions amounted to little in terms of extensive turmoil, engagement of the civilian population, or loss of life (Fowler 2000).

6. See Rodríguez (1997:17–19) for a useful overview of this history. For a more detailed discussion, see Meyer and Sherman (1979).

7. Initially and briefly, these councils were appointed; then elected; and then sold as a means of increasing revenue for the Spanish Crown.

8. In particularly Mexican fashion, regional strongmen ceded power to the center and the president in exchange for opportunities for personal enrichment. See Rodríguez (1997:19).

9. On the free municipality and the revolution, see Womack (1969).

10. The military sector was later eliminated, but the other three sectors remained as the central "pillars" of the PRI regime. The "popular sectors" referred to a variety of middle-class groups such as government employees (including teachers), merchants, artisans, and others.

11. Rodríguez (1997:35).

12. See Courchene, Díaz-Cayeros, and Webb (2000:123–8).

13. Foster (1967:169).

14. Foster (1967:170), emphasis in the original.

15. Courchene, Díaz-Cayeros, and Webb (2000:126).

16. The 1983 reform was presented to congress by President de la Madrid in late 1982, passed in 1983, and put into effect in 1984. Thus, some refer to the reform of 1982, while others identify it with 1983 or 1984. On the reform, see Campbell (2005:chap. 3); Mizrahi (2004); and Shirk (2005:38–39).

17. On municipal service provision, see García del Castillo (2003).

18. In addition, in his efforts to alter the relationships among levels of government, de la Madrid set up new institutions for coordinating planning and budgeting. For example, through his National Development Plan, he created mechanisms for transferring resources to state governments through individual agreements, known as the Convenio Unico de Desarrollo.

19. State planning committees, COPLADEs, had been established in the mid-1970s.

20. Mizrahi (2004); Santín del Río (2004). As a student, de la Madrid had written his thesis on Article 115, which might help explain why decentralization was chosen as a response to a problem of regime legitimacy.

21. Nickson (1995:200).

22. Mizrahi (2004); Willis, Garman, and Haggard (1999:45).

23. Cámara de Diputados (1983:8–9), quoted in Rodríguez (1997:73); see also Aspe Armella (1988).

24. This institution replaced the Centro Nacional de Estudios Municipales, which had been created in 1983 and whose responsibilities had been primarily those of research rather than operations.

25. See, in particular, Cornelius, Craig, and Fox (1994).

26. It was subsequently assigned to a newly created ministry of social development, SEDESOL.

27. Fox and Aranda (1996). Guillén López (1995) shows that in a number of cities, federal PRONASOL programs made direct alliances with local citizen groups and excluded municipal governments.

28. See Grindle (2004).

29. Grindle (1996:chap. 4).

30. This was a historic benchmark in terms of the number of state governments affected.

31. See Mizrahi (2004); and Ward and Rodríguez (1999).

32. The law was passed in 1995 and put into effect the following year.

33. Cabrero Mendoza and Martínez-Vázquez (2000:160–61).

34. See Guigale and Webb (2000) for extensive discussion of the fiscal relationships among levels of government in Mexico.

35. Rodríguez (1997:115); Estados Unidos Mexicanos (2000a).

36. Rodríguez (1977:115). See also Guigale and Webb (2000).

37. See Ward and Rodríguez with Cabrero (1999:24).

38. In 1987, a revision to this electoral law provided additional representation to the party winning the largest number of seats.

39. For an overview of these activities and their relationship to democratization in Mexico, see Cadena-Ros (2003); and Santín del Río (2004). On urban movements in Mexico City, see Davis (1994). See also Eckstein (1989).

40. For analyses of the election, see Domínguez and Lawson (2004). For a discussion of trends, see Alvarado (1998). On the history of the PAN at the na-

tional level, see Shirk (2005); and for a history of the party at the state level, see Beer (2004). On local democracy, see Merino (1994).

41. The state of Coahuila increased this span to four years during the Fox administration.

42. Elected officials on the *cabildo* are voting members; appointed officials can participate in discussions, but cannot vote.

43. In some states, the position of *oficial mayor* has become a department for administration. The secretary is usually a close confidant of the mayor and substitutes for this official when he or she is out of the office.

44. On *usos y costumbres*, see Van Wey, Tucker, and McConnell (2005).

45. Estados Unidos Mexicanos (2000b:166).

46. INAFED 2002. See also Cabrero Mendoza (2003: chap. 5).

47. Nickson (1995:201–3); Rodríguez (1997); Guigale, Nguyen, Rojas, and Webb (2000).

48. Prior to 2000, presidents in Mexico had been cabinet officials in the outgoing administration. Vicente Fox, representing the PAN, had been governor of the state of Guanajuato. Candidates for the 2006 presidential election included a former CEO of a state-owned enterprise, an ex-governor, and an ex-mayor.

49. See Santín del Río (2004).

50. See, for example, Rodríguez (1997: chap. 7).

51. Cabrero Mendoza (2000:175). See also Mizrahi (2004).

52. Merino (2003:9). Author's translation.

53. INAFED (2002).

54. Interview, June 27, 2004, Santo Domingo de Tehuantepec, Oaxaca.

55. Tonatiuh Guillén López has undertaken a study of this type, in which he and his collaborators document significant conflicts in a number of municipalities in northern Mexico that involved decision making by local governments. See Guillén López (1995).

56. Some of this information was available in the Municipal Census 2002, for example.

57. Data from the Municipal Census of 2002 were used for this question.

58. Data from the Municipal Census of 2002 were used for this question. While some governments changed administrations after the census, these data were the most reliable available at the time of the research.

59. In a number of municipalities they governed, PAN mayors introduced "Citizen Wednesdays," when municipal officials would set up shop in public places to hear complaints, respond to questions, and follow up on promises made. These proved popular enough that some non-PAN mayors introduced "citizen Mondays" or other days for the same purpose. See Shirk (2005:181).

Chapter 3
Competitive Elections and Good Governance

1. Interview, June 17, 2004, González, Tamaulipas.

2. See, for example, Kettl (2000).

3. See especially Rodríguez and Ward (1994).

4. Interview, June 23, 2004, Santo Domingo Tehuantepec, Oaxaca.

5. Interview, July 7, 2004, San Juan Guichicovi, Oaxaca.

6. Interview, August 23, 2004, San Fernando, Tamaulipas.

7. Fox and Aranda (1996:50).

8. Crook and Sverrisson (2001); Bruhn (1999:44).

9. Rose-Ackerman (1980).

10. Interview, June 28, 2004, San Pedro Cholula, Puebla.

11. Interview, June 29, 2004, Rosario, Sinaloa.

12. Interview, June 23, 2004, Rosario, Sinaloa.

13. Interview, July 7, 2004, San Juan Guichicovi, Oaxaca.

14. Cabrero Mendoza (2000:182).

15. Ward (1995:141).

16. Interview, June 22, 2004, San Pedro Cholula, Puebla.

17. The *dedazo* (literally, "big finger") is an expression used in Mexico to refer to the practice of presidents, governors, and party bosses choosing the candidates who will replace the existing ones. Interview, July 7, 2004, San Juan Guichicovi, Oaxaca.

18. Interview, July 17, 2004, Acatlán de Pérez Figueroa, Oaxaca. A similar situation was described at another site: interview, June 21, 2004, Coronango, Puebla.

19. Interview, July 9, 2004, San Juan Guichicovi, Oaxaca.

20. Interview, June 19, 2004, Santo Domingo Tehuantepec, Oaxaca. In fact, in this case, a local election resulted in an opposition win, but the federal government refused to recognize the election, froze the powers of the municipality, and sent a temporary administrator to govern the town until new elections could be held.

21. Interview, October 12, 2004, Ticul, Yucatán.

22. Interview, August 25, 2004, Santiago Juxtlahuaca, Oaxaca.

23. Many contend that the PRD actually won the elections but that voter fraud by the PRI was so great as to deny the new party the presidency. On the emergence of the PAN, see Shirk (2005).

24. Interview, July 24, 2004, Acatlán de Pérez Figueroa, Oaxaca.

25. Interview, June 21, 2004, Santo Domingo Tehuantepec, Oaxaca.

26. Interview, July 9, 2004, San Juan Guichicovi, Oaxaca.

27. Interview, July 21, 2004, Iztacamatixlán, Puebla.

28. Interviews: August 23, 2004, Umán, Yucatán; July 29, 2004, Santa Cruz de Juventino Rosas, Guanajuato.

29. Interview, June 18, 2004, Santo Domingo Tehuantepec.

30. Interview, July 17, 2004, Acatlán de Pérez Figueroa.

31. Interview, August 19, 2004, Umán, Yucatán.

32. Interview, July 15, 2004, El Progreso, Yucatán.

33. Interview, July 16, 2004, Mocorito, Sinaloa.

34. Interview, June 28, 2004, San Pedro Cholula, Puebla.

35. Interview, October 15, 2004, Ticul, Yucatán.

36. Interview, June 23, 2004, Rosario, Sinaloa.

37. Interview, July 5, 2004, Aldama, Tamaulipas.

38. Interview, June 23, 2004, Rosario, Sinaloa. Some mayors were reported to be earning as much as $4,000 a month.

39. Since the late 1990s, mayors of capital cities in Argentina, Ecuador, Venezuela, Bolivia, Mexico, and elsewhere have been strong candidates for president, winning elections in Argentina and Ecuador.

40. Interview, June 21, 2004, Santo Domingo Tehuantepec, Oaxaca. For example, in Sinaloa, an official referred to the municipal presidency as a "stairway to other things" (interview, June 19, 2004, Escuinapa). In Yucatán, a local resident reported that the current state legislator had used the municipality "as a platform to jump to more important positions" (interview, June 28, 2004, Valladolid).

41. This initiative was linked to the emergence of the COCEI (Coordinadora Obrera Campesina Estudiantil del Istmo) in Juchitán de Zaragoza, Oaxaca. See Rubin (1997) for an analysis of this movement.

42. According to one account, the "official" faction of the party told party members that if they didn't vote for the "official" candidate, they would lose their lands.

43. Interview, July 16, 2004, Acatlán de Pérez Figueroa, Oaxaca.

44. Interviews: July 20, 2004, Yuriria, Guanajuato; June 22, 2004, Abasolo, Guanajuato.

45. Interviews: July 7, 2004, Manuel Doblado, Guanajuato; July 27, 2004, Santa Cruz de Juventino Rosas, Guanajuato.

46. Interview, August 19, 2004, San Fernando, Tamaulipas.

47. Two interviews, June 29, 2004, Manuel Doblado, Guanajuato.

48. Interview, July 5, 2004, Manuel Doblado, Guanajuato.

49. Teachers belong to a very strong union in Mexico that has long been aligned with the PRI. Interview, October 12, 2004, Ticul, Yucatán.

50. Interview, June 16, 2004, Abasolo, Guanajuato.

51. Interview, August 24, 2004, San Fernando, Tamaulipas.

52. In a municipality in Yucatán, for example, the candidate of the PAN was simply sacrificed by his party when PRD officials offered it seats in the municipal council in exchange for support at the polls. The PRD candidate won. Interview, June 28, 2004, Valladolid, Yucatán.

53. Interview, June 23, 2004, Santo Domingo Tehuantepec, Oaxaca.

54. Interviews: June 18, 2004, González, Tamaulipas; June 24, 2004, Santo Domingo Tehuantepec, Oaxaca.

55. Interview, June 23, 2004, Santo Domingo Tehuantepec, Oaxaca.

56. Interview, July 27, 2004, Acatlán de Pérez Figueroa, Oaxaca.

57. Interview, June 26, 2004, Valladolid, Yucatán.

58. Interview, June 29, 2004, Manuel Doblado, Guanajuato.

59. Interview, June 19, 2004, Santo Domingo Tehuantepec, Oaxaca.

60. Interview, June 23, 2004, Santo Domingo Tehuantepec, Oaxaca.

61. Interview, June 24, 2004, Santo Domingo Tehuantepec, Oaxaca.

62. Interview, July 17, 2004, Yuriria, Guanajuato.

63. Interview, August 5, 2004, San Luis de la Paz, Guanajuato.

64. Interview, July 20, 2004, Acatlán de Pérez Figueroa, Oaxaca.

65. Interview, August 4, 2004, Miguel Alemán, Tamaulipas.

66. Interview, June 26, 2004, San Pedro Cholula, Puebla.

67. Interview, June 23, 2004, Santo Domingo Tehuantepec, Oaxaca.

68. Interview, June 21, 2004, González, Tamaulipas.

69. For example, a federal employee related, "My boss at SEDESOL is running for mayor of a small municipality. . . . I'm helping him in the campaign and he'll give me a job in the administration. I'll just go every two weeks to sign for my check, so I can keep my job at SEDESOL." Interview, July 17, 2004.

70. Interviews: July 17, 2004, Acatlán de Pérez Figueroa, Oaxaca; August 6, 2004, Santiago Pinotepa Nacional, Oaxaca; July 5, 2004, Manuel Doblado, Guanajuato.

71. Interviews: July 15, 2004, Tula, Tamaulipas; August 19, 2004, Umán, Yucatán.

72. Interviews: July 8, 2004, Manuel Doblado, Guanajuato; June 22, 2004, Abasolo, Guanajuato; August 19, 2004, Umán, Yucatán.

73. Interview, June 21, 2004, González, Tamaulipas.

74. Interviews: June 29, 2004, Manuel Doblado, Guanajuato; July 13, 2004, Valladolid, Yucatán.

75. Interview, June 22, 2004, San Pedro Cholula, Puebla.

76. Interview, June 23, 2004, Coronango, Puebla.

77. Interview, July 28, 2004, Chignahuapan, Puebla.

78. Interview, July 8, 2004, Salvador Alvarado, Sinaloa.

79. OLS (ordinary lease squares) regressions of municipal performance scores (table 2.10) and four measures of threat of electoral loss (table 3.1) failed to produce any significant correlation. On average, for every additional unit in political competitiveness, there was a positive difference of 0.72932 in performance. However, political competitiveness explained only 3.26 percent of the variation found in performance and this relationship was not statistically significant at a 90 percent level ($t = 0.97$; $p = .3395$). This result, of course, might be explained by the limited number of observations. Cleary (2001) analyzes political competition and data on services and finances for all municipal elections between 1980 and 2000 and finds a small effect of competition on performance and concludes that "elections alone are less influential on government performance than is commonly thought, and are not sufficient to induce more responsive or efficient government" (Abstract). Moreno (2005) uses different measures of performance and generates a statistically significant relationship between competitiveness and performance.

80. This was true, for example, of low-performing municipalities in Guanajuato and Puebla.

81. This is consistent with findings of innovations in Mexican local governments (Cabrero 2000:178).

82. See Shirk (2005) on the governance orientation of the PAN.

83. Interview, June 6, 2004, Escuinapa, Sinaloa.

84. Interview, July 21, 2004, Yuriria, Guanajuato.

85. Interview, June 29, 2004, Manuel Doblado, Guanajuato.

86. Interview, July 21, 2004, Yuriria, Guanajuato.

87. Interview, August 19, 2004, San Fernando, Tamaulipas; June 19, 2004, Escuinapa, Sinaloa.

88. Keina Jiménez (2004: n. p.).

89. Interview, July 19, 2004, Acatlán de Pérez Figueroa, Oaxaca.

90. Interview, June 16, 2004, Abasolo, Guanajuato.

91. Interview, June 16, 2004, Abasolo, Guanajuato.

92. Interview, June 23, 2004, Santo Domingo Tehuantepec, Oaxaca.
93. Interview, August 13, 2004, San Luis de la Paz, Guanajuato.
94. Interview, July 8, 2004, Manuel Doblado, Guanajuato.
95. Interview, June 29, 2004, Manuel Doblado, Guanajuato.
96. Interview, July 23, 2004, Yuriria, Guanajuato.
97. Interview, July 12, 2004, San Juan Guichicovi, Oaxaca.
98. Interview, July 9, 2004, San Juan Guichicovi, Oaxaca.
99. Interview, August 18, 2004, Santiago Juxtlahuaca, Oaxaca.
100. Interview, July 22, 2004, Ixtacmaxtitlán, Puebla.
101. Ward and Rodríquez with Cabrero (1999:17).

CHAPTER 4
AT WORK IN TOWN HALL

1. Until 2001, no party had come within the "threat zone" of the PRI in Chignahuapan (see table 3.1).
2. Interview, July 23, 2004, Chignahuapan, Puebla.
3. Interview, July 26, 2004, Chignahuapan, Puebla.
4. For a longer version of this history and its outcome, see Schlefer (2006).
5. See, for example, Domínguez (1997); González-Rosetti (2001); Grindle (2004); Williamson (1994).
6. See, in particular, Domínguez (1997); Grindle (2004); Wallis (1999).
7. Campbell (1997:14).
8. Campbell (1997:14).
9. "First, charismatic mayors have moved beyond hierarchy to new styles of leadership by organizing cooperative networks that generate a change in the dynamic of local government. Second, some mayors have learned to organize and work with networks of NGOs, thereby creating new mechanisms of interaction between the municipal government and the citizenry . . . Third, municipal leaders have strengthened intergovernmental relations to affect change . . . Finally, management teams in some municipalities have implemented new management systems to enhance service delivery" Cabrero Mendoza (2000:177).
10. Interview, July 19, 2004, Yuriria, Guanajuato.
11. Interviews: August 18, 2004, San Fernando, Tamaulipas; September 11, 2004, Ticul, Yucatán.
12. Interview with mayor of Mérida, capital of the state of Yucatán, October 12, 2004, Mérida.
13. Interview, July 24, 2004, Acatlán de Pérez Figueroa, Oaxaca.
14. Interview, July 21, 2004, Ixtacamaxtitlán, Puebla.
15. Interview, July 8, 2004, Salvador Alvarado, Sinaloa.
16. Interview, July 23, 2004, Culiacán, Sinaloa.
17. Interview, October 12, 2004, Ticul, Yucatán.
18. Interview, July 19, 2004, Yuriria, Guanajuato.
19. Interview, July 23, 2004, Yuriria, Guanajuato.
20. Interview, October 17, 2004, Oxkutzcab, Yucatán.
21. Quoted in Schlefer (2006:24).

22. Interview, July 29, 2004, San Ignacio, Sinaloa.

23. Interview, October 23, 2004, Oxkutzcab, Yucatán.

24. Interview, July 21, 2004, Ixtacamaxtitlán, Puebla.

25. Interview, June 27, 2004, Aldama, Tamaulipas.

26. Interview, July 22, 2004, Ixtacamaxtitlán, Puebla.

27. Interview, June 30, 2004, Abasolo, Guanajuato.

28. Interview, July 8, 2004, Aldama, Tamaulipas.

29. For a comparison, see Fox and Aranda (1996:25).

30. Interview, July 20, 2004, Tula, Tamualipas.

31. Interviews: July 13, 2004, Mocorito, Sinaloa; August 12 and 13, 2004, Santiago Pinotepa Nacional, Oaxaca; June 22 and 28, 2004, San Pedro Cholula, Puebla; June 18, 2004, Abasolo, Guanajuato; August 20, 2004, Ixtamaxtitlán. Puebla. Mayors were criticized for their failure to delegate in a number of municipalities. Interviews: August 23, 2004, Umán, Yucatán; July 21, 2004, Ixtcmaxtitlán, Puebla; August 19 and 23, 2004, Libres, Puebla; June 17, 2004, González, Tamaulipas; July 13, 2004, Mocorito, Sinaloa; July 12, 2004, San Juan Guichicovi, Oaxaca; July 19, 2004, Tula, Tamaulipas; October 12, 2004, Ticul, Yucatán.

32. Interviews: October 23, 2004, Oxkutzcab, Yucatán; October 12, 2004, Ticul, Yucatán.

33. Interview, August 8, 2004, Miguel Aleman, Tamaulipas.

34. Interview, June 22, 2004, Escuinapa, Sinaloa.

35. Interview, June 23, 2004, González, Tamaulipas.

36. OLS (ordinary least squares) regression showed no significant correlation between municipal income and municipal poverty.

37. Interview, July 15, 2004, Tula, Tamaulipas.

38. As indicated in chapter 2, fiscal control of municipalities was micromanaged by many states. For example, when a budget was submitted and then approved or altered, municipalities received a monthly allotment for current expenditures for salaries, lights, maintenance of town hall, state level programs carried out by the municipality, gasoline for municipal vehicles, and other basic expenses. They had to submit receipts for all these expenditures to the state secretariat of finance. And, money for many projects and programs was available only when specific proposals were submitted to particular state or federal agencies.

39. Interview, July 6, 2004, Aldama, Tamaulipas.

40. Interview, August 18, 2004, San Fernando, Tamaulipas.

41. Interview, June 22, 2004, Valladolid, Yucatán.

42. Interview, July 16, 2004, Tula, Tamaulipas.

43. Interview, June 19, 2004, González, Tamaulipas.

44. Interview, June 22, 2004, Santo Domingo Tehuantepec, Oaxaca.

45. The governor was also important for municipal officials concerned about securing their job futures; in several cases, those who developed good relationships with the governor were able to parlay this experience into jobs in the state capital.

46. Interview, June 28, 2004, Santo Domingo Tehuantepec, Oaxaca. State secretaries are the equivalent of ministers for state level ministries. They are appointed officials.

47. Interview, June 18, 2004, Santo Domingo Tehuantepec, Oaxaca.
48. Interview, June 17, 204, González, Tamaulipas.
49. Interview, July 16, 2004, Rosario, Sinaloa.
50. Interview, June 28, 2004, Santo Domingo Tehuantepec, Oaxaca.
51. Interviews: July 22, 2004, Ixtacamaxtitlán, Puebla; June 23, 2004, Rosario, Sinaloa.
52. Interview, summarized by interviewer, July 23, 204, Tula, Tamaulipas.
53. Interview, summarized by interviewer, August 9, 2004, Miguel Alemán, Tamaulipas.
54. Interview, summarized by interviewer, June 27, 2004, Aldama, Tamaulipas.
55. Two interviews, June 21, 2004, González, Tamaulipas.
56. Interview, July 7, 2004, Salvador Alvarado, Sinaloa.
57. Interview, June 23, 2004, González, Tamaulipas.
58. Interview, June 22, 2004, Valladolid, Yucatán.
59. Interview, August 19, 2004, San Fernando, Tamaulipas.
60. Interview, August 11, 2004, Santiago Pinotepa Nacional, Oaxaca.
61. Interview, July 9, 2004, San Juan Guichicovi, Oaxaca.
62. Interview, June 22, 2004, Santo Domingo Tehuantepec, Oaxaca.
63. Interview, June 23, 2004, Abasolo, Guanajuato.
64. Interview, July 28, 2004, Santa Cruz de Juventino Rosas, Guanajuato.
65. Interview, June 15, 2004, Abasolo, Guanajuato.
66. Interview, July 7, 2004, Manuel Doblado, Guanajuato.
67. Interview, August 12, 2004, San Luis de la Paz, Guanajuato.
68. Interview, July 17, 2004, Acatlán de Pérez Figueroa, Oaxaca.
69. Interview, July 6, 2004, Aldama, Tamaulipas.
70. These were known as the Bartlett Laws, after the governor in office at the time they were passed.
71. Interview, June 19, 2004, Escuinapa, Sinaloa.
72. For example, the federal government ruled that particular social development funds could not be used for scholarships, according to a director in Yucatán, causing the municipality to have to renege on promises it had made to constituents. Interview, October 28, 2004, Oxkutzcab, Yucatán.
73. Interview, July 11, 2004, Manuel Doblado, Guanajuato.
74. Interview, August 24, 2004, San Fernando, Tamaulipas.
75. Interview, June 21, 2004, Santo Domingo Tehuantepec, Oaxaca.
76. Interview, July 19, 2004, San Ignacio, Sinaloa.
77. Interview, July 21, 2004, San Ignacio, Sinaloa.
78. Merino (2004). See also Guillén López (1995).
79. Interview, July 21, 2004, Chignahuapan, Puebla.
80. Interview, June 19, 2004, Esquinapa, Sinaloa.
81. Interviews, June 21 and 22, 2004, Rosario, Sinaloa.
82. Interviews, June 27, 2004, Aldama, Tamaulipas.
83. Interview, July 7, 2004, Aldama, Tamaulipas.
84. Interview, August 4, 2004, Miguel Aleman, Tamaulipas.

Chapter 5

Modernizing Town Hall

1. For NGOs and international development agencies, capacity-building initiatives are additionally attractive because they *appear* to be free from politics. That is, they provide technical and organizational responses to inefficiencies, ineffectiveness, and lack of responsiveness that do not imply interventions in party politics, policy decision-making processes, or public debates. Capacity-building initiatives offer the possibility of getting to the heart of government and governance with the appearance of rationality and technical problem solving. See Hewitt de Alcántara (1998). See also Ward (1998).

2. Interviews: July 6, 2004, Manuel Doblado, Guanajuato; June 15, 2004, Abasolo, Guanajuato.

3. Interview, June 26, 2004, Valladolid, Yucatán.

4. Interview, July 24, 2004, Acatlán de Pérez Figueroa, Oaxaca.

5. One municipal comptroller, for example, complained that his predecessor had employed a bricklayer to carry out professional fiscal responsibilities. Interview, July 7, 2004, Manuel Doblado, Guanajuato.

6. Interview, June 29, 2004, Manuel Doblado, Guanajuato.

7. Interview, July 27, 2004, Santa Cruz de Juventino Rosas, Guanajuato. Table 2.3 indicated that only 20 percent of the research municipalities had public security regulations in 2002.

8. Interview, July 8, 2004, Manuel Doblado, Guanajuato.

9. The municipalities were Abasolo, Santa Cruz de Juventino Rosas, and Manuel Doblado in Guanajuato; Acatlán de Pérez Figueroa in Oaxaca; Chignahuapan and Libres in Puebla; Escuinapa and Mocorito in Sinaloa; Miguel Aleman in Tamaulipas; and Valladolid in Yucatán.

10. In one municipality in Sinaloa, for example, the department of markets and slaughterhouses disappeared and responsibility for tax collection and monitoring of the two areas was given to the treasurer.

11. Interview, July 29, 2004, Santa Cruz de Juventino Rosas, Guanajuato.

12. Interview, July 23, 2004, Chignahuapan, Puebla.

13. Interview, July 17, 2004, Acatlán de Pérez Figueroa, Oaxaca.

14. In fact, many municipalities were without such basic information and organizing tools as employee lists and standard operating procedures.

15. Interview, August 13, 2004, San Luis de la Paz, Guanajuato.

16. Interviews: June 22, 2004, Valladolid, Yucatán; June 29, 2004, Manuel Doblado, Guanajuato.

17. Interview, August 23, 2004, San Fernando, Tamaulipas.

18. Interviews: July 27, 2004, Santa Cruz de Juventino Rosas; June 30, 2004, Abasolo, Guanajuato; September 11, 2005, Ticul, Yucatán.

19. Interview, July 22, 2004, Acatlán de Pérez Figueroa, Oaxaca.

20. Interview, July 22, 2004, Chignahuapan, Puebla.

21. Interview, August 22, 2004, San Fernando, Tamaulipas.

22. Interview, October 12, 2004, Ticul, Yucatán.

23. Interview, July 23, 2004, Chignahuapan, Puebla.

24. Interviews: July 23, 2004, Chignahuapan, Puebla; June 20, 2004, Abasolo, Guanajuato; July 13, 2004, Mocorito, Sinaloa.

25. Interview, July 18, 2004, Progreso, Yucatán.

26. I am grateful to Alexi Canaday-Jarrix for this description of a program in Progresso, Yucatán.

27. Interview, June 19, 2004, Escuinapa, Sinaloa.

28. Interview, June 22, 2004, Rosario, Sinaloa.

29. Interview, August 12, 2004, San Luis de la Paz, Guanajuato.

30. Interview, July 29, 2004, San Ignacio, Sinaloa. In Tamaulipas, a former director of public works was denigrated because he was a biologist, and the treasurer, although a professional, was similarly disdained for not being an accountant. Interview, August 6, 2004, Miguel Aleman, Tamaulipas.

31. Interview, July 22, 2004, Acatlán de Pérez Figueroa, Oaxaca.

32. Interview, June 15, 2004, Abasolo, Guanajuato.

33. Interview, August 25, 2004, San Fernando, Tamaulipas.

34. Interview, August 4, 2004, Santiago Pinotepa Nacional, Oaxaca.

35. Interview, July 13, 2004, Valladolid, Yucatán.

36. Interview, June 15, 2004, González, Tamaulipas.

37. Interview, July 9, 2004, San Juan Guichicovi, Oaxaca.

38. Interviews: July 30, 2004, Santa Cruz de Juventino Rosas, Guanajuato; July 23, 2004, Progreso, Yucatán; July 13, 2004, Valladolid, Yucatán.

39. Interview, August 24, 2004, Santiago Juxtlahuaca, Oaxaca.

40. Interview, June 15, 2004, Abasolo, Guanajuato.

41. Interviews: June 21, 2004, Coronango, Puebla; June 27, 2004, Aldama, Tamaulipas.

42. Interviews, July 22 and 23, 2004, Chignahuapan, Puebla.

43. Interview, June 21, 2004, González, Tamaulipas.

44. Interview, June 29, 2004, Manuel Doblado, Guanajuato.

45. Interview, July 29, 2004, Santa Cruz de Juventino Rosas, Guanajuato.

46. Interview, June 17, 2004, Abasolo, Guanajuato.

47. Interview, August 13, 2004, San Luis de la Paz, Guanajuato.

48. Interview, July 29, 2004, Santa Cruz de Juventino Rosas, Guanajuato.

49. Http://www.sq.pue.gob.mx/servicios/n3servicios/Cedm.html.

50. Interviews: July 24 and 28, 2004, Chignahuapan, Puebla; June 29, 2004, Escuinapa, Sinaloa.

51. Interview, June 26, 2004, Santo Domingo Tehuantepec, Oaxaca.

52. Interview, August 10, 2004, Santiago Pinotepa Nacional, Oaxaca.

53. Interview, July 23, 2004, Mocorito, Sinaloa.

54. Interview, August 4, 2004, Miguel Aleman, Tamaulipas.

55. Interview, July 16, 2004, Tula, Tamaulipas.

56. Interview, August 23, 2004, San Fernando, Tamaulipas.

57. Interview, June 27, 2004, Escuinapa, Sinaloa.

58. Interviews: August 18, 2004, Libres, Puebla; June 19, 2004, Escuinapa, Sinaloa; July 16, 2004, Tula, Tamaulipas; October 8, 2004, Umán, Yucatán.

59. Interview, July 7, 2004, Aldama, Tamaulipas.
60. Interview, July 14, 2004, Mocorito, Sinaloa.
61. Interviews, July 13 and 14, 2004, Mocorito, Sinaloa.
62. Interview, August 12, 2004, Miguel Alemán, Tamaulipas.
63. Interview, June 22, 2004, Valladolid, Yucatán.
64. Interview, August 6, 2004, Miguel Alemán, Tamaulipas.
65. Interview, July 27, 2004, Santa Cruz de Juventino Rosas, Guanajuato.
66. Interview, July 30, Santa Cruz de Juventino Rosas, Guanajuato.
67. Interviews: July 13, 2004, Mocorito, Sinaloa; July 30, 2004, Santa Cruz de Juventino Rosas, Guanajuato.
68. Interview, July 30, 2004, Santa Cruz de Juventino Rosas, Guanajuato.
69. Interview, June 15, 2004, Abasolo, Guanajuato.
70. Interview, July 13, 2004, Valladolid, Yucatán.
71. Interview, July 5, 2004, Valladolid, Yucatán.
72. Interviews: August 4, 2004, Santiago Pinotepa Nacional, Oaxaca; June 29, 2004, Escuinapa, Sinaloa; July 15, 2004, Mocorito, Sinaloa; July 19, 2004, Tula, Tamaulipas.
73. Sinaloa was the only research state in which there was broad compliance with state level mandates. In Tamaulipas, the freedom of information requirements established by the federal government were consistently ignored at the local level.
74. Interview, August 6, 2004, Miguel Alemán, Tamaulipas.
75. Interview, August 18, 2004, San Fernando, Tamaulipas.
76. Interview, July 15, 2004, Mocorito, Sinaloa.
77. Interviews, June 22, 23, and 28, 2004, Rosario, Sinaloa.
78. Interview, July 16, 2004, Rosario, Sinaloa.
79. Interview, August 23, 2004, San Fernando, Tamaulipas.
80. Interview, October 19, 2004, Oxkutzcab, Yucatán.

CHAPTER 6
CIVIL SOCIETY

1. Interview, July 22, 2004, Acatlán de Pérez Figueroa, Oaxaca.
2. Thus, for the purposes of this discussion, I am excluding the possible influence of political parties—an important part of civil society. The ways in which citizens are engaged in parties and electoral activities are dealt with in detail in chapter 3.
3. A general overview of civic associations in Mexico is found in Puga (2004). According to this author, associational life in Mexico became stronger when economic crises robbed governments of resources that could be distributed to keep the political peace, when presidents became less powerful leaders in the country, when political competition increased, and when horizontal associations simultaneously grew stronger (5).

4. The social development fund program known initially as PRONASOL and later as SOLIDARIDAD was an important innovation in this regard.

5. Interview, June 23, 2004, Abasolo, Guanajuato.

6. Interview, June 29, 2004, Manuel Doblado, Guanajuato.

7. Interview, June 28, 2004, Rosario, Sinaloa.

8. Interview, July 6, Salvador Alvarado, Sinaloa.

9. Interview, June 24, 2004, Abasolo, Guanajuato.

10. Interview, July 16, 2004, Mocorito, Sinaloa.

11. Interview, August 10, 2004, San Luis de la Paz, Guanajuato.

12. Many individual programs required local participatory mechanisms, a component of development projects that could be traced back to community development programs in the 1960s and 1970s and that again became popular in the 1990s and 2000s. In 2003, the Law of Social Development guaranteed that programs focused on social development would be accompanied by "social participation forms in the formulation, implementation, evaluation, and control of social development programs" as a way of promoting the organizational capacity of Mexican society. Quoted in Puga (2004:11).

13. Paraphrase of interview, June 6, 2004, Rosario, Sinaloa.

14. Interview, August 11, 2004, Santiago Pinotepa Nacional, Oaxaca.

15. Interview, June 19, 2004, Santo Domingo Tehuantepec, Oaxaca.

16. Interview, July 8, 2004, Salvador Alvarado, Sinaloa.

17. Interview, July 5, 2004, Manuel Doblado, Guanajuato.

18. Interview, August 8, 2004, San Fernando, Tamaulipas.

19. I am grateful to Orazio Belletini for the report on this process.

20. Sometimes, the donation of land would be in exchange for an agreement to employ local residents in the construction of the project, thus responding to a problem of employment.

21. Interview, June 19, 2004, Santo Domingo Tehuantepec, Oaxaca.

22. Interview, June 28, 2004, Santo Domingo Tehuantepec, Oaxaca. The federal government, after establishing a secretariat for public administration, began to encourage the creation of municipal planning institutes, whose purpose was to increase the capacity of citizens to oversee the functions of local government. These institutes, composed of citizens and local officials, would watch for factors such as abuse of power and authority, favoritism, and corruption. At the time of the research, however, these institutes existed only in sixteen relatively large cities. See http://www.funcionpublica.gob.mx/paraleer/g17_e/art-operacion.html.

23. Interview, June 20, 2004, Acatlán de Pérez Figueroa, Oaxaca.

24. Interview, August 20, 2004, Santiago Juxtlahuaca, Oaxaca.

25. Thus, a councilor responsible for overseeing public works in a Oaxaca municipality indicated that "Town hall is always open to the possibility that the community offer *tequío*, which means that it would be possible to reduce the cost of labor" and project resources could go further. Interview, July 12, 2004, San Juan Guichicovi, Oaxaca. On the relationship among local labor obligations, migration, and remittances, see Van Wey, Tucker, and McConnell (2005).

26. Such leadership positions could have an important place in promoting greater local level democracy. In one municipality, for example, the secretary of a local social development committee had never held a leadership position before and was proud that people would come to him with their problems. Meetings were held at his home every two weeks. He was grateful to the municipality for responding to his requests because it legitimized his position locally. He was successful because he knew whom to contact and how to proceed.

27. Interview, June 21, 2004, Santo Domingo Tehuantepec, Oaxaca.

28. Interview, August 25, 2004, Santiago Juxtlahuaca, Oaxaca.

29. Interview, June 16, 2004, González, Tamaulipas.

30. Interview, June 17, 2004, González, Tamaulipas.

31. Interview, July 6, 2004, Mocorito, Sinaloa. On the role of home town associations (HTAs) in local development, see Burgess (2005); Levitt (2001).

32. Interview, August 26, 2004, San Fernando, Tamaulipas.

33. Interview, July 27, 2004, Salvador Alvarado, Sinaloa.

34. Stevens (1974:94).

35. I am grateful to Elizabeth Coombs for this history.

36. I am grateful to Alberto Saracho-Martinez for this history.

37. This included $100 for the hookup and a $20 contribution to buy land for a community well and water tank.

38. I am grateful to Orazio Belletini for this history.

39. Interview, July 20, 2004, Acatlán de Pérez Figueroa, Oaxaca.

40. Interview, July 22, 2004, Acatlán de Pérez Figueroa, Oaxaca.

41. I am grateful to Elizabeth Coombs for this history.

42. Interview, July 22, 2004, Chignahuapan, Puebla.

43. Interview, October 17, 2004, Oxkutzcab, Yucatán.

44. Interview, July 22, 2004, Ixtacamaxtlán, Puebla.

45. Interview, July 7, 2004, San Juan Guichicovi, Oaxaca.

CHAPTER 7
WHAT'S NEW?

1. On the concept of innovation, see Altshuler and Behn (1997).

2. I am grateful to Enrique Cabrero of CIDE for helping us think through this definition. In this perspective, an innovation might be mandated by another level of government, but not implemented until some local officials or citizens take the initiative to put it into effect. Many of the innovations considered in this chapter also used state level resources as they were implemented.

3. Most of the innovations chosen by the researchers for further study were those around which there was some consensus in the interviews that the change had been important and positive. These, for example, would be the kinds of changes that many would mention when asked, "Is there anything new in how your municipality is working?" However, some of the innovations were those that seemed intuitively interesting, surprising, or unusual to the researcher, such as the digitalization of property tax records or a sewage treatment plant providing recycled water for local irrigation.

4. Guanajuato had eight innovations; Oaxaca, twelve; Puebla, twelve; Sinaloa, eight; Tamaulipas, fifteen; and Yucatán, nine. Guanajuato and Puebla each had one municipality that provided no evidence of innovation. I am grateful to Orazio Bellettini, Karla Breceda, Alexi Canaday-Jarrix, Sergio Cárdenas-Denham, Elizabeth Coombs, Xóchitl León, and Alberto Saracho-Martínez for the histories of these innovations.

5. The annual municipal innovation prize in Mexico, awarded by the Centro de Investigaciones y Docencia Económicas and the Ford Foundation, has also found no clear distinction among innovators on the basis of party. This is an important issue for further research, as the PAN is regularly considered to be the political party most interested in good governance, and is often credited with important actions to improve it.

6. Hirschman (1981).

7. One of the succeeding administrations represented the PRI and one the PVEM.

8. Schlefer (2006b).

9. As indicated in chapter 6, "Citizen Wednesdays" (or Mondays or Tuesdays, etc.) were days set aside for the mayor and municipal officials to set up shop in some public area so that citizens with problems could have direct access to those with the capacity to solve them.

10. Interview, July 22, 2004, Mocorito, Sinaloa.

11. "I obey but I do not carry out."

CHAPTER 8
THE PROMISE OF GOOD GOVERNANCE

1. Stevens (1974:94).
2. Fox (2001); Tendler (1997).
3. Moore (2004).
4. Tendler (1997); Fung (2004).

BIBLIOGRAPHY

Abers, Rebecca. 1998. "From Clientelism to Cooperation: Local Government, Participatory Policy, and Civic Organizing in Pôrto Alegre, Brazil." *Politics and Society* 26 (4): 511–37.

Alatas, Vivi, Lant Pritchett, and Anna Wetterberg. 2002. "Voice Lessons: Local Government Organizations, Social Organizations, and the Quality of Local Governance." Policy Research Working Paper No. 2981. Washington, DC: World Bank (March).

Altshuler, Alan A., and Robert D. Behn, eds. 1997. *Innovation in American Government: Challenges, Opportunities, and Dilemmas.* Washington, DC: Brookings Institution.

Altshuler, Alan A., and Marc D. Zegans. 1997. "Innovations and Public Management: Notes from the State House and City Hall." In Alan A. Altshuler and Robert D. Behn, eds., *Innovation in American Government: Challenges, Opportunities, and Dilemmas.* Washington, DC: Brookings Institution.

Alvarado, Arturo. 1998. "Unraveling from Above: A Reexamination of Mexican Federalism: From One Party Presidential Dominance to Partisan Federalism?" Washington, DC: Woodrow Wilson Center, Latin American Program Working Papers.

Angell, Alan, Pamela Lowden, and Rosemary Thorp. 2001. *Decentralizing Development: The Political Economy of Institutional Change in Colombia and Chile.* Oxford: Oxford University Press.

Aspe Armella, Pedro. 1988. *Descentralización.* Mexico, DF: Cuadernos de Renovación Nacional.

Bailey, John. 1995. "Fiscal Centralism and Pragmatic Accommodation in Nuevo León." In Victoria Rodríguez and Peter M. Ward, eds., *Opposition Government in Mexico.* Albuquerque: University of New Mexico Press.

Baiocchi, Gianpaolo. 2001. "Participation, Activism, and Politics: The Pôrto Alegre Experiment and Deliberative Democratic Theory." *Politics and Society* 29 (1):43–72.

Barzelay, Michael. 2001. *The New Public Management: Improving Research and Policy Dialogue.* Berkeley: University of California Press.

Beer, Caroline C. 2004. "Electoral Competition and Fiscal Decentralization in Mexico." In Alfred P. Montero and David J. Samuels, eds., *Decentralization and Democracy in Latin America.* Notre Dame, IN: University of Notre Dame Press.

———. 2003. *Electoral Competition and Institutional Change in Mexico.* Notre Dame, IN: University of Notre Dame Press.

Behn, Robert D. 1997. "The Dilemmas of Innovation in American Government." In Alan A. Altshuler and Robert D. Behn, eds., *Innovation in American Government: Challenges, Opportunities, and Dilemmas.* Washington, DC: Brookings Institution.

Binswanger, Hans P., and Swaminathan S. Aiyar. 2003. "Scaling Up Community-Driven Development: Theoretical Underpinnings and Program Design Implications." Policy Research Working Paper No. 3039. Washington, DC: World Bank (April).

Blair, Harry. 2000. "Participation and Accountability at the Periphery: Democratic Local Governance in Six Countries." *World Development* 28 (1): 21–39.

Blockhus, Jill. n.d. "Policy-Oriented Learning and the Potential for Trickle Up: How Local Actors' Experiments Influence Forest Policy Planning." Dissertation Proposal, Department of Political Science, Massachusetts Institute of Technology.

Bruhn, Kathleen. 1999. "PRD Local Governments in Michoacán: Implications for Mexico's Democratization Process." In Wayne A. Cornelius, Todd A. Eisenstadt, and Jane Hindley, eds., *Subnational Politics and Democratization in Mexico*. La Jolla: Center for U.S.–Mexican Studies, University of California, San Diego.

Burgess, Katrina. 2005. "Migrant Philanthropy and Local Governance in Mexico." In Barbara Merz, ed., *New Patterns for Mexico: Remittances, Philanthropic Giving, and Equitable Development*. Cambridge, MA: Harvard University Press.

Burki, Shahid Javed, Guillermo Perry, and William Dillinger. 1999. *Beyond the Center: Decentralizing the State*. Washington, DC: World Bank.

Cabrero Mendoza, Enrique. 2003. "Políticas de modernización de la adminsitración municipal. Viejas y nuevas estrategias para transformar a los gobiernos locales." In Enrique Cabrero Mendoza, ed., *Políticas públicas municipales: Una agenda en construcción*. Mexico City: Miguel Angel Porrua.

———. 2000. "Mexican Local Governance in Transition: Fleeting Change or Permanent Transformation?" *American Review of Public Administration* 30 (4): 374–88.

Cabrero Mendoza, Enrique, and Martínez-Vázquez. 2000. "Assignment of Spending Responsibilities and Service Delivery." In Marcelo M. Guigale, and Steven B. Webb, eds., *Achievements and Challenges of Fiscal Decentralization: Lessons from Mexico*. Washington, DC: World Bank.

Cadena-Ros, Jorge. 2003. "State Pacts, Elites, and Social Movements in Mexico's Transition to Democracy." In Jack A. Goldstone, ed., *States, Parties, and Social Movements*. Cambridge: Cambridge University Press.

Campbell, Tim. 2005. *The Quiet Revolution: Decentralization and the Rise of Political Participation in Latin America's Cities*. Pittsburgh, PA: University of Pittsburgh Press.

———. 1997. "Innovation and Risk Taking: The Engine of Reform in Local Government in Latin America and the Caribbean." World Bank Discussion Paper No. 357. Washington, DC: World Bank.

Cheema, G. Shabbir, and Dennis A. Rondinelli, eds. 1983. *Decentralization and Development: Policy Implementation in Developing Countries*. Beverly Hills, CA: Sage Publications.

CIDAC (Centro de Investigaciones para el Desarrollo, A.C.). 2005. http://www.cidac.org.

Cleary, Matthew R. 2001. "Electoral Competititon and Government Performance in Mexico." Paper prepared for the 23rd International Congress of the Latin American Studies Association, Washington, DC (September 6–8).

Coase, Ronald H. 1960. "The Problem of Social Cost." *Journal of Law and Economics* (October): 1–44.

Cornelius, Wayne A. 1999. "Subnational Politics and Democratization: Tensions between Center and Periphery in the Mexican Political System." In Wayne A. Cornelius, Todd A. Eisenstadt, and Jane Hindley, eds., *Subnational Politics and Democratization in Mexico*. La Jolla: Center for U.S.–Mexican Studies, University of California, San Diego.

Cornelius, Wayne A., Ann L. Craig, and Jonathan Fox, eds. 1994. *Transforming State-Society Relations in Mexico: The National Solidarity Strategy*. La Jolla: Center for U.S.–Mexican Studies, University of California, San Diego.

Cornelius, Wayne A., Todd A. Eisenstadt, and Jane Hindley, eds. 1999. *Subnational Politics and Democratization in Mexico*. La Jolla: Center for U.S.–Mexican Studies, University of California, San Diego.

Courchene, Thomas, Alberto Díaz-Cayeros, and Steven B. Webb. 2000. "Historical Forces: Geographic and Political." In Marcelo M. Guigale and Steven B. Webb, eds., *Achievements and Challenges of Fiscal Decentralization: Lessons from Mexico*. Washington, DC: World Bank.

Crook, Richard C., and James Manor. 1998. *Democracy and Decentralisation in South Asia and West Africa: Participation, Accountability and Performance*. Cambridge: Cambridge University Press.

Crook, Richard C., and Alan Sturia Severrisson. 2001. "Decentralization and Poverty Alleviation in Developing Countries." IDS Working Paper 130. Brighton, UK: Institute of Development Studies.

Davis, Diane E. 1989. *Urban Social Movements and Political Change in Mexico: The Paradox of Austerity*. New York: Columbia University Press.

———. 1994. *Urban Leviathan: Mexico City in the Twentieth Century*. Philadelphia, PA: Temple University Press.

de la Cruz, Rafael, et al. 1998. *Descentralización en perspectiva*. Caracas: Ediciones IESA.

de la Cruz, Rafael and Armando Barrios, eds. 1994. *Federalismo fiscal: El costo de la descentralización en Venezuela*. Caracas: Nueva Sociedad.

Diamond, Larry. 1999. *Developing Democracy: Toward Consolidation*. Baltimore: Johns Hopkins University Press.

Dillinger, William, and Steven B. Webb. 1999. "Fiscal Management in Federal Democracies." World Bank Policy Research Working Paper 2121. Washington, DC: World Bank.

Domínguez, Jorge I., ed. 1997. *Technopols: Freeing Politics and Markets in Latin America in the 1990s*. University Park: Pennsylvania State University Press.

Domínguez, Jorge I., and Chappell Lawson, eds. 2004. *Mexico's Pivotal Democratic Election: Candidates, Voters, and the Presidential Campaign of 2000*. Stanford, CA: Stanford University Press.

Earle, Rebecca, ed. 2000. *Rumours of Wars: Civil Conflict in Nineteenth-Century Latin America*. London: Institute of Latin American Studies.

Eaton, Kent. 2004. *Politics beyond the Capital: The Design of Subnational Institutions in South America*. Stanford, CA: Stanford University Press.

———. 2001. "Political Obstacles to Decentralization: Evidence from Argentina and the Philippines." *Development and Change* 32 (1): 101–27.

Eckstein, Susan. 1989. *Power and Popular Protest in Latin America*. Berkeley: University of California Press.

Escobar-Lemmon, María. 2001. "Fiscal Decentralization and Federalism in Latin America." *Publius: The Journal of Federalism* 31 (4): 23–42.

Espinosa Valle, Víctor Alejandro. 1999. "Alternation and Political Liberalization: The PAN in Baja California." In Wayne A. Cornelius, Todd A. Eisenstadt, and Jane Hindley, eds., *Subnational Politics and Democratization in Mexico*. La Jolla: Center for U.S.–Mexican Studies, University of California, San Diego.

Estados Unidos Mexicanos. 2002. *Ley de Coordinación Fiscal.*

———. 2000a. *Programa para un nuevo federalismo, 1995–2000, Balance Sexenal*. Mexico, DF: Talleres Gráficos.

———. 2000b. *Programa especial para un auténtico federalismo, 2000–2006.* Mexico, D.F.: Talleres Gráficos.

Fagen, Richard, and William S. Touhy. 1972. *Politics and Privilege in a Mexican City*. Stanford, CA: Stanford University Press.

Faguet, Jean-Paul. 2000. "Does Decentralization Increase Responsiveness to Local Needs? Evidence from Bolivia." Unpublished paper, Centre for Economic Performance and Development Studies Institute, London School of Economics.

Faletti, Tulia G. 2003. "Of Presidents, Governors, and Mayors: The Politics of Decentralization in Latin America." Paper prepared for the 2003 meeting of the Latin American Studies Association, Dallas, March 27–29.

Foster, George M. 1967. *Tzintzuntzán: Mexican Peasants in a Changing World*. Boston: Little, Brown.

Fowler, Will. 2000. "Civil Conflict in Independent Mexico, 1821–57: An Overview." In Rebecca Earle, ed., *Rumours of Wars: Civil Conflict in Nineteenth-Century Latin America*. London: Institute of Latin American Studies.

Fox, Jonathan. 2001. "Vertically Integrated Policy Monitoring: A Tool for Civil Society Policy Advocacy," *Nonprofit and Voluntary Sector Quarterly* 30 (3): 616–27.

———, 1994. "Latin America's Emerging Local Politics." *Journal of Democracy* 5 (2): 105–16.

Fox, Jonathan, and Josefina Aranda. 1996. *Decentralization and Rural Development in Mexico: Community Participation in Oaxaca's Municipal Funds Program*. La Jolla: Center for U.S.–Mexican Studies, Monograph Series No. 42, University of California, San Diego.

Fukasaku, Kiichiro, and Ricardo Hausmann. 1998. *Democracy, Decentralization, and Deficits in Latin America*. Paris: OECD.

Fung, Archon. 2004. *Empowered Participation: Reinventing Urban Democracy*. Princeton, NJ: Princeton University Press.

García del Castillo, Rodolfo. 2003. "La política de servicios municipales en México: Casos y tendencies recientes." In Enrique Cabrero Mendoza, ed., *Políticas públicas municipales: Una agenda en construcción*. Mexico City: Miguel Angel Porrua.

Gibson, Edward L. 2004. *Federalism and Democracy in Latin America*. Baltimore: Johns Hopkins University Press.

Golden, Olivia. 1997. "Innovation in Public Sector Human Services Programs: The Implications of Innovation by 'Groping Along.'" In Alan A. Altshuler and Robert D. Behn, eds., *Innovation in American Government: Challenges, Opportunities, and Dilemmas*. Washington, DC: Brookings Institution.

Goldfrank, Benjamin. 2002. "The Fragile Flower of Local Democracy: A Case Study of Decentralization/Participation in Montevideo." *Politics and Society* 30 (1): 51–83.

González-Rosetti, Alejandra. 2001. The Political Dimension of Health Reform: The Case of Mexico and Colombia. PhD diss., Department of Public Health Policy, London School of Hygiene and Tropical Medicine.

Grandvoinnet, Helene, Mattia Romani, and Monica Das Gupta. 2003. "Fostering Community Driven Development: What Role for the State?" Policy Research Working Paper 2969, World Bank (January).

———. 2000. "State-Community Synergies in Development: Laying the Basis for Collective Action." Policy Research Working Paper No. 2439, World Bank (September).

Grindle, Merilee S. 2004a. *Despite the Odds: The Contentious Politics of Education Reform*. Princeton, NJ: Princeton University Press.

———. 2004b. "Good Enough Governance: Poverty Reduction and Reform in Developing Countries." *Governance: An International Journal of Policy and Administration* 17, 4 (October): 525–48.

———. 2000. *Audacious Reforms: Institutional Invention and Democracy in Latin America*. Baltimore: Johns Hopkins University Press.

———. 1996. *Challenging the State: Crisis and Innovation in Latin America and Africa*. Cambridge: Cambridge University Press.

Guigale, Marcelo M., Vinh Nguyen, Fernando Rojas, and Steven B. Webb. 2000. "Overview." In Marcelo M. Giugale and Steven B. Webb, eds., *Achievements and Challenges of Fiscal Decentralization: Lessons from Mexico*. Washington, DC: World Bank.

Guigale, Marcelo M., and Steven B. Webb. eds., 2000. *Achievements and Challenges of Fiscal Decentralization: Lessons from Mexico*. Washington, DC: World Bank.

Guillén López, Tonatiuh, ed. 1995. *Municipios en transición: Actores sociales y nuevas políticas de gobierno*. Tijuana: Colegio de la Frontera Norte.

Haggard, Stephan, and Steven B. Webb. 2004. "Political Incentives and Intergovernmental Fiscal Relations." In Alfred P. Montero and David J. Samuels, eds., *Decentralization and Democracy in Latin America*. Notre Dame, IN: University of Notre Dame Press.

Heller, Patrick. 2001. "Moving the State: The Politics of Democratic Decentralization in Kerala, South Africa, and Porto Alegre." *Politics and Society* 29 (1): 131–163.

Hewitt de Alcántara. 1998. "Uses and Abuses of the Concept of Governance." Paris: UNESCO.

Hirschman, Albert O. 1981. "Policymaking and Policy Analysis in Latin America—A Return Journey." In Albert O. Hirschman, *Essays in Trespassing: Economics to Politics and Beyond*. Cambridge: Cambridge University Press.

Hirst, Paul. "Democracy and Governance." In Jon Pierre, ed., *Debating Governance: Authority, Steering, and Democracy*. Oxford: Oxford University Press.

Hiskey, Jonathan T., and Mitchell A. Seligson. 2003. "Pitfalls of Power to the People: Decentralization, Local Government Performance, and System Support in Bolivia." *Studies in Comparative International Development* 37 (4): 64–89.

Huntington, Samuel. 1968. *Political Order in Changing Societies*. New Haven, CT: Yale University Press.

Hutchcroft, Paul D. 2001. "Centralization and Decentralization in Administration and Politics: Assessing Territorial Dimensions of Authority and Power." *Governance: An International Journal of Policy and Administration* 14 (1): 25–54.

Hyden, Gøran, and Julius Court. 2002. "Comparing Governance across Countries and over Time: Conceptual Challenges." In Dele Olowu and Soumana Sako, eds., *Better Governance and Public Policy: Capacity Building and Democratic Renewal in Africa*. Bloomfield, CT: Kumarian Press.

IDD (International Development Department). 2004. "Building Municipal Capacity in Finance." *IDD Research News*. Birmingham, UK: University of Birmingham.

INAFED (Instituto Nacional de Federalismo). 2002. *Dirección del Sistema Nacional de Información Municipal*.

INAFED (Instituto Nacional de Federalismo). 2004, 2005. http://www.inafed .gob.mx.

INEGI (Instituto Nacional de Estadísticas y Geografía). 2000. *Censo General de Población y Vivienda, 2000*. Mexico, DF: INEGI.

Jones, R. J. Barry. 2000. *The World Turned Upside Down? Globalization and the Future of the State*. New York: Manchester University Press.

Kamarck, Elaine Ciulla. 2000. "Globalization and Public Administration Reform." In Joseph S. Nye, Jr., and John D. Donahue, eds., *Governance in a Globalizing World*. Washington, DC: Brookings Institution.

Keina Jiménez. 2004. Discontinuidad en las gestiones municipales: Causas y consecuencias en el Município de Tehuantepec. PhD diss. Autonomous University of Chiapas, Mexico.

Kettl, Donald. 2000. *The Global Management Revolution: A Report on the Transformation of Governance*. Washington, DC: Brookings Institution.

Khemani, Stuti. 2001. "Decentralization and Accountability: Are Voters More Vigilant in Local than in National Elections?" Policy Research Working Paper No. 2557. Washington, DC: World Bank.

King, Elizabeth M., Peter F. Orazem, and Darin Wohlgemuth. 1998. "Central Mandates and Local Incentives: The Colombia Education Voucher Program." Working Paper Series on Impact Evaluation of Education Reforms No. 6. Washington, DC: World Bank.

Lafourcade, Olivier. 2000. "Preface." In Marcelo M. Guigale and Steven B. Webb, eds., *Achievements and Challenges of Fiscal Decentralization: Lessons from Mexico*. Washington, DC: World Bank.

Lall, Somik V., Use Deichmann, Mattias K. A. Lundberg, and Nazmul Chaudhury. 2002. "Tenure, Diversity, and Commitment: Community Participation for Urban Service Provision." Policy Research Working Paper 2862. Washington, DC: World Bank.

Latinobarómetro. 2005. "Confianza en instituciones, America Latina, 1996–2004." Santiago, Chile: Latinobarómetro.

Levitt, Peggy. 2001. *The Transnational Villagers*. Berkeley: University of California Press.

Litvack, Jennie, and Jessica Seddon, eds. 1999. *Decentralization Briefing Notes*. Washington, DC: World Bank.

Lynn, Jr., Laurence E. 1997. "Innovation and the Public Interest: Insights from the Private Sector." In Alan A. Altshuler and Robert D. Behn, eds., *Innovation in American Government: Challenges, Opportunities, and Dilemmas*. Washington, DC: Brookings Institution.

Manor, James. 1999. *The Political Economy of Democratic Decentralization*. Washington, DC: World Bank.

McConnell, Grant. 1966. *Private Power and American Democracy*. New York: Knopf.

Merino, Mauricio. 2004. "Los gobiernos municipales de México: El problema del diseño institucional." Documento de Trabajo No. 145. Mexico, DF: CIDE.

———. 2003. "Prólogo." In Enrique Cabrero Mendoza, ed., *Políticas públicas municipales: Una agenda en construcción*. Mexico City: Miguel Angel Porrua.

———. 1994. *En busca de la democracia municipal: La participación ciudadana en el gobierno local mexicano*. Mexico, DF: El Colegio de México.

Meyer, Lorenzo, and William Sherman. 1979. *A Compact History of Mexico*. Mexico, DF: El Colegio de México.

Mizrahi, Yemile. 2004. "Twenty Years of Decentralization in Mexico: A Top-Down Process." In Philip Oxhorn, Joseph S. Tulchin, and Andrew D. Seele, eds., *Decentralization, Democratic Governance, and Civil Society in Comparative Perspective: Africa, Asia, and Latin America*. Baltimore: Johns Hopkins University Press.

Mohrir, Vasant. 2002. "Governance and Policy Analysis." In Dele Olowu and Soumana Sako, eds., *Better Governance and Public Policy: Capacity Building and Democratic Renewal in Africa*. Bloomfield, CT: Kumarian Press.

Montero, Alfred P. 2001. "After Decentralization: Patterns of Intergovernmental Conflict in Argentina, Brazil, Spain, and Mexico." *Publius: The Journal of Federalism* 31 (4): 43–64.

Montero, Alfred P., and David J. Samuels. 2004. "The Political Determinants of Decentralization in Latin America: Causes and Consequences." In Alfred P. Montero and David J. Samuels, eds., *Decentralization and Democracy in Latin America*. Notre Dame, IN: University of Notre Dame Press.

Moore, Michael P. 2004. "Revenues, State Formation, and the Quality of Governance in Developing Countries." *International Political Science Review* 25 (3): 297–319.

Moreno, Carlos Luis. 2005. Decentralization, Electoral Competititon and Local Government Performance in Mexico. PhD diss. University of Texas at Austin.

Nickson, R. Andrew. 1995. *Local Government in Latin America*. Boulder, CO: Lynne Rienner.

Oates, Wallace. 1977. *The Political Economy of Fiscal Federalism*. Lexington, MA: Lexington Books.

———. 1972. *Fiscal Federalism*. New York: Harcourt Brace Jovanovich.

Olowu, Dele. 2002. "Introduction: Governance and Policy Management Capacity in Africa." In Dele Olowu and Soumana Sako, eds., *Better Governance and Public Policy: Capacity Building and Democratic Renewal in Africa*. Bloomfield, CT: Kumarian Press.

O'Neill, Kathleen. 2003. "Decentralization as an Electoral Strategy." *Comparative Political Studies* 36 (November): 1068–91.

Oxhorn, Philip. 2004. "Unraveling the Puzzle of Decentralization." In Philip Oxhorn, Joseph S. Tulchin, and Andrew D. Selee, eds., *Decentralization, Democratic Governance, and Civil Society in Comparative Perspective: Africa, Asia, and Latin America*. Baltimore: Johns Hopkins University Press.

Oxhorn, Philip, Joseph S. Tulchin, and Andrew D. Selee, eds. 2004. *Decentralization, Democratic Governance, and Civil Society in Comparative Perspective: Africa, Asia, and Latin America*. Baltimore: Johns Hopkins University Press.

Peters, B. Guy. 2000. "Governance and Comparative Politics." In Jon Pierre, ed., *Debating Governance: Authority, Steering, and Democracy*. Oxford: Oxford University Press.

Peterson, George E. 1997. *Decentralization in Latin America: Learning through Experience*. Washington, DC: World Bank.

Pierre, Jon. 2000. "Introduction: Understanding Governance." In Jon Pierre, ed., *Debating Governance: Authority, Steering, and Democracy*. Oxford: Oxford University Press.

Pierson, Paul. 2000. "The Limits of Design: Explaining Institutional Origins and Change." *Governance: An International Journal of Policy and Administration* 13 (1): 475–99.

Portes, Alejandro, and Patricia Landolt. 1996. "Unsolved Mysteries: The Toqueville Files II: The Downside of Social Capital." *The American Prospect* 7, 26 (May-June): 18–22.

Prud'homme, Remy. 1995. "The Dangers of Decentralization." *The World Bank Research Observer* 10, 2 (August): 201–20.

Puga, Cristina. 2004. "Associations and Governance in Mexico." Paper prepared for the 25th International Congress of the Latin American Studies Association. Las Vegas, NV, October 7–9.

Putnam, Robert. 1993. *Making Democracy Work: Civic Traditions in Modern Italy*. Princeton, NJ: Princeton University Press.

Ribot, Jesse C. 2000. "Decentralization, Participation, and Representation: Administrative Apartheid in Sahelian Forestry." In Pauline E. Peters, ed., *Development Encounters: Sites of Participation and Knowledge*. Cambrdge, MA: Harvard University Press for the Harvard Institute for International Development.

Riker, William H. 1964. *Federalism: Origin, Operation, Significance*. Boston: Little, Brown.

Rodríguez, Victoria E. 1997. *Decentralization in Mexico: From Reforma Municipal to Solidaridad to Nuevo Federalismo*. Boulder, CO: Westview Press.

Rodríguez, Victoria E., and Peter M. Ward. 1995. "Introduction: Governments of the Opposition in Mexico." In Victoria Rodríguez and Peter M. Ward, eds., *Opposition Government in Mexico.* Albuquerque: University of New Mexico Press.

———. 1994. *Political Change in Baja California: Democracy in the Making?* La Jolla: Center for U.S.–Mexican Studies, University of California, San Diego.

Rondinelli, Dennis A. 1989. "Decentralizing Public Services in Developing Countries: Issues and Opportunities." *Journal of Social, Political and Economic Studies* 14 (1): 77–98.

Rondinelli, Dennis A., and G. Shabbir Cheema, eds. 2003. *Reinventing Government for the Twenty-First Century: State Capacity in a Globalizing Society.* Bloomfield, CT: Kumarian Press.

Rondinelli, Dennis A., James S. McCullough, and Ronald W. Johnson. 1989. "Analyzing Decentralization Policies in Developing Countries: A Political-Economy Framework." *Development and Change* 20 (1): 57–87.

Rondinelli, Dennis A., John R. Nellis, and G. Shabbir Cheema. 1984. *Decentralization in Developing Countries: A Review of Recent Experience.* Washington, DC: World Bank.

Rose-Ackerman, Susan. 1980. "Risk Taking and Reelection: Does Federalism Promote Innovation?" *The Journal of Legal Studies* 9 (3): 593–616.

Rubin, Jeffrey W. 1997. *Decentering the Regime: Ethnicity, Radicalism, and Democracy in Juchitán, Mexico.* Durham, NC: Duke University Press.

Santín del Río, Leticia. 2004. "Decentralization and Civil Society in Mexico." In Philip Oxhorn, Joseph S. Tulchin, and Andrew D. Selee, eds., *Decentralization, Democratic Governance, and Civil Society in Comparative Perspective: Africa, Asia, and Latin America.* Baltimore: Johns Hopkins University Press.

Schlefer, Jonathan. 2006a. "Change in Chignahuapan: Reforming a Municipal Government in Mexico." Teaching Case, Kennedy School of Government, Harvard University.

———. 2006b. "Change in Chignahuapan: Sequel." Teaching Case Sequel, Kennedy School of Government, Harvard University.

Schönwälder, Gerd. 1997. "New Democratic Spaces at the Grassroots? Popular Participation in Latin American Local Government." *Development and Change* 28: 753–70.

Seligson, Mitchell A. 2006. "Can Social Capital Be Constructed? Decentralization and Social Capital Formation in Latin America." In Lawrence Harrison and Jerome Kegan, eds., *Developing Cultures—Instruments of Cultural Transmission and Change.* London: Routledge.

Shirk, David A. 2005. *Mexico's New Politics: The PAN and Democratic Change.* Boulder, CO: Lynne Rienner.

Snyder, Richard. 2001. "Scaling Down: The Subnational Comparative Method." *Studies in Comparative International Development* 36 (1): 93–110.

———. 1999. "After the State Withdraws: Neoliberalism and Subnational Authoritarian Regimes in Mexico." In Wayne A. Cornelius, Todd A. Eisenstadt, and Jane Hindley, eds., *Subnational Politics and Democratization in Mexico.* La Jolla: Center for U.S.–Mexican Studies, University of California, San Diego.

Stepan, Alfred. 2001. *Arguing Comparative Politics*. Oxford: Oxford University Press.

Stevens, Evelyn P. 1974. *Protest and Response in Mexico*. Cambridge, MA: MIT Press.

Stone, Deborah A. 1997. "State Innovation in Health Policy." In Alan A. Altshuler and Robert D. Behn, eds., *Innovation in American Government: Challenges, Opportunities, and Dilemmas*. Washington, DC: Brookings Institution.

Stoner-Weiss, Kathryn. 1997. *Local Heroes: The Political Economy of Russian Regional Governance*. Princeton, NJ: Princeton University Press.

Straface, Fernando. 2003. "Latin American and Caribbean Award for Innovations in Government." Unpublished paper, Kennedy School of Government, Harvard University (March).

Teaford, Jon C. 1984. *The Unheralded Triumph: City Government in America, 1870–1900*. Baltimore: Johns Hopkins University Press.

Tiebout, Charles M. 1956. "A Pure Theory of Local Expenditures." *Journal of Political Economy* 64 (5): 416–24.

Tendler, Judith. 1997. *Good Government in the Tropics*. Baltimore: Johns Hopkins University Press.

Toqueville, Alexis De. 1848. *Democracy in America*. 1988 edition. New York: Perennial Library.

VanWey, Leah K., Catherine M. Tucker, and Eileen Diaz McConnell. 2005. "Community Organization, Migration, and Remittances in Oaxaca." *Latin American Research Review* 40 (1): 83–107.

Wallis, Joe. 1999. "Understanding the Role of Leadership in Economic Policy Reform." *World Development* 27 (1): 39–53.

———. 1995. "Policy Making and Policy Implementation among Non-PRI Governments: The PAN in Ciudad Juárez and Chihuahua." In Victoria Rodríguez and Peter M. Ward, eds., *Opposition Government in Mexico*. Albuquerque: University of New Mexico Press.

Ward, Peter M. 1998. "From Machine Politics to the Politics of Technocracy: Charting Changes in Governance in the Mexican Municipality." *Bulletin of Latin American Research* 17 (3): 34–65.

Ward, Peter M., and Victoria E. Rodríguez with Enrique Cabrero Mendoza. 1999. *The New Federalism and State Government in Mexico: Bringing the State Back In*. Austin, TX: U.S.–Mexican Policy Report No. 9, Lyndon B. Johnson School of Public Affairs, University of Texas at Austin.

Weingast, Barry R. 1995. "The Role of Political Institutions: Market-Preserving Federalism and Economic Growth." *Journal of Law, Economics and Organization* 11:1–31.

Wibbels, Eric. 2004. "Decentralization, Democracy, and Market Reform: On the Difficulties of Killing Two Birds with One Stone." In Alfred P. Montero and David J. Samuels, eds., *Decentralization and Democracy in Latin America*. Notre Dame, IN: University of Notre Dame Press.

Wiesner, Eduardo. 2003. *Fiscal Federalism in Latin America: From Entitlements to Markets*. Washington, DC: Inter-American Development Bank.

Williamson, John, ed. 1994. *The Political Economy of Policy Reform*. Washington, DC: Institute for International Economics.

Willis, Eliza, Christopher da C. B. Garman, and Stephan Haggard. 1999. "The Politics of Decentralization in Latin America." *Latin American Research Review* 34 (1): 7–56.

Womack, John. 1969. *Zapata and the Mexican Revolution*. New York: Random House.

World Complete, Harvard Maps Collection, May 2003, CD 1/3 GFK Macon.

Wunsch, James S., and Dele Olowu. 1990. *The Failure of the Centralized State: Institutions and Self-Governance in Africa*. Boulder, CO: Westview.

Ziccardi, Alicia. 2003. "El federalismo y las regione: Una perspectiva municipal." *Gestión y Política Pública* 12 (2) (Mexico City: CIDE).

Index

AAMLAC (Asociación de Autoridades Locales de México, A.C.), 42

Abasolo: area of, 14, 44; competition to PRI in, 68; economy of, 45; government performance in, 60; income of, 94; innovation in, 145; marginalization index for, 44; population of, 14, 44, 94; social infrastructure of, 46

Acatlán de Pérez Figueroa: area of, 14, 44; citizens' benefit extraction in, 136–37; competition to PRI in, 68; economy of, 45; government performance in, 60; income of, 94; marginalization index for, 44; population of, 14, 44, 94; social infrastructure of, 46

accountability: and citizen involvement, 12, 18, 21, 22, 124, 125, 139–40, 141–42, 174–75, 177, 178; and competitive elections, 63, 83; and electoral cycle, 120, 121; for funding, 165; future improvement of, 180; government imposition of, 18; lack of, 3; to mayor, 101; and municipal planning institutes, 201n22; and taxes, 7; through decentralization, 2; through elections, 143. *See also* monitoring

administration, political: changes in, 51–52, 70, 85–86, 88–90, 104, 108–9, 118, 142, 159, 165, 171, 174; decentralization of, 167, 168; innovations by, 159, 160, 161; priority setting in, 109, 110, 165, 171; programs of, 171; and sustainability of programs, 159; three-year tenure of, 18

administration/management: autonomy of local, 27; conflict in, 78; contracting out by, 109, 111–12; and decentralization, 4, 6, 7, 9; efficiency in, 166; and electoral competition, 77; expenditures on, 50; fiscal, 4, 6, 7, 8, 19, 28, 30, 42, 116, 167, 168; freedom to change, 171; of funding, 99–100; and funding contacts, 98–99; of human resources, 101, 110, 172; infrastructure of, 40; innovation in, 147, 148, 150–52, 154–55, 160; by

mayor, 100–101; measuring performance of, 57; modernization of, 106–22, 172–73, 176, 180; of municipal property, 101, 111; and office space, 81; plans for, 41; reorganization of, 20, 109, 110–12; standardization of, 103

agriculture, 53, 55

alcohol, 41, 53

Aldama: area of, 14, 44; citizens' benefit extraction in, 133–35; competition to PRI in, 68; economy of, 45; government performance in, 60; income of, 94; innovation in, 154; marginalization index for, 44; population of, 14, 44, 94; social infrastructure of, 46

AMMAC (Asociación de Municípios de México, A.C.), 42

aportaciones (grants), 33, 36

Aranda, Josefina, 12, 64

Article 115. *See* Constitution of 1917

Asociación de Municípios de México, A.C., 42

auditing, 101

authoritarianism, 25, 30, 174, 176

autonomous agency, use of, 151

ayuntamiento, 38. *See also* government, local; officials, local

Aztec empire, 26

Bando de Policía y Buen Gobierno (municipal code), 41, 57–58

benefit extraction, 18, 21, 125, 133–41, 142, 174, 175, 177, 181. *See also* services

Blair, Harry, 6

block grants, 42

budget/budgeting: and councils, 172; innovation in, 151, 155; monitoring of by *síndicos,* 38; in Oaxaca, 53; and partisan conflicts, 81; and post-election chaos, 88; preparation of, 51; as pressing problem, 154; public availability of, 57, 58; state oversight of, 196n38

cabildazos, 80

cabildo. See councils, local